AN HISTORICAL SKETCH
OF THE

TOWN OF DEER ISLE
MAINE

WITH NOTICES OF ITS
SETTLERS AND EARLY INHABITANTS

George L. Hosmer

HERITAGE BOOKS
2010

HERITAGE BOOKS
AN IMPRINT OF HERITAGE BOOKS, INC.

Books, CDs, and more—Worldwide

For our listing of thousands of titles see our website
at
www.HeritageBooks.com

A Facsimile Reprint
Published 2010 by
HERITAGE BOOKS, INC.
Publishing Division
100 Railroad Ave. #104
Westminster, Maryland 21157

Copyright © 1905 Abel Hosmer

Original cover illustration by Deborah L. Riley

— Publisher's Notice —
In reprints such as this, it is often not possible to remove blemishes from the original. We feel the contents of this book warrant its reissue despite these blemishes and hope you will agree and read it with pleasure.

International Standard Book Numbers
Paperbound: 978-0-7884-1282-0
Clothbound: 978-0-7884-8449-0

CONTENTS.

                                    PAGE

CHAPTER I 5
    Introduction. — Discovery. — Settlements. — Mills. — Marriages.

CHAPTER II 24
    First Settlers. — The Revolution. — Land-Titles. — Incorporation.

CHAPTER III 39
    Notices of Settlers and Early Inhabitants. — Physicians. — Men and Vessels Lost at Sea. — A List of Aged Persons.

CHAPTER IV 211
    Municipal and Miscellaneous, 1789–1882. — Ecclesiastical. — Origin of the Names of the Different Localities in the Town. — Conclusion.

AN HISTORICAL SKETCH

OF THE

TOWN OF DEER ISLE.

CHAPTER I.

INTRODUCTION. — DISCOVERY. — SETTLEMENTS. — MILLS. — MARRIAGES.

FOR some years past it has been my purpose to write an historical sketch of this town, with notices of its settlers and early inhabitants. When I came here a young man, nearly half a century ago, there were but few of the early settlers remaining, the last of whom, Mr. Joseph Sellers, died in 1844 at the age of ninety-two years. My information has been derived from those who were contemporary with them, and they in their turn have passed away. Although the means I have had for such a work were scanty, yet it was all that could be obtained, as I had nothing but verbal information: but I may reasonably judge that it is in the main correct. I have thought it best to preserve it, in order that those who are now living, and those who may come hereafter, may have some knowledge of the hardships endured by their ancestors. The history of the early settlement of any country is a history of toil, privations, and suffering, and of these the persons noticed here have had their full share. It was with them a hard struggle for a subsistence, and had it not been for the seafowl, sea and shellfish, it could not have been obtained by them, and had those means been wanting elsewhere, the seacoast could never have been settled where it was in this State. I have hopes that what is here written may prove of interest to the descendants of those whose notices are here recorded. It is, or should be, a matter of interest to every one, to have some knowledge of the history of his native place, or of the town in which he resides. In too many cases it is not felt until the sources from which such information might have been obtained no longer exist, and I wish to improve this opportunity for its preservation, for otherwise it will soon have passed from memory and be lost beyond recovery.

DISCOVERY.

We have no authentic information by whom, and at what time, the islands on which this town is situated were discovered. It has been stated that, in 1556, André Thevit, a Catholic priest, sailed in a French ship along the entire coast; that he entered Penobscot Bay, where he spent five days and had numerous conferences with the natives. The first Englishman who visited this locality was Martin Pring, who sailed from Bristol in 1603, and visited Penobscot Bay and islands. Seeing some foxes on the shore of one island, he named it Fox Island, and that was the name by which those islands, on which the towns of North Haven and Vinalhaven are situated, were formerly known; one as the North, and the other as the South, Fox Island. He was well pleased with the scenery of the bay, with the excellence of the fisheries, and with what animals were seen by them. When he returned to England, he carried an Indian canoe with him, but while here saw but few inhabitants. It is probable that he sailed up the bay lying between the towns of Deer Isle and Isle au Haut on the one side, and the towns of North Haven and Vinalhaven on the other. From its height the Isle au Haut would have been a prominent landmark, as it can be seen about thirty-five miles at sea, and is the outermost island of any considerable size in this vicinity. If he sailed up the bay, as we have supposed, he must have seen Deer Island. We may regard him as the first Englishman who saw it, if not the first European, for if Thevit had seen the bay and published his discovery, it seems reasonable to us that he would have been followed by others of his countrymen and possession taken.

In 1604 Champlain visited this region, and is said to have landed upon its shores, but there is little information respecting this. In 1605 the bay and islands were visited by James Rozier. It has been stated that the latter sailed up the passage now known as Eggemoggin Reach, between Deer Isle on the one side and the towns of Brooklin, Sedgwick, and Brooksville on the other, and that he anchored near the cape lying at the southwestern extremity of the town of Brooksville, which bears his name. If this account be correct, he must have passed very near Deer Island, as the passage is, in its narrowest part, not more than half a mile in width. In June of the same year Weymouth visited the bay and river, but from the account given us, we believe that he sailed up the western side, between the towns of Islesborough and Camden, and anchored opposite the hills now known as Camden Hills. Here a party of them went on shore and afterward going, in a pinnace, farther up the bay they reached a part which, according to their description of it, must have been near where the city of Belfast is now situated.

From the account given us, they appeared to have been as well pleased with what they saw as was Pring two years earlier. The intercourse of Weymouth with the natives was at first friendly, but, unfortunately for his reputation, he kidnapped five and carried them to England, three of whom he delivered to Sir Ferdinand Gorges (to whom the Province of Maine was chartered in 1639), who kept them in his family three years.

It is not probable that Weymouth went to that part of the bay in which this town is situated, or, if he did, nothing is said about it, and as the records made of their discoveries by those early voyagers are very brief, conjecture must supply the vacancy; but we may come to the conclusion that, at least, Pring and Rozier must have seen Deer Island. In 1614 Captain John Smith, of Virginia, visited this region and reported a settlement as having been made, but he must have referred to that made by the French on the island of Mount Desert, as it is said that was occupied by them as early as 1604. Others came to it in 1609, and Madame de Guerchville's colony was there in 1613, a year before Smith came to this coast. No English settlement is reported to have been made anywhere in this vicinity, until that of 1626 by Isaac Allerton, under the direction of the Plymouth Colony, for purposes of trade, upon the peninsula on which the town of Castine now stands. This was continued till 1635, when it was taken possession of by the French. It was retaken in 1654 and retained till 1670, when it was surrendered to the French, and by them retained most of the time until 1704, when it was captured by Captain Church of the Plymouth Colony. No other settlement which was permanent, was made by the English anywhere in this neighborhood, until about the year 1760, which was the date of the settlement of Castine. We have no account of who gave this island its name, or when it was given, but it has been said that deer were found upon it in abundance, and that it was so called from this circumstance. This is very probable, as those animals could easily visit it in the winter by crossing the Reach on the ice, and they have been known to cross that passage by swimming. I have been told that, in one instance, in the early years of the settlement here, one was seen so coming over by the members of a family who then resided near the shore, and on its landing was killed by them, and that it was a providential occurrence, as at the time they were suffering from hunger. Several have been killed since I have resided here, and within twenty years past I saw an old one and her young near the highway about half a mile from the Northwest Harbor.

SETTLEMENTS.

When the first settlers came here the island was an unbroken wilderness. No evidences were found indicating that it had ever been occupied by white men, and probably but few had ever landed upon its shores. The Indians had made some parts of it places of residence for the purpose of obtaining a supply of food from the clam-flats, and the proofs of their occupancy, in many instances, also, covering a considerable space, were to be found wherever those shellfish were in great abundance, while the depth of the shells in the ground showed that they must have been centuries in accumulating. When the land was plowed, the spots upon which they had built their wigwams were easily discernible. It is probable that the times of these visits were those in which other food was not so readily procurable. Occasionally skeletons have been found, and at one time two were discovered under the roots of a hard-wood tree which had grown to a large size, and was in a state of decay when it was blown over during a storm. One was that of a person of ordinary size, the other of one who was at least eight feet in height, and between the ribs of the larger one was found the head of a dart made of copper. They lay nearly side by side, and had been probably engaged in mortal conflict, the larger one fatally wounded by the smaller, and the smaller falling by the hands of the larger. This conflict must have happened a long time before discovery, as they must have lain upon the ground, and the tree which grew over them would have been a long time in attaining its growth. They were found nearly sixty years ago, and a medical man then residing in the town gathered up the skeleton of the larger one and preserved it. Upon putting the bones together, he calculated that the height of the man was what is above stated.

When the settler came, his first care was to provide a shelter for his family. A hut, the sides of which were built of logs, and the roof of bark, unless he had boards, which he probably had not, as then there were no sawmills anywhere in the vicinity; a wall of stones laid up for a fireplace, with a hole in the roof to let out the smoke and let in the light and air, and a floor, if any it had except the ground, made of small trees sided with an axe. The walls were plastered with clay or mud in the spaces between the logs, or caulked with moss to keep out the cold. His first habitation was near the shore, as it was more convenient than farther back from it, causing him less distance for the transportation of the articles of food. In the months of May, June, July, and a part of August, the bark used for roofing could be peeled from the trees; at other times it was fast to them and could not be obtained for the purpose. When he had opportunity, a house was built of logs of more convenient size, and if boards could be had, they could be used for roofs and floors; the chimney of rocks was carried farther up and topped out with sticks and clay, and a few squares of glass might be obtained to admit light into his dwelling. This second class was a great improvement upon the first. In time that kind of houses gave way to framed ones as there was opportunity to procure lumber, sawmills having been erected here, and they in their turn were succeeded by better ones. In such rude dwellings, as I have in the first and second places described, were many of their children born and families reared. A very few of the second class were standing fifty years ago, but none now remain, as boards have taken the place of logs in their erection. A large portion of the dwelling-houses that were standing when I first came here are not now, and a great improvement in that direction has taken place. We who live in dwellings so convenient, roomy, and elegant, can hardly conceive, many of us, how they could have lived in such places as they did, and on such fare as they had; but a more healthy and robust generation was produced in those times than is now with us. Many of them were remarkable for their physical strength and powers of endurance.

His next task was to clear his land so that crops might be raised, and if he arrived in the month of June, it was the proper time to fell the trees, as that month is the most suitable for the purpose. A few acres could be cut down the first summer, and when the trees were down the limbs could be lopped, as it is termed, so that the brush could be near the ground. In the first of the fall, when dry, fires could be set and the limbs burnt. After that, the trunks were cut into pieces of proper length to be moved into piles and burnt. They were set on fire before the fall rains came, and about all consumed except the stumps, and the next year he was ready to put in his seed for such crops as he wished to raise. Usually corn was planted at first, as it could be conveniently grown, and in fair seasons it grew bountifully, the land being new and the ashes a powerful stimulant. In those days but few potatoes were raised, as they were not so highly esteemed as at present. If grain were sown it had to be stacked, and afterward it was threshed. No gristmills were here until some years after the first settlers came. Corn then was the favorite crop, as it could be prepared for food by pounding in what was called a samp-mortar. This was made of a hard-wood log with one end hollowed out for the use of a heavy pestle, into the bottom of which nails were thickly driven to enable it to break up the corn more thoroughly. It was then termed samp, and when thus made ready for boiling, formed a valuable addition to their other food. It was also a favorite article of food with the Indians, who raised corn, and thus prepared it, and oftentimes cooked it with green beans, which dish was called succotash.

It was a work of years to clear the land for the plow, as it took a long time for the stumps to rot so that they could be taken out; but usually when they were dried sufficiently, they were set on fire, and the roots, when rotten, could be dug up. As soon as fodder could be raised, cattle were procured, and a cow was a valuable animal to them. Sheep were kept as soon as they could be by them, as their wool was necessary for purposes of manufacture for clothing; flax was also raised for the same purpose, and the cloth was durable if not fine. The implements used in its manufacture are now nearly obsolete; the flax-wheel and hand-card are no longer in use, and the spinning-wheel and hand-loom are soon destined to follow.

As years passed along, his circumstances improved; more land was cleared and greater crops raised, and he could also increase his stock and, consequently, his means of living. In a few years mills were built to grind his grain and corn. Upon every lot of land were logs suitable for lumber, which could be drawn out by oxen to the shore and towed to the sawmill for manufacture. Cordwood could be sold to be carried to Boston or other places in Massachusetts, and the proceeds exchanged for articles of necessity. At first, before he was enabled to keep oxen, it was cut in places convenient to the landings and drawn on hand-sleds. This was a slow and toilsome process, but it was better than to waste it by burning upon the ground, for the little he was paid for it was a help to him. After he could keep a team, he could chop and draw it out in the winter in considerable quantities. Although the price was small, sometimes not exceeding one dollar per cord for the best hard wood, yet it was better than nothing. I recollect hearing an old gentleman say that once he was obliged to sell such wood at the small price of fifty cents per cord upon the landing, and at the same time cloth, then known as India cotton, was fifty cents a yard. In these times perhaps sixty yards of much better cloth might be purchased with the proceeds of one cord of such wood.

In those days there were no roads; the inhabitants lived near the shore, and in order to visit each other they must follow that or go in boats. There were footpaths through the woods in those places where the shore could not be used as a road, which were marked by trees spotted to guide the traveler. It was about twenty-six years after the town was settled before it was incorporated, and until that time every person, if he needed a road, was obliged to make it himself. If a farmer had a grist to carry to mill, and could not go by water, he was obliged to carry it upon his shoulder. I once heard one who was here quite early say that he had at one time three bushels of corn that he was obliged to carry to the Northwest Harbor to mill, which was six miles from his house. He put it into two bags and, starting with one, carried it until he was tired, laid it down, walked back to the place where the other was left, took that up and carried it till he was tired, then rested and started with the other, and in that way transported his corn to, and his meal from, the mill. He was a perfectly reliable man, and I have no doubt of the truth of his statement, for he was of large size and great strength. These little incidents show us what hardships were endured by those who were before us. The chief article of food upon which they relied at first was the clams which were then very abundant in the flats in front of the lots occupied by them, and the seacoast of New England has abounded with them. It was at times the chief reliance of the Pilgrims who settled at Plymouth, without which they would doubtless have perished by starvation. Although it is not a very nourishing kind of food if confined to it, nor so palatable as some other kinds, still there was no fear of the supply being exhausted. It was considered of so much consequence that, in 1641, the Colony of Massachusetts passed an ordinance that, whatever right the owner of land had to the flats left bare at low water in front of his land, he had no exclusive right to the shellfish that might be taken from them; nor had he a right to prevent any one from taking fowl, these being considered rights which others had in common with the owners of the land. This is yet the law of our State. The taking of them for bait for the cod-fisheries has since been quite an important business, and the quantity that has been dug from the flats in this town within the last fifty years has amounted to many thousand barrels, and furnished employment for many. At this time they are put up in cans by the packing companies in their factories in the town. It needed but little time to enable the settler to procure what he needed from day to day, as the supply must be taken at the time of their use, for if kept very long they became unwholesome. During the months of May, June, July, and August they were not so suitable for food as at other times. In the winter and early spring, when the ice covered the shores, it had to be cut through to dig them, which made the labor severe.

The seafish at that time were very abundant; a man could load a small boat in one day, at times. Their boats were made of a large log of wood hewn into proper shape, and dug out, and were termed "log canoes." They have long since gone out of use, and their places supplied by boats of a better kind and much more convenient. A few of the former kind were to be seen sixty years ago, but it is a long time since I have seen one. The fish were at that time much nearer the shore than at present, and it was but little labor to row out where they were and take what was wanted. The chief difficulty was in obtaining salt. There was no place of trade nearer than Fort Point, which was the only place until the British took possession of Bagaduce in 1779, where a market was opened for what they had to sell, and such goods as they needed could be purchased. Salt was manufactured here by boiling sea-water, of which two per cent. only is salt. In order to manufacture it, large kettles or iron pans were set by the shore, the water was pumped up at high water and led into them by spouts and boiled down. The wood used for fuel was conveniently near in abundance, but it was a slow process, as about four hundred gallons of water were necessary to produce one bushel of salt weighing sixty pounds, — but it was an article they must have. One man, Mr. Jonathan Eaton, was for several years engaged in the business, and what he made during the summer he carried up to the towns above Newburyport, on the Merrimack River, the locality whence he came, and sold or exchanged it for produce. The price here was never less than one dollar per bushel, and its quality was about equal to the Liverpool salt at present.

Other kinds of fish were taken, — the herring in weirs made by enclosing the mouth of a creek or cove by brush woven between stakes set or driven into the flats above low-water mark. The top of the hedge was low enough to admit them at high water, but upon the ebb of the tide below the top of it they were detained, and were taken when the flats were bare; they were salted, the larger ones in casks, the smaller cured by smoking. In the winter the frost fish, as they were termed, were taken in considerable quantities at the mouths of brooks, and were acceptable, as it was not the season of fresh fish of other kinds. The smelts could be taken in the same way in the spring, and when lightly salted and cured by drying made a very palatable article of food.

The other source of supply upon which they relied was the seafowl, particularly of the duck kind; they were taken by shooting, netting, and driving. Every one who could procure a gun and ammunition did so, that enabling him easily to secure an abundance of them from the surrounding waters. The practice of netting was by setting large nets on the flats, fastened to stakes, in such a manner as to float and rise with the tide horizontally upon the surface, and when spread covering considerable space; when the fowl swam near the shore, as is their practice, and, diving, came up under the nets, they became entangled, and could be taken. Large quantities were taken in this way, and when dressed, those not wanted for present needs were salted for future use. The feathers were valuable for beds, and were salable, six full-grown ones furnishing one pound of them. The other method was styled duck-driving, and as it has not been practised within the memory of any but the very oldest of our inhabitants, it will be proper to give a description of the manner in which they were taken. For a very few days in the month of August they could not fly, as they were then shedding their quills, or larger feathers. The time was well known to the inhabitants in the places around, in other settlements, and all who could come did so from Penobscot River, from Penobscot, and around the bay, in boats. First a circle of boats was formed so as partially to surround them, and they were also stationed so as to prevent their taking a wrong direction. Duck Harbor, on the southwestern part of Isle au Haut, was the place selected to drive them into, as it was well suited for the purpose, being narrow and extending half a mile or more into the land. Beginning at the upper part of the bay, below Eagle Island, they were driven in for several miles; as this went on, others were overtaken, and by the time they had reached the place of destination a large number were included in the drive. Narrowing the flock as they went along, they were driven into the mouth of the harbor and up to the head of it; when the fowls reached the shore they were taken and killed, and every one engaged in it could have all he needed.

The water, and not the land, is their element. They can swim quite rapidly, but when on landing they attempted to walk they could easily be taken. At one time a very large drive was made, and many, attempting to walk over the land from the head of the harbor to the southern shore of the island, perished in the woods, where their remains were seen for a long time. Such unrestrained slaughter soon had its effect, and they decreased or sought other places in which they could be free from this wholesale destruction. No drive has been made for perhaps eighty years or more. My informant, the late Captain David Thurlow, a man well known here in his day, was present at several of the " drives," and from him I obtained the information given above. He died in 1857, at the age of eighty-two years, and they were a common practice when he was young. From an account given me many years ago, I judge that wild fowls, when they escape from danger, often shun the place afterward. Among the early years of the settlement here the wild geese, going on their flights toward the north, frequently halted and landed upon a particular part of the island, near what is called " Dunham's Point " (the locality of the silver mine which has been opened here), and they also did so on their return in the fall. As this became known persons would lie in wait for the chance to shoot at them; after it had been done a few times they landed there no longer, and for years whenever they passed over that spot, they would rise so much higher than usual upon approaching it as to be above the reach of any shot, coming down again when safely beyond it, to their usual level.

MILLS.

I have no means of ascertaining the date of the erection of the first mill here, but I am inclined to think that it was by Mr. Nathaniel Kent, of Boston, on the site of the mills afterward occupied by Stephen Holt and Richard Warren. Messrs. Mark Haskell & Sons also put up a saw and gristmill at the Northwest Harbor. They purchased the land they occupied there in 1772, of Ezekiel Marshall, who was here before them; but they did not come until a few years after that, and from what information I have been able to obtain it was not until 1778. In the notice of them I shall state more fully about them. Jonathan Greenlaw, who came as early as 1762 or 1763, one of the family of that name who came shortly after, and, next to William Eaton, the first settler, gave a deed to Kent of a tract of land containing a square mile, in consideration of the erection and maintenance of a gristmill. The date of the deed I have never learned, but, if it ever was put on record, it must have been done in the records of the county of Lincoln, in which county we then were, as Hancock County was not incorporated till 1789. Greenlaw had, of course, no title to the land he conveyed, as the title then was in Massachusetts. The mill was afterward occupied by Joseph Tyler, Esq., a native of Dedham, Massachusetts, who came during the latter part of the Revolutionary War. A sawmill was built, whether by Kent or Tyler I do not know. It stood for some years, occupied by Esquire Tyler, and manufactured boards and other lumber from the logs which were then standing in that vicinity. After Tyler moved into another part of the town, the place was occupied by Stephen Holt, who rebuilt the gristmill and ran it till 1842. After his removal the late Hon. Richard Warren built mills there, which were destroyed by fire. The "Kent Claim," as it was called, was a subject of litigation for several years. It covered the land settled by Mr. Joseph Colby, who came here not far from 1766, and the lawsuit was prolonged for several years in the courts of Lincoln County. Mr. Colby had frequently to attend court, and, as the practice was then, the jurors were chosen and could serve as often as they were returned, and he was, while his case was in court, a juryman, as it enabled him to meet his expenses of travel to and from the shire-town, which was Pownalborough, near the towns of Dresden and Wiscasset. He at length prevailed, and the Kent Claim was reduced to 200 acres, the lots occupied by Messrs. Joseph and Belcher Tyler. It afterward passed into the ownership of Mr. Nathaniel Bishop, of Medford, Massachusetts, and some time not far from 1820 he contracted to sell the land to Mr. Stephen Holt, of Andover, Massachusetts, who occupied it till 1842, when he was ousted by Mr. Bishop for non-payment for the land, and it afterward passed into the hands of the late Richard Warren. The saw and gristmill at the Northwest Harbor stood till about 1860. A gristmill was built at the Reach shore in 1837 by Captain John Torrey which has been discontinued some ten years or more, and there is now no saw or gristmill in the town. One of the latter is much needed, for if there were one a considerable amount of grain would be raised in the town; but as it has to be carried out of the town to be ground, the farmers have nearly discontinued its production. It can be as easily raised here as in the towns in the vicinity, and might be with profit. Other sawmills were built: one on Thurlow Island as early as 1800, or before, by Joseph Colby, Jr., and David Thurlow, which manufactured a good deal of lumber in its day. It was destroyed by being blown down in a violent squall, in the early part of the year 1839. Another was maintained several years, known as "Crockett's Mill," till about thirty years ago. Another was formerly standing on Stinson's Neck, near the residence of Mr. Josiah C. Webb, and another on what was known as the Emersons' Mill Pond, not far from the house of Captain Benjamin J. Sylvester. It was built about the year 1790, and went down in 1807.

The first framed dwelling-house in the town was built by Mr. Ezekiel Morey, who came in 1767. I made inquiries of the oldest people, and they all stated that it was standing when they could first remember. The eldest son of the builder, Mr. Elias Morey, who was born in 1761, informed me that he was ten years of age when it was built. That would fix the date at 1771. It was standing less than twenty years ago on the spot at present occupied by the house of Mr. James Jordan, and was known as the Hallet house. The next oldest now standing is the ell part of the house formerly occupied by the late Joseph Raynes, which was put up prior to 1790. It has been repaired within a few years. The next oldest are the houses occupied by Mr. Levi Greenlaw and that of the late Mr. Nathan Eaton. The next is the house built at some time about the years 1793 or 1794, and occupied by the late Ignatius Haskell, Esq., which is still in a good state of preservation. It is at present the property of his granddaughter, Mrs. Rebecca Haskell.

MARRIAGES.

The marriages solemnized between parties residing in the place before the settlement of a minister here in 1773, must have been at the fort on what is now known as Fort Point, by the chaplain of the garrison, Dr. William Crawford. He was the nearest person by whom the ceremony could be performed, and is said to have been the first one who married couples according to Protestant forms on Penobscot River. The fort was named Fort Pownal, and was built in 1759. He was a surgeon as well as chaplain, and served in both capacities under General Wolfe at Quebec. It was some ten years after the settlement was commenced here, till the establishment of a church and the employment of a minister, and during the occupation of Bagaduce by the British, those intending marriage from this place went there for the purpose, as there was a chaplain there. At that time there were no justices of the peace here, for there was no authority to appoint them, as Massachusetts had no governor during the war of the Revolution. Afterward the war appointments were made, and the first ones here were Messrs. Joseph Tyler, Thomas Stinson, and Ignatius Haskell, Esquires.

The first child born of white parents here was Mr. Timothy Billings, in May, 1764. He was born near the shore, on the lot formerly owned by the late Captain Jonathan Torrey, and by his descendants at the present time. His father removed here in 1763, but did not remain long. It has been claimed by some that Mr. John Closson was the first, but it is a mistake. His mother, prior to his birth, went over to the other side of the Reach, and he was born in what is now the town of Sedgwick, March 5, 1764. The first child born at the Northwest Harbor, according to the best information I have, was Joseph Eaton, who settled in Sedgwick, and died there. He was the son of Mr. Jonathan Eaton, and was born in the latter part of the year 1767. Near the Southeast Harbor Mr. Thomas Colby was the first white child born, in April, 1768, and at the Southwest Harbor Thomas Small was born about the same time.

It is worthy of note that the first children born of English parents in this and the two nearest towns, as originally incorporated, lived to a great age. Mr. Billings died in 1854, aged ninety; Mr. Reuben Gray, born in Penobscot, in the present town of Castine, near the site now occupied by the stores in that place, in May, 1763, died in 1859, aged ninety-six; and Elizabeth Black, born in that part of Sedgwick now Brooklin, about 1760, died at the age of nearly one hundred years. At the time of her death she was Mrs. Freethy.

In another part of this book will be found a record of all the persons who have lived to the age of ninety years and upward, since I came here, in 1835. The oldest died in 1879, aged ninety-seven, and there is evidence that only one other person arrived to so great an age before 1835 — Mrs. Colby, the wife of Mr. Joseph Colby, in 1833. She will be further noticed, as she carried the news of the surrender of Lord Cornwallis to Bagaduce, which was the first information the officers of the army stationed there had of the event.

From what has been written we can have some idea of the condition of those who first came here; it required courage to face what they did, and resolution to go through it. We who talk of poverty now should compare our surroundings with theirs. The poorest among us at this day have means to procure what to them would have been luxuries. Their food at best was coarse and often scanty, their clothing would now be considered insufficient to protect the wearer from the cold. We little consider that we are enjoying the fruits of their labors, for their hands cleared the fields we cultivate, and the foundation of our privileges was laid by them. We can show them no gratitude, but we can respect their memories. The worth of too many is not appreciated until they are gone. There are many things in life which cannot be understood unless they come within our experience, and if understood at all, they are so but imperfectly, which makes it difficult for one who lives in other times to correctly write the histories of the past.

I come now to the period of the Revolution, and in another chapter will give the names of such male inhabitants as were here, according to the best information I have been able to acquire. It will be a list of such as were at that time twenty years of age, or nearly, and upward, and the date of their coming, as correctly as I can from what information I have obtained.

CHAPTER II.

FIRST SETTLERS. — THE REVOLUTION. — LAND-TITLES. — INCORPORATION.

THE year 1775 brought the Revolution, and found the Island with a number of settlers. The first permanent settlement was made in 1762 by William Eaton, although he was not the first who began one. The following is a list of the persons referred to at the close of the last chapter. The dates of their coming are as correct as they can now be made.

Eaton, William, Sr.,	1762	Pressey, Chase (son),	1765
Eaton, Eliakim (son),	,,	Pressey, John, Jr. (son),	,,
Eaton, Jeremiah (son),	,,	Richards, Wm., about	,,
Eaton, William, Jr. (son),	,,	Stinson, Thomas, Sr.,	,,
Greenlaw, Alexander,	,,	Stinson, Thomas, Jr. (son),	,,
Greenlaw, Charles,	,,	Thompson, Thomas,	,,
Greenlaw, Ebenezer,	,,	Trundy, Samuel,	,,
Greenlaw, Jonathan,	,,	Webb, Samuel, about	,,
Greenlaw, William,	,,	Webb, Seth,	,,
Billings, John,	1763	Whitmore, Joseph,	,,
Closson, Nathan,	,,	Babbidge, William,	1766
Torrey, J'than, about	,,	Dunham, Elijah, Sr.,	,,
Torrey, David, ,,	,,	Dunham, Elijah, Jr. (son),	,,
Weed, Benjamin, ,,	,,	Dunham, Joseph (son),	,,
Freeze, George, ,,	,,	Colby, Joseph,	,,
Freeze, John, ,,	,,	Dow, John,	1767
Staples, Joshua,	1764	Dow, Nathan,	,,
Staples, Moses,	,,	Eaton, Jonathan,	,,
Linn, Robert,	1765	Hooper, John.	,,
Pressey, John, Sr.,	,,	Morey, Ezekiel,	,

Small, Thomas,	1767	Saunders, Thomas,	1771
Carman, Levi,	1768	Raynes, John, Sr.,	1772
Crockett, Josiah,	,,	Raynes, James (nephew),	,,
Eaton, Theophilus,	,,	Raynes, John, Jr. (son),	,,
Marshall, Ephraim,	,,	Raynes, Sam'l (nephew),	,,
Marshall, Ezekiel,	,,	Sellers, Charles,	,,
Small, Job,	,,	Sellers, Joseph,	,,
Bray, Nathaniel, about	,,	Babbidge, Courtney, Sr.,	1773
Colby, Ambrose, ,,	,,	Robbins, Thomas,	1775
Cole, Benjamin, ,,	,,	Curtis, Lot, date unknown.	
Nason, Robert, ,,	,,	Hardy, Peter, Sr., ,,	,,
Haskell, Francis,	1770	Howard, Ezra, ,,	,,
Haskell, Abijah (son),	,,	Howard, John (son),,	,,
Haskell, Jonathan (son),	,,	Tuttle, Zebulon, ,,	,,
Haskell, Mark, Sr.,	,,	Sixty-nine in all.	

Most of the persons above named were friendly to the American cause, but a few were loyalists, or, as they were then termed, "Tories." Three from this place entered the army, for which they obtained a pension under the first act providing one for the soldiers of the Revolutionary army. Their names were Joseph Whitmore, Samuel Stinson, and Courtney Babbidge, Jr. Mr. Whitmore died in 1841, aged eighty-six; Mr. Stinson in 1847, aged eighty-eight, and Mr. Babbidge not far from the year 1833, in the town of Vinalhaven, over seventy years of age. After the war, Mr. Solomon Barbour, Mr. George Gross, and Mr. James Gibson moved here, where they remained till their deaths; and later, two others came, Mr. John Harvey, who died in 1837, aged eighty-six, and Mr. Judah Coville, who died in 1843, aged eighty-nine years. Mr. Barbour lived, while he resided here, upon what has been known as the "Barbour Farm," owned by Ignatius Haskell, Esq., a part of which has since been owned and occupied by Mr.

Edwin P. Cole. In 1784 came Mr. Micajah Lunt from Newburyport, who was in the naval service; he died in 1827 or 1828, and I believe Mr. Barbour died not far from that time. The wives of all, except Mrs. Harvey, survived their husbands, and some received pensions. Only one person ever resided here, to my knowledge, who was in what is known as the " Old French War," — Mr. Benjamin Weed, who was among the first that came. He was engaged in the siege of Louisburg, on the Island of Cape Breton, the second time an expedition was fitted out from New England to take it from the French, not far from the time that Quebec was taken.

In 1779 the British took possession of the peninsula of Bagaduce, on which the village of Castine now stands, and commenced the erection of a fort. All the inhabitants within their reach were required to perform labor upon it for a certain number of days, which number I never heard, nor did I ever hear that any compensation was paid for it. It was called "working out their tour." In my younger days I used frequently to hear it spoken of by those who were contemporaries with those of that day. It was not safe for any one to refuse, unless a reasonable excuse could be made. The work was hurried on, as the Americans fitted out an expedition for the purpose of retaking it, the fleet composing it arriving in about five weeks after possession was taken, which was in the month of June. It failed of its object, but it is not within the scope of this work to give the reasons of its failure or a history of the expedition. Any one who wishes, may read the History of Castine, by Dr. Wheeler, which gives an account, at considerable length. They also required the inhabitants of the settlements around them, and those on the Penobscot River, to take an oath of allegiance or of neutrality. In most cases this was compulsory, and it might be by some regarded as not morally binding. It was not safe for any to refuse this oath, as it would be likely to render the person refusing an object of suspicion, if not of persecution or arrest. There were some in other settlements who, rather than take it, abandoned their homes and moved away, some of whom returned after the peace, as did William Eaton, the first permanent settler here; but that was not always so easy to do, for all the settlers had was here, and they did, no doubt, the best thing they could under the circumstances. One man named Page, who lived in what is now the town of Brewer, was notified to come and take the oath. He refused, and sent an answer to their summons accordingly, and word was sent him that if he did not come a file of soldiers would be sent to burn his house. To this he replied: " Come on, for I have two loaded guns in my house, and two at least who come will never go back." He was not molested.

Those persons who were loyalists paid frequent visits to Castine, and were suspected of giving information relative to the other settlers who might be considered friendly to the American cause, which obliged them to exercise great caution in all their conduct. Although they were assured by the officers that if they gave no cause for suspicion they would not be molested, yet to be an object of suspicion was too often a reason for arrest, and when taken they might be subjected to such cruel punishments as were inflicted. I do not remember hearing of any person in this place being arrested, but some were in other places and suffered most severely by whipping. One was a Mr. Williams, of Islesborough; another, Mr. Nathaniel Carson, who lived on Cape Rozier. Mr. Jonathan Eaton, of Sedgwick, a son of Mr. Theophilus Eaton, of this place, was informed against by a Tory and was arrested in the evening by a file of soldiers who were guided by the one who gave the information. They started to carry him to Castine; on their way the road led near the top of a high bank by the shore, which was thickly covered with trees, and on their arrival there, he, being a powerful man, shook off those who were on each side of him, jumped down the bank, and in the darkness escaped. In a few minutes he returned to his house, took a few things, and went to Isle au Haut which was then a wilderness, and remained there all the season, not returning until the danger was over.

The punishments that were then given might well have been dreaded. The prisoner was tied up and lashes laid upon his bare back, sometimes by hundreds, with a whip styled a "cat-o'-nine-tails," which had nine lashes and in each lash nine knots. When inflicted in the open air, the screams of the victims might, in calm weather, be heard a long distance, for their sufferings were terrible; often a bullet or something like it was put into their mouths to prevent them from chewing their tongues in their agony. A surgeon stood by in such a severe whipping, to pronounce when it was unsafe to carry it any further; and, if the whole number had not been laid on, he must, after his wounds were healed, receive the remainder. We would not now allow such cruelty, but that was the manner in which their soldiers were punished for some offenses, and what Williams, and Carson, and others as unfortunate, endured. It would have been more merciful to shoot them at once, for their pain would have been short. At most, it would have been murder, but such whippings were worse than murder. The subjects of them ever after felt the consequences; the sense of manhood was crushed out of them, and they became dispirited and morose.

I recollect, some twenty-five years or more ago, making the acquaintance of an old gentleman who then resided on the coast of York County near Wood Island, who had served many years in the capacity of sailmaker in the British navy. He was on board the *Northumberland*, the ship which conveyed Napoleon to St. Helena, and he gave me a description of his personal appearance which corresponded with what has been written concerning it. He was the coxswain of the barge which carried him from the ship to the shore. I asked him concerning the punishments by whipping, which were said to have been practised then on board their ships-of-war, and how it was possible in some cases, that any one could come out of them alive. He informed me that he once witnessed a punishment of five hundred lashes given for desertion, which was a crime most severely punished. The prisoner was sentenced to be flogged "through the fleet," and the manner of its infliction was thus: A large boat was used, upon which a platform was laid, and the frame raised to which the prisoner was lashed. The number of lashes was divided by the number of ships in the fleet that were there at the time; he was rowed from ship to ship, and the boatswain's mate of each administered its quota of lashes. He also informed me that when any one on board was to be whipped, the sailors supplied him with brandy in abundance, with which gunpowder was mixed, so that when the time arrived for the punishment, he was so far intoxicated as to be hardly able to stand, and the operation of what was administered to him enabled him to go through it with little pain comparatively to what it would have been had he been sober. What has been written above may be deemed a digression, but may well be worth remembering as it shows us what those who were here had to fear, if they were subjects of arrest.

In 1781 Cornwallis surrendered, which virtually ended the war, and the news of his surrender was carried to

Castine by a lady of this place, to whom allusion has been made, — the wife of Mr. Joseph Colby. A neighbor of hers, Mr. Seth Webb, who has settled on Kimball's Island in the present town of Isle au Haut, and who also had a residence here a part of the time, — sometimes his family being at one and sometimes at the other place, — happened to be at Isle au Haut when an American vessel anchored in the harbor, the captain of which had a number of handbills which were printed for distribution, announcing the event in its details. One of these he gave Mr. Webb, and he gave it to Mrs. Colby. The inhabitants here were then in the practice of going to Castine to trade, as while the British were there it became a place of considerable importance, and its merchants did, for those times, a large amount of business. Happening to go the next day, she carried the handbill with her, starting in the night, as the weather was favorable, with her two sons to row her up in a boat so as to enable her to reach that place early in the day, the distance from her residence by water being about twenty-five miles. Upon her landing, she was very politely accosted by an officer with: "Well, madam, what news this morning?" Her reply was: "Not much, only there is a rumor that my Lord Cornwallis has surrendered." He instantly checked her, saying, "It will not do to bring such news here." Asking her for her authority, she instantly drew out her paper and handed it to him; on reading it, he requested her to loan it to him for an hour, promising to return it, and soon a messenger was sent to request the lady who brought it to go with him before the officers, who, after they had read it, said: "We fear the news is too true."

One great cause of annoyance was the practice that there was of plundering the inhabitants on the seacoast in this vicinity, by persons who went about for that purpose in boats which were then styled "shaving-mills." They committed their depredations in places where they were not known. They would land upon the shore, visit the houses of the inhabitants, and steal whatever they could lay their hands on, which was a cause of distress to the persons plundered, as they had but little, and that little they wanted themselves. It was useless to make any complaint, as there was then no redress to be had. The British, it is true, held possession here, but it was military possession. If any one in their service committed such acts, he was severely punished by whipping upon proof sufficient to procure conviction, for to their honor it must be said that their officers strictly prohibited plunder of the inhabitants, and any one who was detected well knew what were the consequences. It was done by lawless persons from other places. I recollect hearing an old gentleman, who, during that period, was a child, say that upon one time such a boat landed near the house of his father, and upon the entering of the house by the persons who came in it, they saw his father's gun standing near the fireplace, which they took and carried away. His mother was alone in the house, with the exception of her little children. Upon his father's return, when he found his gun was gone, he was enraged, saying that he had rather parted with a cow, as a gun was necessary for his procuring a living by shooting fowl and game. The practice was not confined to the seacoast, for I heard another old gentleman say that during the war his father was visited by such people, led by a Tory in the vicinity, who took his oxen from him and drove them away, and the next spring he had to dig up his ground with his hoe to put in the seed. This took place in what is now Brooksville, near Walker's Pond.

In 1783 peace was proclaimed; the British troops abandoned Castine, and those who were loyalists here went with them. They left behind the fruits of twenty years' toil, which to them was labor lost. Only two, the sons of one of them, returned, who remained here till death. They doubtless feared that the results of the prejudice existing against them here might be to their annoyance, if not to their injury; but perhaps had they remained and accepted the situation under the new order of things, it would have gradually worn away. In a few years they would have acquired a title to their lands, which were as valuable for farming purposes as any in the town. Many other Tories from other parts of the country abandoned their estates and went into the Provinces. Their possessions, in some cases large, were confiscated, and they lost all. They were then styled refugees, and many of the present inhabitants of New Brunswick and Nova Scotia are their descendants. They were rewarded for their loyalty by grants of land, but it was in the wilderness of New Brunswick and among the rocks of Nova Scotia. They carried with them an intense hatred of the government here, which has in some degree been transmitted to their posterity. During the war for the suppression of the great rebellion a stronger sympathy for the South was nowhere manifested than there, and in some places and at some times it was not safe for any one to avow Union sentiments.

I have sometimes thought that sufficient charity was not exercised toward the Tories, for there can be no doubt as to their sincerity, and we must consider that there are always two sides to a question. Loyalty was to them a sacred principle, in which they had been early educated and had grown up. The injunction of St. Peter, to " honor the king," coupled as it is with that to " fear God," had to them great significance, for if the one was binding, as we must all admit, why was not the other? We can afford to be charitable and just in the matter, even if we do not indorse their principles, for there was another light in which it might have been viewed that is entitled to consideration. The British government had, within the memory of the oldest among them, crushed out two rebellions with great severity, and when the Revolution commenced, they might well consider that there was no reasonable prospect of its success. In their opinion it was a contest between weakness and power, and in the event of its failure they would have been on the safe side, and what could those on the other hope for? Had it failed, could we have reasonably expected that such men as John Hancock and Samuel Adams would have been permitted to die in their beds, should the British government have obtained possession of them? Although there were acts of violence between the Whigs and Tories in other places, I never learned of any here, as there was too great a disproportion between them, for the Tories were but few in comparison to their opponents, and all they could do was to carry information to the officers at Castine. The others were kept in awe in consequence of the fears entertained of the troops there, who would speedily retaliate if any injury were inflicted upon their loyal friends. Only one act of injury ever came to my knowledge, which was that of the crew of an American privateer upon one of the Tories here, a member of that family which moved away at the close of the war, who was either carried or enticed on board of the vessel, while she lay at anchor not far from his place of residence. He was forced to go into the main-top, where he was fired at, not with the intention to kill, but to see how near the bullets could go and not hit him, — an act of cruelty and cowardice. His terror while it was being done was so great as to cause insanity.

LAND-TITLES.

When the settlers first came here it was not altogether certain to whom the territory belonged. The first grant in which its description is included was that made by James the First, in 1620, to the Plymouth Company in England, as that embraced all the land lying between the 40th and 48th parallels of latitude. Afterwards the Earl of Sterling had a grant of all the State as far west as Pemaquid, now in the town of Bristol. It was surrendered in 1686 to the Province of Massachusetts, and in a few years after conferred on her. In 1783, some twenty years after settlements were begun here, it was secured to her by the treaty of that year, and that fully established the ownership. Not far from the year 1788 the General Court of Massachusetts passed a resolve granting one hundred acres of land to each of the persons who had settled on Deer Island and Sheep, now Jordan's, Island, previous to the first day of January, 1784; and Messrs. Joseph Tyler and George Tyler, Esquires, were appointed a committee to cause said lots of land to be surveyed and allotted to the several persons entitled to receive them, and were empowered to give deeds of the same which lots were to include the improvements made by each settler, and the sum of thirty shillings was required to be paid by each to defray the expense of the survey. Those persons who had purchased the right of such as would have been entitled to said lots were included in the allotments. The deeds of the Messrs. Tyler that I have seen bear date January 1, 1789. The survey was made by William Tupper, and the lots were laid out large, actually containing more than one hundred acres each. Most of the persons named in the list just given received their allotments, excepting some who had sold their rights, and their assigns received them, and some others who had moved in since 1775, and others who had become of age and taken up lots. Those persons who are above described were styled "proprietors," in speaking of whom, they or their assigns will be meant. Another class who had lands allotted to them, who had settled after the first day of January, 1784, and before a certain date, were called "young settlers," and had one hundred acres each upon the payment of one dollar per acre. The Messrs. Tyler obtained a grant of the remainder of the island, which gave great dissatisfaction, as the settlers had held a meeting and chosen a committee to go to the General Court at Boston for the purpose of purchasing the land remaining after the settlers' lots had been set off. The committee appointed were Messrs. Joseph Tyler and Thomas Thompson. They being unable to attend, Messrs. George Tyler and Levi Carman were appointed in their stead, but the latter, being at the time master of a vessel, was also unable to attend and committed the business to George Tyler, Esq., who instead of acting for the settlers, obtained a grant in the name of himself and his brother as above stated. The price was small for the quantity of land (I am now unable to ascertain it without trouble), but they failed to pay according to the contract in the grant, and the proprietors afterward purchased it. They caused a survey of the most valuable lots and sold them; the balance, amounting to thirty-four acres for each proprietor, was afterward surveyed in lots of nineteen and fifteen acres, and each one drew one of each quantity. The first survey of proprietors' lands was made by Mr. William Young, not long after the year 1800, and the second by a surveyor named Flye in about 1815; but previous to this, in 1798, a survey of the settlers' lots was made the second time by Mr. John Peters, Jr., of Bluehill, who cut down each settler's lot to one hundred acres exactly, which was a deduction from the amount allotted in the survey made by Tupper, by order of the Messrs. Tyler as a committee, as named before. In the grant to the Tylers the "Kent Claim" was made valid, but before the proprietors obtained theirs, the case of Kent *v.* Colby had been decided in favor of Mr. Colby, the defendant.

INCORPORATION.

In January, 1789, the town was incorporated, the act of incorporation including "Great Deer Island, Little Deer Island, Isle au Haut, and Sheep Island," but between Great Deer Island and Isle au Haut were several islands, some of which had been settled prior to that time. Merchant's Island had been settled in 1772 by Mr. Anthony Merchant, who came from York in the State of Maine, then Massachusetts; Kimball's Island was settled as early as the Revolutionary War by Mr. Seth Webb, whom we shall notice; but Isle au Haut was not settled till 1792 by Mr. Peletiah Barter, who came from Baxter's Island in the present town of Boothbay; Wreck Island was occupied by Mr. Joseph Colby, Jr., and Thurlow's Island by Mr. David Thurlow prior to 1800. The inhabitants of all lying between Deer Island and Isle au Haut had all the privileges of citizens here; their schools were maintained by the town; they were considered as gaining a legal settlement in the town after five years' residence, and such persons as fell into distress in other towns, by residence upon those islands were considered as chargeable to this town, and no question was ever raised, notwithstanding they were not included in the act of incorporation until after the late war, when the burdens of taxation were heavy, in consequence of the large expense incurred. They then — after substitutes had been put into the army and the quota of men furnished by the town for their benefit as well as that of others — attempted to resist the payment of their share of taxes, on the ground of not being included in the act of incorporation, when the amount paid by them for war purposes was small in proportion to their numbers in comparison with that paid by the town at large; and none of them ever entered into the service of the United States, which they would have been obliged to do, if drafted, as they would have received no town bounty (which was not less than one hundred dollars, and at the last call for troops, in 1864, it was three hundred), had they not been considered as belonging in the town.

In order to prevent any litigation, the selectmen drew up a petition to the Legislature, which was acted upon in 1868, and the territorial limits of the town were established, embracing those islands, and legalizing the assessment and collection of all taxes otherwise legally assessed upon their inhabitants. The limits of the town as then established were as follows: " Beginning at the middle of the Reach opposite the northwestern end of Little Deer Island; thence southeasterly by the middle of said passage to the southeastern end of same, including Conary's, York's, or White, Islands, and Gibson's Island; thence southwesterly so as to include Great Spoon Island; thence to the southwestern extremity of Isle au Haut; thence up the Ship Channel northerly to the western end of Great Deer Island, and thence northerly to the place begun at, excluding Pickering's, Eaton's, and Pumpkin Islands." In 1874 the town of Isle au Haut was incorporated, which included all islands within the above limits, with Merchant's and all islands lying southerly of it.

The grant to the settlers provided that four hundred acres of land should be reserved for ministerial, and the same quantity for school, purposes; and when the proprietors had their survey made by John Peters, Jr., the " parsonage lot," so called, was set off in one body near the Northwest Harbor, of which the first settled minister was to have one hundred; and the lands allotted for the use of schools were in separate lots in different places. The first census taken after incorporation in 1790 found the town containing 682 inhabitants; the numbers for 1800, 1810, and 1820, I have never seen; in 1830 there were 2,217; in 1840, 2,841; in 1850, 3,037; in 1860, 3,592; in 1870, 3,414; and the number for 1880 was 3,268, besides Isle au Haut, 270. I have, in what has been written, given some idea of what was the condition of the settlers here up to 1789. With them things had improved from 1762 till that time, and they have been going on in that direction since, and in no other particular so great as in the means of transportation and communication; for, instead of the slow sailing-vessels of those times, which sailed occasionally from here, we now have some five or six steamers touching here at least twice each week on their passages each way. One can start at noon on one day and be in Boston the next morning, while under the state of things since my remembrance, it was sometimes a passage of ten days in a "wood coaster." We can now send by mail for two cents what in former days cost twenty-five, and in ten days or less it can be carried from Maine to California; and we now have the telegraph here. Although the improvement has been so great in almost everything, still we perhaps do not enjoy life better than they did. An increase of means brings with it one of wants, and as our incomes increase, so do our expenses.

CHAPTER III.

Notices of Settlers and Early Inhabitants.

MICHAEL CARNEY. — He was said to have been the first white man who attempted a settlement in the town. He was a native of Ireland, and was here as early as 1762, at least. He made his settlement on what is now the farm of Mr. George C. Hardy, on the northern shore of the island. The place where his habitation stood is still known, and was shown to me by Mr. Hardy a few years ago. How long he remained here is not known, as very few seem to have heard anything about him, and what little is known is through tradition. How long he came before Mr. William Eaton is not known, but in all probability it was not long, perhaps the same year. He moved from the place of his settlement to an island lying between Great and Little Deer Islands, which to this day bears his name; and from that place he removed, and all traces of him have been lost. Whether he had a family or not is not known.

WILLIAM EATON was the first man who made a permanent settlement here, and it was said to be in 1762. I have judged that his native place might have been Haverhill, Massachusetts, or that vicinity, as he was a cousin to Theophilus and Jonathan Eaton, who were born there, and he was about the age of the first named. He was married in York, Maine, to a member of the family of Mr. Eliakim Wardwell of that place, in 1742. I have been told that her maiden name was Ruth, but the records of York show that the marriage was between Mr. William Eaton and Miss Meribah Wardwell. There is a tradition that before her birth her mother was taken captive by the Indians, and while in captivity was compelled to become the wife of one of the chiefs, and that Mrs. Eaton was the fruit of their union. Some of her descendants seem to show the probability of such an origin. Mr. Eaton was described to me by one of his granddaughters as a man of a light complexion; she was born in 1776, and well remembered him.

On the return of peace between the tribe by which she was held in captivity and the white people, Mrs. Wardwell was delivered up to her husband with her child. She afterward had children, the youngest of whom, Mr. Daniel Wardwell, settled in the town of Penobscot, where he died in 1803. He was the father of Colonel Jeremiah Wardwell, a man of note there, who died in 1825. A sister of Mrs. Eaton was the mother of Captain Joseph Perkins, one of the settlers in Castine, who was there in 1779 when the British took possession of the place. He was one of the most prominent men of that town till his death in 1818, and was, with Colonel Wardwell, one of the first board of selectmen in the town of Penobscot, in 1787. The father of Eliakim Wardwell was Mr. Samuel Wardwell, who suffered death during the delusion of witchcraft. He was a resident of Andover, Massachusetts; his father, whose name was Thomas Wardwell, was the first of the family who came over from England. Mr. Eaton, or, as he was called, Major Eaton, settled on what is now the Scott farm, near the steamboat landing. He resided there several years, when he sold out his possession to Mr. Nathaniel Scott, of what was then the town of Ward, now Auburn, in the county of Worcester, Massachusetts. He was the ancestor of all of that name here. His son, Mr. John Scott, occupied the farm after him. A daughter, Martha Scott, was the wife of Mr. Asa Green, who came here from Worcester County, and who will be noticed hereafter.

After the sale of his right to Mr. Scott, Major Eaton moved to Little Deer Island, where he occupied the farm that was owned by Mr. Peter Hardy, Jr., at the time of his death in 1859. What time he moved there I never knew, nor do I know the time of his death. His farm there, after he died, passed into the possession of Mr. Benjamin Weed, his son-in-law. Major Eaton left four sons and two daughters: Eliakim, who settled on Little Deer Island and died there; Jeremiah, who settled on the farm since owned and occupied by the late Captain Amos Howard, and now by his widow; William, who settled on the lot now owned and occupied by Mr. William E. Powers and Mr. Francis M. Holden, dying not far from the year 1841; and Samuel, whose descendants live in the town of Brooklin. His daughters were the wives of Mr. Jonathan Torrey and Mr. Benjamin Weed.

GREENLAW. — The next persons who came were five by the name of Greenlaw. They settled on Campbell's Neck, now the farm of Mr. Samuel W. Campbell, and that of Mr. William Foster's heirs — in all about five hundred acres. Their names were Jonathan, Charles, Alexander, Ebenezer, and William, and whether they were all brothers or not I do not know. They were natives of Scotland, who had emigrated from that country not long before, and were endeavoring to find a place to settle upon with which they might be suited. The places they took up were satisfactory and they commenced settlements. After the occupation of Bagaduce by the British in 1779, they made frequent visits there, as they were zealous loyalists, and were suspected of carrying information,— a cause of displeasure to their neighbors, who were almost all friendly to the American cause. They were the persons before spoken of as going with the British in 1783 to the Provinces, where they settled, and where their descendants still reside.

Some time after, two of the sons of Jonathan Greenlaw, Messrs. William and Richard Greenlaw, came back and remained till their deaths. They were brought back by the brothers-in-law of Mr. William Greenlaw, — Messrs. Joseph Whitmore and Captain Seth Hatch, — who went after them in a vessel.

JOHN BILLINGS. — He was the person who settled the lot lying southeasterly of, and adjoining that of Mr. Eaton, on the shore of the Reach. He came here from Boston in 1763, and was the father of Mr. Timothy Billings, noticed as the first child born of white parentage in the town. How many years he resided here is not known, but it could not have been many, as his name does not appear among those who were styled proprietors. Whom he sold his right to we do not know, but at the time of Peters' survey, in 1798, Mr. Josiah Closson held it. Whether the precise spot occupied by him can now be pointed out is to us unknown. From what information we have we should judge that he removed to Sedgwick. His sons were: Benjamin, who lived in that town, at what is called Sargentville, on the farm since occupied by his son, Mr. Nathan Billings; Abel, who lived and died in Sedgwick; Isaac, and Solomon, both deacons of the Baptist Church, who lived and died in Brooksville, the former on the place now occupied by Frederick Billings, Esq., his son; the latter on the northwest side of Walker's Pond; Timothy, who occupied the northwestern lot on Little Deer Island, now owned by Mr. Michael D. Snowman; and Daniel, his youngest son, who lived on the land now occupied by his son, Mr. Edward C. Billings. There was another son, John Billings, who died a young man, and a daughter was the wife of Mr. Samuel Howard who took up the farm lying between those of Messrs. Timothy and Daniel Billings, afterward owned by Captain John Gray.

NATHAN CLOSSON. — He settled upon the lot of land adjoining that of Mr. Billings, on the southeast. He came, as has been understood, from Connecticut in 1763. He died not many years after that, but the date is to us unknown. His widow was entitled to a settler's right, which was occupied by her son, Mr. John Closson. Their children were: John, Josiah, and Nehemiah, who will be noticed. One of the daughters was the wife of Mr. Benjamin Billings, of Sedgwick; another was Mrs. Long, mother of the late Mr. Joel Long, who lived in East Bluehill, and owned a sawmill there, and another was the wife of Mr. John Carter, of Sedgwick.

It was the family of Mr. Closson who captured the deer which was seen swimming across the Reach, of which an account has been before given. His son, Mr. John Closson, whose first wife was a Miss Tobin, and his second a Miss Snow, remained upon the place until his death in March, 1854, aged ninety years. His sons by the former were: Captain John Closson, who lived in Bluehill and died there, and Mr. Isaac Closson, who resided in Searsport; and by his last wife the present Franklin Closson, Esq. His daughters were the wives of Mr. Ephraim Crockett, Captain Jonathan Bray, Mr. John Saunders, and Mr. Isaac Bray, and another married in Boston. They are all now dead, with the exception of the last, who was living a few years ago. Mr. Josiah Closson remained here some years, and his wife was a sister of the first wife of Mr. John Closson. He sold his farm to Captain Jonathan Torrey and removed to Sedgwick, where he died. One of his sons was Mr. Ephraim Closson, who traded near the meetinghouse in North Sedgwick, where he died several years ago. The youngest son of Mr. Nathan Closson was Deacon Nehemiah Closson, who filled that office for many years in the First Congregational Church here. He was a man much respected, and was considered a true Christian. By trade he was a blacksmith, and many years ago had a shop situated between the place now occupied by the house of Mr. William H. H. Spofford and the Masonic Building, but which was afterwards removed and placed near his house. This house, where he died not far from thirty years ago, is still standing beside that of Dr. F. B. Ferguson. His wife was Miss Sophia Johnson, who survived him several years, dying at the age of ninety-one years, as did the wife of Mr. John Closson, who died in 1862 at the same age. The son of Deacon Closson was Mr. George C. Closson, who removed from this town to the town of Fairfield, Somerset County, in this State, nearly forty years ago. His daughters were the wives of Mr. Joshua Chatto; of a Mr. Carter, in Bluehill, or Brooklin; of Captain John C. Bray, and afterward of Mr. Samuel Candage, of Bluehill; and the youngest, of Mr. Carruth, of Boston.

THOMAS THOMPSON. — He settled upon the land adjoining that of Mr. Closson on the southeast. He removed here from Massachusetts not far from the year 1765. He was a man of a great deal of energy, and in his time was one of the most prominent and enterprising citizens of the town, and one of its selectmen. He was of small stature, but he possessed a great share of courage, being perfectly fearless, was very active in what he undertook, and what he lacked in size he made up in what is generally termed " pluck."

He was the owner of more than one allotment of land — about three hundred acres — as appears by the plan of Peters' survey. His death took place not far from the year 1824, at the age of more than eighty years. His wife, a very worthy woman, the sister of Mr. William Foster, died at the age of ninety-one. They were the parents of the late Mr. Adam Thompson, whose family consisted of nine sons and five daughters, all of whom lived to the age of manhood and womanhood. They were the late Messrs. John, Solomon, Adam, Jr., and Edward B. Thompson, and Captains Dudley and Hiram Thompson, with others who are now deceased. Another son of Mr. Thomas Thompson was Captain John Thompson, who was in his day an enterprising master-mariner, and who died in Philadelphia; and another, who was named Thomas, died when a young man. The daughters were the wives of Major Nathan Low, Mr. Joseph Sellers, a Mr. Hazen, who lived in Bridgton, Cumberland County, Mr. Nathaniel Kennison, of Sedgwick, Colonel Edward Barnes, of Boston, and Mr. John Howard, Jr.

STAPLES. — The occupant of the land adjoining that of Mr. Thompson on the southeast was a man named Staples. His widow, Mrs. Mercy Staples, with Joshua and Moses Staples, seems to have been here very early, not far from 1764. In all probability the sons above named were then quite young. Mr. Joshua Staples, in whose name the lot appears on the Peters' plan, married a daughter of Mr. John Raynes, Sr., and had one daughter, Jane Staples, the wife of Mr. Elias Morey, Jr., who lived and died on Swan's Island. Mr. Moses Staples moved to Swan's Island, where he died in 1845, aged over ninety years. Mrs. Mercy Staples herself had a settler's right, since known as the "Granny Lot," she having been called "Granny Staples." She had a deed from the Tylers, and it passed from her to her son-in-law, Mr. Thomas Conary, by whom it was conveyed to the late Pearl Spofford, Esq., and is now held by his heirs. The lot set off to Joshua Staples afterward became the property of Mayor Nathan Low, and is now held by his heirs.

There was another son of Mrs. Staples who must at that time have arrived at manhood, — the father of Mr. Samuel

Staples, who died at Green's Landing in 1841, aged seventy-three years. He had a younger son also, named William, and two daughters, — one the wife of Mr. Stephen Babbidge, and the other the wife of Mr. Timothy Saunders. He was impressed on board of an English ship-of-war during the Revolution, when that iniquity was practised. He was never heard of after that, and probably died while in the service. His wife afterwards married a Mr. Hutchinson, of Sedgwick, by whom she had two sons and one daughter. The sons were Rev. David Hutchinson, a presiding elder in the Methodist Episcopal Church, in the western part of the State, and Mr. Timothy Hutchinson, who lived here many years and died on Little Deer Island; and the daughter was Susan, the wife of Captain Benjamin Gray, of Penobscot.

ROBERT LINN was the occupant of the lot adjoining the Staples lot on the south. Of him we know comparatively little, for he left no descendants here. He came in 1765, and probably lived a number of years on his lot, but at some time he conveyed his property to Joseph Tyler, Esq., for his support. Mr. Tyler lived many years upon it and died there, as will be stated more particularly when we notice him among the inhabitants of that part of the town where he first had his residence. The farm is now occupied by Mr. James Tyler, and upon it are large quantities of marble. The Marble Company some years ago purchased the right on the property of Mr. Tyler, erected a large building upon the premises, and put in machinery, but it proved a failure and was abandoned after some two or three years of operation. Whether it is of value or not we cannot say, but there are large quantities of it in the vicinity.

JONATHAN TORREY. — He was the settler nearest to Mr. Linn on the southeast, but not on the adjoining lot, for that was afterward the property of Mr. Thompson. Mr. Torrey lived about three fourths of a mile from Mr. Linn.

He came from Falmouth, Maine, which then embraced the city of Portland and the present towns of Deering, Westbrook, and Falmouth. There are persons of that name now in the town of Deering. He came in about the year 1763, and in 1767 married a daughter of Mr. William Eaton, and after her death married a Mrs. Robinson, a daughter of the Mrs. Mercy Staples before spoken of. Another person named David Torrey was here, who had a settler's right, but did not stop many years, as no separate lot was assigned him. He was perhaps a brother of the subject of this sketch. In all probability he assigned his right to Jonathan Torrey, as he had a two-hundred-acre lot. Mr. Jonathan Torrey lost his life by the capsizing of a boat near Cape Rozier, when returning home from Castine. His oldest son, David, was in the boat, and, being more vigorous, was able to keep upon its bottom, and for a while kept his father upon it with him; as the water was cold, Mr. Torrey became chilled, fell off, and was drowned, but David was soon after rescued. It has been stated that a certain man belonging to the town, who is now dead, passed them when they were both upon the bottom of the boat, but made no effort to save them, and afterward admitted that he saw them. By his first wife Mr. Torrey had five sons. David (born in 1768), who left no children and whose widow died in 1879 at the age of ninety-seven years. Another was William who married a daughter of Mr. Ambrose Colby; after his death she became the wife of Mr. Amos Gordon. Their children were Mr. Hezekiah Torrey, who was the representative from this town in 1822; Mr. William Torrey, formerly well known here, who died on his passage to California around Cape Horn; and Eliza, who was the first wife of John P. Johnson, Esq. A third son was Captain Jonathan Torrey who was born in 1774 and died in 1848, of smallpox.

He was the father of the present Mr. David and of Captains William and Belcher T. Torrey. Another of the sons was Mr. Daniel Torrey, who was the father of the late Captains Samuel, Daniel S., George W., Davis H., and Francis H. Torrey, and of Mr. John Torrey, who lived and died on Newbury Neck in the town of Surry. One of his daughters who was formerly the wife of Mr. Johnson, is now the widow of the late Captain Jeremiah Hatch. The fifth brother was the late Captain John Torrey, who left no children. By his second marriage Mr. Torrey had four sons: James, the father of Messrs. Amos, James, the late Charles S., and Henry Torrey, and of one daughter, who was the first wife of Mr. George C. Hardy. His other sons were Mr. Levi Torrey, who lived and died on Swan's Island; Deacon Asa Torrey, who died in Ellsworth, and the late Captain Ebenezer Torrey, the father of Mr. Nelson Torrey, and of the wife of Franklin Closson, Esq. By the first marriage there were three daughters, who were the wives of Nathan Haskell, Esq., Mr. Jonathan Eaton, and Mr. Nathaniel Webster who removed to Cape Elizabeth. Two of the daughters were afflicted with insanity — Mrs. Haskell and Mrs. Webster — and what was very singular, the one was rational while the other was insane. A part of the time one would be afflicted, and, when she recovered, the other would be taken insane. The real estate of Mr. Torrey is still owned and occupied by his descendants; the larger part was owned by the late Captain Daniel S. Torrey, and is now owned by members of his family.

WILLIAM FOSTER was the nearest settler to Mr. Torrey on the southeast. He came, as we have understood, from Dedham, Massachusetts, and was by trade a blacksmith. In those days that trade was employed in the manufacture of many articles that are now by machinery made a specialty. Axes, both broad and narrow, and other edge-tools, hoes, pitchforks, ox-chains, and plow-irons, — for those were the days of the clumsy wooden plows, which have long since gone out of use, — and other articles which were rudely manufactured in comparison with those of our day. Of him Deacon Nehemiah Closson learned his trade, at which he wrought almost all his days. Mr. Foster settled upon a part of the land formerly occupied by the Greenlaw family; whether he came here before they left or not is unknown to us, but as he had a two-hundred-acre lot it is probable that he purchased the rights of one of them at least, which with his own would entitle him to that quantity. Both he and his wife died here many years ago, leaving a large family, for they were the parents of thirteen children, as I have understood. Only two of his sons remained, who both died here, — Messrs. William and Samuel H. Foster, the former the father of Mr. George Foster, and the latter of Mr. William H. and Charles H. S. Foster, and of two daughters, one the present wife of Mr. Admiral G. Sawyer, and the other a Mrs. Smith, now residing in Boston. Mr. Foster, Sr., had one daughter, who was the wife of Captain John Howard, Jr., who died about fifty years ago of a cancer. Another was the wife of Mr. David J. Waters, who published a newspaper in Castine about the year 1800. After his death she married a Mr. Stephen Kidder, not a resident here, by whom she had a daughter. Upon his death, she removed to this town, and for many years kept a boarding-house in what was known as " the Aaron Haskell house," near that occupied by the late William S. Green, Esq. She afterwards married Mr. Samuel Obear, of Sedgwick, and they went to live at Lowell, Massachusetts, where Mrs. Susan MacIntire, the daughter above mentioned, resided, and where she remained until her death. The real estate of Mr. Foster is now only in part occupied by his descendants.

JOHN CAMPBELL. — He was the occupant of the lot adjoining that of Mr. Foster on the south. He was a large landed proprietor, owning one lot of two hundred acres, another known as the Campbell's Neck lot of seventy-seven, and the island near known as Campbell's Island, of eighty-eight acres. It is probable that he purchased the rights of some of the Greenlaw family, as he would of his own right be entitled to but one hundred acres. He was a native of Argyleshire in Scotland, and born, according to the inscription on his gravestone, about the year 1730, as he died in 1820 aged ninety years, as is there stated. He served for several years on board an English ship-of-war, but before his coming here resided in Portsmouth, New Hampshire. The name of his wife was Mary Blunt. After the commencement of the Revolutionary War he wished to remain neutral, alleging that the struggle with such a power as Great Britain would be vain, as the Americans were too weak to be successful in the contest with her; but those were times when neutrality was not tolerated, and as he became an object of suspicion from such a desire he prudently removed from that place. Whether he came here directly after leaving there is to us unknown, nor is the time of his coming, but it was probably during the latter part of the war, for the Greenlaws left in 1783, and it must have been prior to their leaving if he purchased the rights of any of them. He remained here till his death. There has been some doubt as to his age, some considering that he was over one hundred years of age from his stating that he had known of two rebellions in his time, one of which was in 1745. If he meant that the other was that of 1715, he must have been much older than ninety years, but it is probable that one which he styled a rebellion was the Revolution. It is to be presumed that his family knew more than others about the matter, and that the date of his birth was what is above stated. He left three sons, Messrs. Robert, George, and James Campbell, and two daughters, one was the wife of Captain Peter Hardy, Jr., and the other was first the wife of Mr. Dudley Carlton, of Sedgwick, and afterward of Mr. Frederick Carman. Captain George Campbell was a resident of Newburyport, Massachusetts, at the time of his death, in 1828, at the age of forty-eight years, and the time of the death of Mr. James Campbell is to us unknown. Mrs. Hardy died not far from 1841, and Mrs. Carman in 1874, aged ninety years. Captain Robert Campbell was the occupant of the larger part of his father's estate. He died in 1866, at the age of ninety-two years. He was the father of the present Mr. Samuel W. Campbell and of a daughter, Mrs. Mary Foss, who died in Dubuque, in the State of Iowa. He was for many years a master-mariner, and, we believe, sailed from Newburyport, where he married his wife. He made several voyages to the West Indies, and after he quitted that business resided the remainder of his life upon his farm. There were not many years' difference in the death of himself and that of his wife, and she was over eighty years of age at her death. They had another son, Captain Robert Campbell, Jr., who resided near New York, and who died many years ago. His son, Mr. Samuel W. Campbell, now owns and occupies his real estate.

THOMAS STINSON, Esq., was the first settler on what is known as Stinson's Neck. He came from Woolwich, Maine, in 1765. He used to say that he might have secured a far more valuable claim than the one he did, for the most desirable parts of the island, later, were not then taken up; but the place he selected was very convenient for the procuring of seafowl and fish, both sea and shell, much more so than on some other parts. That was a great object with them, for the time it required to put the land in order to obtain crops was long, and in the meantime a supply must be had which could be procured as it was needed. In the vicinity of his residence was a very convenient place to take fowl by netting, the process of which has before been explained; the method was far preferable to the taking of them by shooting, for when shot at many times they became more shy and avoided the place where it was done. He was a man of piety, and was one of the deacons of the church when first established here in 1773, and it has been said of him that the first religious meeting that ever assembled in the town, was held by him. Its occasion was the regret of his wife, expressed one Sabbath day, that they could not have the privilege of attending one as in the place they came from, and he answered that she might have it on the next Sabbath day, and accordingly when the day came he took his wife and family with him to the place where a large tree stood near his house, and under its shade he performed the services usual on such occasions, reading a sermon. He was one of the first persons, as before mentioned, who held the commission of a justice of the peace here. In his day he was considered a man of integrity, and had considerable influence. His sons were: Thomas, Samuel, William, and John. One of his daughters was the wife of Mr. Thomas Robbins, Jr., and the mother of the late Mr. William G. Robbins, and of the wives of the late Mr. Richard Greenlaw, 2d, and Captain Asa Richardson, who is now, in 1881, living at the age of eighty-six years. Another daughter was the wife of Mr. George Adams, and the mother of the wife of Mr. Henry W. Hallett who died here nearly forty years ago, and also the mother of the present Mrs. Saunders, the widow of the late Mr. Asa Saunders. The real estate of Mr. Stinson passed into the hands of his son, the late Mr. John Stinson, and is now the property of Mr. Hardy Lane.

His son, Mr. THOMAS STINSON, Jr., will be noticed in another place.

SAMUEL STINSON settled upon the lot adjoining that of his father. His birth took place not far from the year 1758, and he enlisted in the military service during the war of the Revolution. It has been told of him that when placed as a sentry at one time, he was ordered, if he heard or saw anything that was suspicious, to challenge by saying, " Who goes there? " three times, and if no answer was made to fire, and that while on duty one night he had occasion to challenge; instead of saying it three different times, he said, " Who goes there three times? " and upon receiving no answer fired. After his term of service had expired he returned home, married Miss Hannah Babbidge, and settled upon the lot he occupied till his death, which took place not far from the year 1847. He was an upright and reliable man, and for fifty years a church member. His sons were: James, Thomas, Samuel, Aaron, and Simon. All, with the exception of Thomas, remained here. His daughters were the wives of Mr. George Freeze, of Ellsworth, of Mr. Solomon Crockett, of Prospect, and of Mr. Josiah Barbour, of this town.

WILLIAM STINSON took up a lot of land lying south of that of his brother Samuel, and occupied it till his death, in 1848, or about that time. His first wife was a Miss York, by whom he had his family; after her death he married a Miss Polly Calef, and when she died he married the widow of Mr. William Webb. He was one of the deacons of the Congregational Church for many years, and when I first came here, he, with his colleague, Deacon

Closson, used to occupy the deacons' seat, as it was called, in front of, and below, the high, old-fashioned pulpit in the meetinghouse that was burnt down, which stood on the spot now occupied by the present one. He was a man of dignified appearance, and had a good share of what is called " common sense," the most valuable of all kinds of sense. He represented the town in 1825 in the Legislature at Portland, and through all his long life was much respected. The men of those days were more rigid than men are now in doctrinal matters, but as a general thing they were as much so in their integrity. The sons of Mr. Stinson were the late Benjamin Stinson, Esq., of Swan's Island, and the present Mr. William Stinson. The daughters were the former wife of Mr. Josiah Barbour; of the late Captain John Toothaker; of Mr. John Buckminster, and afterward of Mr. Moses S. Finney; of Captain Jeremiah Hooper, of North Haven; of Mr. Solomon York, of Brooklin, and of Mr. Seth Whitmore, of Trenton. The real estate of Mr. Stinson is now owned and occupied by Mr. Johnson Billings.

JOHN STINSON was the youngest son, and his wife was Miss Isabel Dyer, of Castine, now Brooksville, on Cape Rozier. After her death he married the widow of Mr. Thomas Trundy. He lived on his father's farm until about thirty years ago, when it was sold to Mr. Lane, the present occupant. Mr. Stinson died in Rockland, where he removed after the sale of the place. He was a man of good reputation, and was more communicative than either of his brothers, who were rather taciturn, particularly Mr. William Stinson. He was for many years a church member, and took much interest in that direction. His sons were John, Thomas, David, and George W., of all whom removed from this town. The daughters were the wives of Messrs. James and Ebenezer Joyce, and Alexander Staples, all of Swan's Island, and Mrs. Staples afterward became the wife of Mr. Joseph Small. By his second marriage Mr. Stinson had a son, now living near Boston, at the time of whose birth the father was about seventy-six years of age.

THOMAS CONARY was the first settler of what is known as Black Island, lying in the Reach, or, as it is sometimes called, Conary's Island, which, as before stated, was included within the limits of the town by the Act of Legislature of 1868. As has been understood, Mr. Conary was a native of Ireland. He was a very witty person, and in former years I used to hear of many of his droll and comical expressions. His first wife was the daughter, by adoption, of the ancestor of the Limeburner family, now living in Brooksville. Mr. Limeburner emigrated from Scotland before the Revolutionary War, and with him came, besides his own family, two children, a son and a daughter adopted by him. The son was Cunningham Limeburner who died at an advanced age, not far from 1825, in Brooksville, and the daughter, Mrs. Conary, was, I believe, a sister by birth to him. After her death he married a daughter of Mercy Staples, the sister of Messrs. Joshua and Moses Staples, and by both marriages had ten sons, one of whom made this town his permanent residence — Mr. Thomas Conary, Jr., who died at an advanced age. His other sons settled in towns in this vicinity, and all of the name in this and other towns near us are the descendants of Mr. Conary, Sr. He had three daughters of whom I have had knowledge. One was the wife of Mr. Robinson Crockett, Jr., who lived in this town many years, afterward removing to Brooksville, where he died; another was the wife of Mr. Ebenezer Marks, of Brooksville, and another of the late Mr. Amaziah Roberts, of Sedgwick.

BENJAMIN YORK was the person who settled the island now in the limits of the town, known as White, or York's

Island, in the Reach. There is another island known as York's Island lying easterly of, and near, Isle au Haut, and within the limits of that town. About Captain York, as he was called, or whence he came, but little is known to us. A son of his was the father of the late Mr. Rufus York who was drowned in Crockett's Cove, in the spring of 1844. He was on board a vessel loaded with wood to be carried to Rockland, which took fire from the funnel above the fireplace in the night, and when discovered the deck load was on fire, and the flames swept everything on the deck. With him were his son Samuel S. York and Mr. Benjamin Cole. His son was the first who discovered the fire and first on deck. He was delayed in helping his father up the gangway and was badly burned, as were they all. Mr. York was lame, and when they jumped overboard to swim to shore, which was but a short distance from the vessel, he became chilled and sank, but the other two gained the shore. Samuel was unable to walk; as his father's house was near, he crept to it and got in, but lived only a day or two. Mr. Cole was not so badly injured as to be unable to walk, and helped Samuel to reach his home, but his injuries were so severe as to impair his health so that he lived but two or three years. The body of Mr. York was found and buried a few days after the occurrence. Another brother of the family was Mr. Benjamin York, who left town nearly fifty years ago. One of the sisters was the wife of Mr. Richard Crockett, and mother of the present Captain Levi B. Crockett; another was the wife of Mr. Ephraim Crockett, a brother to her sister's husband. Captain York, the subject of this notice, had other sons, whose descendants reside at Naskeag Point, in the town of Brooklin, and all of the name in this vicinity are descendants of his. A daughter of his was the wife of Deacon William Stinson, before noticed, but of the rest of the family, little is known. Captain York, for his last wife, married the widow of a Mr. Richardson, of Falmouth, Maine, who was the father of Captain Asa Richardson, now living here at the age of eighty-four years. She must have been much younger than her last husband.

THOMAS ROBBINS, Jr., was the settler upon the point of Greenlaw's Neck, from which the bar runs to Stinson's Neck. He was the son of another person of the same name, who will be noticed; and in the notice of Thomas Stinson, Esq., his wife and children are there named. Of him but little is known, and but one of his sons remained here, — Mr. William G. Robbins, who sold his property to the present occupant, Mr. William Smith, not long after 1860, and removed to the town of Addison, Maine, where he died. Another brother, Mr. James Robbins, removed East when a young man, and of him nothing is known.

THOMAS WARREN settled on what is known as Warren's, or Freeze's Island, now owned and occupied by the widow of Mr. Billings P. Hardy. It appears, from what information we have had, that he claimed a "settler's right," but that it was disputed on the ground, doubtless, that he had not made a settlement in season to be entitled to one. His wife was the daughter of Mr. George Freeze, and by her he had three children: one was the late Hon. Richard Warren, well known to us all, who died in 1865 at the age of seventy-nine. He represented the town in the Legislature in 1823 and in 1835; he was State senator in 1844 and 1845; was several times one of the selectmen, and was for many years engaged in trade and in the fishing business. His wife, a most excellent woman, died in 1861, much lamented. She was the daughter of Mr. Samuel Trundy, Sr. Another son was William Warren, who died when a young man, and a daughter, Mary Warren, was the wife of a Mr. Spencer, who lived in a town on the Penobscot River, above Bangor. Mr. Thomas Warren was drowned by falling out of a log canoe, and after his death his widow married Mr. William Ring, who occupied the island on which Mr. Warren settled and the land nearest to it on Greenlaw's Neck, which is still known as "Ring Town," and is now owned by the heirs of the late Pearl Spofford, Esq. Mr. Ring afterward removed to the town of Ellsworth, where both he and his wife died.

ELIJAH TOOTHAKER settled on the lot still known as the "Toothaker Place." He was one of those known as "young settlers," and the lot was surveyed to him as appears by Peters' plan made in 1798. Where he came from I never knew, but he had a brother who lived in the town of Phillips, in Franklin County, named John Toothaker whose descendants now live there, and another by the name of Joseph who lived for some time on Swan's Island. The wife of Mr. Toothaker was named Elizabeth Daggett. He was drowned not far from 1810, while coming from the mainland, by accidentally falling overboard. His oldest son, the late Captain John Toothaker, aged about sixteen years, was with him, and came home with the boat. Mr. Toothaker left four sons: John, for many years a master-mariner, dying in 1841, aged forty-eight years; Elijah, who was lost at sea, being knocked overboard by the main boom of the schooner *Charles* of Castine; Ebenezer, a blacksmith by trade, who lived in the town of Holden, at Gilmore's Corner; and Captain Thomas D. Toothaker, who removed to Belfast, and was lost at sea. The daughters were the wives of Mr. Isaac Harding, of Sedgwick; Mr. Benjamin Smith, of Swan's Island; Mr. William G. Robbins, of this town, and a Mr. Full who resided in some town near Bangor. After the death of

Mr. Toothaker, his widow married Captain Belcher Tyler. She was five times a widow. Her third husband was Mr. Thomas Stinson, 2d; the fourth was Mr. Samuel Jordan, of Sedgwick; the fifth was Mr. Dominicus Carman, of this town, she having as many husbands as the woman of Samaria.

WILLIAM GREENLAW was the first settler near what is called " Fish Creek." He was the son of the Mr. Jonathan Greenlaw mentioned before, who went with the British to New Brunswick in 1783. As has been before stated, the two brothers, William and Richard, returned here. The wife of Mr. Greenlaw was Miss Rebecca Babbidge, a daughter of Mr. William Babbidge, and at the time of their marriage there was no person qualified to solemnize marriages nearer than Bagaduce, where the chaplain to the garrison officiated. The person who performed the duties of chaplain, as well as surgeon there, was Dr. John Calef, a refugee from Ipswich, Massachusetts, in which State he was born. When the troops evacuated the place, he went with them into the Province of New Brunswick, where he lived the remainder of his days. Mr. Greenlaw was married in 1780; he and Mr. Joseph Whitmore, with their intended wives, who were sisters, went there for that purpose, and were both joined in marriage on the same day. Mr. Greenlaw and wife were the parents of ten sons and one daughter who lived to manhood and womanhood. The eldest of the sons was William, who was lost at sea on a whaling voyage when a young man. The second son was the late Captain John Greenlaw, a capable and intelligent master-mariner, who died in 1870, at the age of eighty-seven years, after having lived with his wife in wedlock sixty-six years. He was the father of the present Captain Jeremiah H., Ebenezer, and William Greenlaw. Another son was Mr. James Greenlaw, who was drowned not far from 1830, leaving a family. Another was Captain Jonathan Greenlaw who removed to Eastport, out of which place he sailed many years. Another was the late Captain Richard Greenlaw, the father of the present Mr. Thomas R. Greenlaw. Another was Thomas Greenlaw, who was drowned when a young man. Another was Mr. Ebenezer Greenlaw, the father of the present Mr. Eben Greenlaw, 2d. Another was the late Captain Walter Greenlaw, well known in his day, who died at sea in about the year 1847. Another is the present Mr. Levi Greenlaw, the sole survivor, at the age of seventy-nine years in 1882; and the other was the late Mr. William Greenlaw. The daughter was the wife of Mr. Daniel G. Copp, who removed from this place to Castine. He was by trade a ship carpenter and joiner, and from Castine he removed to the city of Ellsworth, where he died.

About this family there was one singularity: of the ten sons there were five who could use no food or drink in which there was anything sweet, it operating upon them as an emetic; while upon the remaining five it had no such effect. Mr. Greenlaw was one of whom every one who knew him spoke in praise, as a quiet, honest, and upright man. The land occupied by him was not a part of that taken up by his father and uncles, as that passed into other hands; but as he was here so early, he was entitled to a settler's right, and the place is still the property of his descendants.

NATHANIEL SCOTT was the person who purchased the settler's right of Major William Eaton. As I have understood, Mr. Eaton left the place while the British had possession of Bagaduce, in order that he might escape the necessity of taking the oath of allegiance or neutrality. He went to the town of York, the place from which he came here, but after peace was proclaimed returned, and it was probably not many years after that he sold his right to Mr. Scott, who came here with a family. His son, John Scott, was married before he came, as was his daughter, Martha, to Mr. Asa Green. There was a son of the name of William Scott who purchased the lot at the Northwest Harbor, on which the house known as the " Green House " now stands, and erected a house upon it. It has since been much improved, and is now a large and elegant house. The house that was standing fifty years ago was built by William Scott, after which he died, and Mr. Green and wife came here from Worcester County, Massachusetts, and occupied it till their death. Ignatius Haskell, Esq., had a claim upon it, which he sold to Mr. Asa Green, and afterward it was transferred to his son, the late William S. Green. The time of Mr. Green's removal I do not know exactly, but it was prior to 1800, as the land was sold to William Scott previous to Peters' survey, and he died not long after his purchase. Mr. Nathaniel Scott died not long after 1790, and Mr. John Scott occupied the farm till his death, which took place not far from 1830. Mr. John Scott and wife were the parents of eight sons and three daughters. The sons were: John, who died a young man; James, who died a young man also; Clark, about whom I never knew anything; Enos who, with his brother Eben, removed to Lubec; William, who resided in Boston some years ago; the present Mr. Levi Scott, and the late Mr. Leonard Scott. The daughters were the wives of Mr. Joseph Clifton and Captain Enoch P. Hazen, and one, Lucinda, died unmarried. The estate is now occupied by the widow of Mr. Leonard Scott, and by Captain William Torrey, John Weed, and William P. Scott. Whether Mr. William Scott is still living is not to us known. Mrs. Hazen, with her husband, removed to Brooklin, where he died, and after his death she went to reside with one of her daughters in Massachusetts. Mrs. Clifton lived to be very aged, leaving three daughters; one, the wife of Captain William Torrey; another the wife of Mr. Thomas Lowe, and another, married, living in Massachusetts.

ASA GREEN, the son-in-law of Mr. Nathaniel Scott, died in 1838, aged over eighty years, and his wife survived him. He was for many years elected constable, and was in former years a deputy sheriff. He was elected, in 1819, with Ignatius Haskell, Esq., a delegate to frame the constitution of the State. Their children were John, a master-mariner, who was, with his brother, Asa Green, Frederick Spofford, Esq., Abner Babbidge, and Amos Angell, a son of Dr. David Angell, wrecked on the Green Islands in February, 1818, in the schooner *Shakespeare*, returning from Boston, and all perished. Another son was the late Captain William S. Green who was well known to us for many years. He was in 1842, 1859, and in 1863, a representative to the State Legislature, and died in 1870 at the age of sixty-five years, leaving a widow who is still living (1882), three sons: Martin, now dead, Thomas B., and John W., and a daughter, Mrs. Kettletas. Another son of Mr. Asa Green was Thomas Green, the father of the present Mr. Asa Green. The daughters of Asa Green, Sr., were Frances, the wife of Mr. Joseph Small; Mary, the wife of Mr. Thomas Haskell, and afterward the wife of Mr. Thomas Dow, Jr., Roxanna, the wife of Captain Francis Haskell, who was lost in the schooner *Commodore Perry* (on board of which were his son and son-in-law), on Long Ledge, off Mount Desert, November 26, 1845. Another daughter was the wife of the late John R. Haskell, and the mother of the present Captain Sylvanus G. Haskell. She afterward married Mr. Moses C. Angell, who removed to Boston, where he died a few years ago, and where his widow still resides. The property of Captain William S. Green was, after his death, occupied by Martin V. B. Green, and is now by Mrs. Kettletas, with whom her mother resides.

PETER HARDY was the settler upon the lot adjoining that of William Eaton on the southwest. He was a native of the county of Worcester, Massachusetts. His wife was a daughter of Deacon Francis Haskell, but whether they were married here, or before they came here, is to me unknown. His son, Peter Hardy, Jr., the eldest of the family, was born in February, 1770, and it is probable that the marriage was before they came here, as his father-in-law did not come till 1770, according to the best information that we have. The land he settled upon was the place occupied by Michael Carney, but Carney had gone before Mr. Hardy came. He was for several years a coroner, and he and his wife died upon the same day, in 1831, and were buried in one grave, having lived together in wedlock over sixty years. There have been but three other instances that have come to my knowledge where both husband and wife occupied the same grave. One was in 1826, of Mr. Jeremiah Pressey and wife; another in 1832–33, of Mr. James Babbidge and wife, who were drowned in attempting to pass through the flood-gates at Holt's milldam, and the other was that of Captain Joseph Raynes and wife, in 1859.

Mr. Hardy and wife were the parents of three sons: the late Captain Peter Hardy, who died in 1863 at the age of ninety-three years; Mr. Jonathan Hardy, who lived and died upon Little Deer Island; and another named Silas, who, when a young man, was lost at sea. One daughter of the family was the wife of a Mr. Wooster, and was the mother of five children at two births, the last being but thirteen months after the first. Another daughter was the wife of a Mr. Adams in Massachusetts. Another was the wife of Captain Jonathan Haskell, 3d, who died in 1873, aged ninety-four years. Another married Captain Jonathan Haskell, Jr., who was known as "Long Metre," as he was a very tall man. The youngest was the wife of Mr. Oliver Lane, Jr., the father of the present Mr. Hardy Lane.

Captain Peter Hardy, Jr.'s wife was Miss Sarah Campbell, daughter of Mr. John Campbell. They had the following-named sons: Peter, who lived on Little Deer Island, and died there in 1859, aged sixty-one years; Silas, who formerly traded on Swan's Island, and who was a master-mariner, and died in Australia a number of years ago. John, who lived in Newburyport, and is now dead; Francis, who formerly was a master-mariner, but who now resides in Massachusetts; George C. Hardy, a well-known citizen, who has been one of the selectmen in former years, and who owns and occupies the farm settled by his grandfather; and another, now dead. There was one daughter, now the widow of Mr. John Thompson. Captain Hardy was for many years a master-mariner. He was a man of enterprise, and accumulated quite a property for those days; was a member of the Legislature in 1834 and in 1839, and was for some years one of the selectmen.

The family of Mr. Jonathan Hardy, whose wife was a Miss Putnam, of Newburyport, was Silas L., who lived on Little Deer Island and died there not far from 1861; Jonathan, who lived there many years, and afterward removed to Winterport, where he died a few years ago; Joseph P., who moved to Winterport, where he was well known for several years, and afterward removed to the State of Illinois, where he is probably now living; Billings P., who moved to Frankfort, but afterward returned and purchased Freeze's Island, where he resided till his death. Another son was Captain Abijah W. Hardy, who resides in Winterport. The daughters were the wives of Major Nathan Low, Joshua Haskell, and Mr. Henry Harris.

JEREMIAH EATON was the first settler upon the farm adjoining that of Mr. Hardy upon the southwest. He was the son of Major William Eaton, and his wife was a daughter of Captain Mark and a sister of Ignatius Haskell, Esq. She survived him, and her second marriage was with Mr. John Howard, who will be noticed. She had no children, and Mr. Eaton adopted two brothers, the children of Eleanor Bray, afterward the wife of Mr. Perry and the mother of the present Mr. Eli Perry. The children took his name, and were known as Mr. Asa B. Eaton and Edward Eaton. He bequeathed his property after his wife's decease to them, but they did not receive it. It became the property of Ignatius Haskell, Esq., and afterward that of Thomas Adams, Esq., of Castine, by whom it was sold to the late Captain Amos Howard, and it is now occupied by his widow. Asa B. Eaton, one of the adopted sons, married Miss Mercy Raynes, daughter of William and sister of the late Captain Johnson Raynes. Three of their children only lived to grow up. One, the present Captain William R. Eaton, who resided for many years here, in 1867 removed to Wakefield, Massachusetts, and now resides in Newburyport. He has been for many years an enterprising master-mariner. Another son was the late Mr. Nathan H. Eaton, and a daughter now dead was the wife of a Mr. Dexter, in Boston. Mr. Eaton died at sea in 1851, and his wife survived him not many years. The other brother, Mr. Edward Eaton, married a daughter of Mr. Chase Pressey, by whom he had one son, Hiram Eaton, who went from here about forty years ago, and two daughters, now dead, one of whom married in Boston. Both Edward Eaton and his wife died more than fifty years ago.

JOHN HOWARD was the settler upon the lot southwesterly of that of Mr. Jeremiah Eaton, though not adjoining, as the land now occupied by Mr. Albion K. Haskell, which was first purchased by Mr. John Scott, Jr., and afterward by the late Captain Ignatius Haskell, Jr., lies between. Mr. Howard was three times married. His first wife was a daughter of Mr. John Pressey, Jr., and their children were John, Joshua C. Michael, Thomas, and Amos Howard, none of whom is now living. His daughters by his first wife were the wife of Captain William Eaton, the son of William Eaton, Jr., — and afterward the wife of Mr. Nathaniel Ingalls, — and the others were the wives of the late Mr. Samuel H. Foster, Pepperell Tyler, and Andrew Tyler; and all, with the exception of the present widow of the last named, are now dead. Mrs. Foster died in 1881, at nearly eighty-nine years of age. Mr. Howard for his second wife married the widow of Mr. Jeremiah Eaton, and after her death married Mrs. Mary C. Small, of Newburyport, Massachusetts, who was many years younger than himself. By her he had one daughter, Mary A., who was the wife of Captain Edmund S. Raynes, of this town, now residing in Newburyport. She is now dead. Mr. John Howard, Jr., married first, a daughter of Mr. Thomas Thompson, and by her had one son, Captain Thomas Howard, now a resident of Newburyport. After her death he married Susan, the daughter of Mr. William Foster, by whom he had six sons and two daughters. One of the sons only remained here, the late Mr. Stephen K. Howard. Three, William, Charles, and John, died when young men. Oliver now resides in Gloucester, Massachusetts, and the place of residence of the other, Darius, is to us unknown. Of his daughters, one was the wife of Mr. Rufus H. Moulton, a master ship-carpenter, who lived for many years in Brooklin, and afterward removed to Massachusetts; the other was the wife of Mr. Pettingill, in Newburyport. Captain Joshua C. Howard, the second son, married Lydia, the daughter of Joseph Tyler, Esq., by whom he had two sons, one of whom was drowned when a child. The other, Mr. Joseph T. Howard, lived in Newburyport, where he died not many years ago. His daughters were the wives of Mr. Michael H. Pressey, of this town, a Mr. Short, in Newburyport, and the youngest was the wife of Captain John J. Raynes, now of Hyde Park, Massachusetts. Captain Howard who was very skillful as a pilot, serving in that capacity on board of one of the first steamers navigating the waters in this vicinity, in 1827, and afterward upon the revenue-boat *Veto* at Castine, came to his death from the effects of arsenic. While serving on board the *Veto*, a revenue-cutter, whose duty was inspection, went to Castine and procured his services as pilot to Bangor. Her captain being a harsh man, a conspiracy was formed by the cook and others to poison him, and while at Bangor arsenic was procured, with which the captain and those who sat at the table with him were poisoned. The dose was so large that it operated speedily; death did not immediately take place, but all died not long after. Captain Howard survived them all, living some six months after the occurrence, which took place in the year 1832. The next brother, Michael Howard, married a daughter of Mr. Chase Pressey, and both are now dead. They occupied the house near that of Mr. Samuel Pickering, and of the family but two remain: Charles, who went into Massachusetts, and a daughter who now occupies the house of her father. The other brothers, Messrs. Thomas and Amos Howard, died but a few years ago, and were well known to us here.

WILLIAM EATON, Jr., settled the lot adjoining that of Mr. Howard on the southwest, and his wife was a daughter of Deacon Francis Haskell. Their sons were William, Jeremiah, and Samuel, all now dead. The daughters were the wives of Dr. Moody Powers; Mr. Amasa Holden, who came from Mendon, Massachusetts, and was for many years a school-teacher; a Mr. Knight, of Newburyport; Mr. John Short, of the same place, who removed from here to Castine, and afterward to Bangor, where he died; Captain Ignatius Haskell, Jr.; another was first the wife of Mr. Avery Small, and after that of Mr. William Greenlaw; and one, Esther, died unmarried. They all, with the exception of Mrs. Greenlaw, are now dead. The farm of Mr. Eaton is now owned by two of his grandsons, Mr. William E. Powers and Mr. Francis M. Holden. The wife of Mr. Eaton died in 1836, and he died not far from the year 1841. Captain William Eaton, his son, married Abigail Howard, the daughter of Mr. John Howard. Their son, the present William Eaton, is a pilot in the revenue service, and resides in Portland; their daughters were the wives of Captain Daniel S. Torrey, Mr. William Low, Captain Francis H. Torrey, and Mr. John Weed, of whom the Mrs. Torreys are living. Captain Eaton was lost in the latter part of the year 1830, on board the sloop *Huntress* of Castine, Captain John Greenlaw, Jr. He acted as pilot on a trip from that place to New York, and on their return was lost. Besides the two above named there were on board Mr. William Buckminster and Joseph Conary, who acted as cook. Mr. Jeremiah Eaton, the next brother, married and lived near the bar on Little Deer Island. He was drowned in 1834, leaving a widow and family, of whom but three are now living. The other brother, Samuel Eaton, was lost at sea when a young man.

ABIJAH HASKELL, a son of Deacon Francis Haskell, settled the lot adjoining that of Mr. Eaton on the southwest, and his wife was a daughter of Mr. Benjamin Cole,

Sr. Their sons were Jonathan Haskell, 3rd, Abijah, Francis, and Joshua Haskell. One of the daughters was first the wife of Captain Benjamin S. Haskell, who was lost in the schooner *Lingun*, about 1822. She afterward became the wife of Doctor Abiel Reed, by whom she had one son, the present Captain William H. Reed, now residing in Portland, and a daughter, who was the wife of Mr. Levi Marshall, Jr. Another was the wife of Mr. Ezekiel Marshall, and another that of Mr. Thomas Dow. Captain Jonathan Haskell, 3d, married a daughter of Mr. Peter Hardy, by whom he had two daughters, — one the widow of the late Edward Y. Haskell, and the mother of the present Captain Caleb W., George D., Albert L., and Edwin L. Haskell; the other the widow of the late Captain Dudley Thompson. Captain Haskell died in 1873, aged ninety-four years. Mr. Abijah Haskell, the next eldest brother, married a sister of Mrs. Jonathan Haskell; he lived on Little Deer Island, where he died at the age of ninety-one years. His wife survived him not long, and they lived together in wedlock sixty-five years. Captain Francis Haskell, the next brother, was lost as has been stated, in 1845, on board the schooner *Commodore Perry*. Joshua, the youngest, died about two years ago. The estate of Mr. Abijah Haskell is still owned and occupied by his descendants.

NATHAN HASKELL, Esq., settled the lot lying southwesterly of the land of Mr. Abijah Haskell, though not adjoining it, and he came here, I judge, prior to 1784, or about that year. He first married a daughter of Captain Mark Haskell, by whom he had one daughter, who became the wife of Rev. Wigglesworth Dale. After her death he married Miss Lucy Torrey, daughter of Mr. Jonathan Torrey. She was the mother of the late Mr. Edward Y. Haskell and of the wife of Mr. Peter Powers, the mother of

Nathan H. Powers, now of Orland. Mr. Haskell at his death left a widow who survived him several years. He was a man of intelligence; was for many years a justice of the peace, and filled offices in the town, and was also a deacon in the Congregational Church. His real estate was, after his death, owned and occupied by his son, whose widow now lives on it.

CALEB HASKELL, a brother of Nathan Haskell, occupied the lot adjoining that of the last-named on the southwest. His wife was not a native of this town, and none of his family after his death remained here, except a daughter, who was the first wife of Mr. Jesse Niles, a carpenter, who came not long after 1800, from New Hampshire, and who occupied the farm for many years. It was sold in about the year 1840, and is now owned and occupied by Mr. William H. Thompson. None of the family of Mr. Niles by his first wife is now living, but after her death, which took place in 1835, he married a daughter of Mr. Naylor Small, by whom he had a family.

NATHAN DOW settled on the lot of land adjoining that of Mr. Caleb Haskell on the southwest. A part of his farm bordered upon the Northwest Harbor, and embraced what is now known as Dow's Point, on the northeast side of the entrance to the harbor. He was the second person who permanently settled in that part of the island, Mr. John Pressey having taken up a lot on the southwest side of the entrance, opposite the land occupied by Mr. Dow. He came in the fall of 1767, and, I presume, came from the town of Brunswick, Maine, or that vicinity, as he was a neighbor of Mr. Theophilus Eaton who came here from that place, then better known as New Meadows River, which runs up into that town. He died here, leaving two sons, John and Nathan Dow, and two daughters, who were married. The elder, Diana, was the wife of Mr. Jonathan

Eaton, who will be noticed, and who came with Mr. Dow. The other was the wife of Mr. Josiah Crockett, who was well known here in his time. Mr. John Dow, his son, married a daughter of Mr. Thomas Saunders, and was the father of the late Mr. Thomas Dow, Mr. Stephen Dow who was drowned over fifty years ago, Mr. Samuel Dow who settled on Mount Desert Island, Ephraim Dow who removed there about forty years ago, and Mr. William T. Dow who removed from here to Tinker's Island. One daughter was the wife of Mr. William Staples, a son of the man who was said to have been impressed on board a British ship-of-war during the Revolution. Another was the wife of the late Joseph C. Stinson, Esq.; another married Captain John Kempton, of Isle au Haut, and another married Captain Jacob Carlton, who for many years resided in the same place, and afterward removed to Winterport, where he died. Captain Carlton represented this town in the Legislature in 1838. Of Nathan Dow, Jr., I knew but little. He left three sons: one, the present Mr. Nathan Dow, who is now (1881) aged eighty-nine years; Joshua, and Ephraim Dow, who have been dead some years. The land of Mr. Nathan Dow, Sr., was mostly occupied by his son Nathan after his decease, and after the death of Nathan, Jr., the three sons of his just named came into possession. Part of it is now owned by the heirs of the late Martin V. B. Green, and the residue by the descendants of the original owner.

THEOPHILUS EATON settled upon the lot of land adjoining that of Mr. Dow on the southeast, and bordered by the waters of the Northwest Harbor. He was a cousin of Major William Eaton, the first permanent settler, and was born in Haverhill, Massachusetts, in the year 1720, and came here in 1768. From Haverhill he removed to the town of Sandown, New Hampshire, and from that place to Brunswick, and from the latter place here. The occasion of his coming was this: A daughter of his, Judith Eaton, married Mr. Edward Howard who afterward lived and died in Brooksville. Mr. Howard came here and commenced a settlement. His wife was taken sick, and he went to Brunswick to bring her mother here to take care of her daughter during her sickness. Mrs. Howard died, and after that Mr. Eaton came here in a boat to take his wife home. This was in 1767. Mr. Howard, after the death of his wife, gave his mother-in-law all his rights to land here, as a compensation for her services. Mr. Eaton was pleased with the location, and the next spring, 1768, came here with his family and remained till his death in 1793. The wife of Mr. Eaton was Miss Abigail Fellows; she died in 1824, at the residence of her son, James Eaton, in the town of Prospect, aged one hundred and two years and eight months. His sons were: Moses, who lived on what is now the place occupied as a village, in the town of Sedgwick; Jonathan, whom we have noticed as making his escape when arrested to be carried to Bagaduce; Ebenezer, who was for many years a minister of the gospel on the island of Mount Desert, and James, who occupied his father's place after his death, and to whom the lot was laid out on Peters' plan, but who later sold it to Captain Jonathan Haskell. The daughters who survived him were, one, the wife of Mr. Harding, in Sedgwick; another was the wife of Mr. Solomon Billings, who lived on the northwest side of what is known as Walker's Pond, in Brooksville, and another was the wife of Captain John Raynes of this place. She died in 1850, at the age of ninety-one years. Mr. Eaton was one of the earlier selectmen of the town, and was a man much respected. The farm occupied by Mr. Eaton was afterward in part occupied by the late Captain John Torrey, and a part of his posses-

Town of Deer Isle, Maine. 73

sion is the property of his adopted daughter, the widow of the late Mr. Joshua Pressey, 2d.

LEVI CARMAN was the person who settled on the lot lying on the southeast of that of Mr. Eaton. He came, as appears by the best information now to be had, in, or about, the year 1768, but from what place is not known. He was a master-mariner, and was engaged in the coasting trade. From the fact that he was chosen one of the committee to obtain a grant of the lands remaining on the island after the settlers had had their lots assigned them, it must have been that he was a man of intelligence and character. The time of his death was before 1798, as on Peters' plan the lot he occupied, containing two hundred acres, was assigned to the " Widow Carman "; and of him but little has been learned. His widow died in 1835, aged ninety-one years. One son was Mr. Dominicus Carman, who lived near what is known as Carman's Rock, a large granite bowlder by the side of the highway leading to the steamboat-landing, about one mile from the Northwest Harbor, and was considered a skillful doctor of cattle, to which he paid considerable attention. His wife was a daughter of Mr. Ezra Howard, who will be noticed. They had one son who lived to manhood, the late Mr. Thomas Carman, the father of Michael P., Edwin, and Abner P. Carman. One of the daughters married Mr. Samuel Saunders; one married Mr. James Jarvis; another married Mr. Francis Haskell; and there was another who went from here many years ago. After the death of his wife, he married Mrs. Elizabeth Jordan, the lady before noticed, who was five times a widow. He was born in 1766 and died not far from 1850. Another son was Mr. John Carman, who died many years ago. His wife was a Miss Choate, a native of Essex County, Massachusetts, and a sister of Mr. George G. Choate, who lived here many years before his removal to Bluehill, where he died, and who is well remembered by older people among us for his wit. Mr. John Carman and wife were the parents of three sons and six daughters. The sons were the present Mr. Levi and Mr. Frederick Carman, and John Carman, who died when a young man. The daughters were the wives of Mr. John Ferguson, who, at the time of his marriage, lived in Massachusetts; of the late Mr. Solomon Haskell, of this town; of the late Jonathan E. Webb, Esq.; of Mr. James Clough, of Bluehill; of Dr. Charles N. Briggs, a dentist, a native of Rhode Island; and of a Mr. Trowbridge. With one or two exceptions they are now dead. The widow of Mr. Carman married Mr. Jeremiah Stover who came here from Penobscot, whom she survived, and died not far from 1852, at an advanced age. One of the daughters of Mr. Levi Carman, Sr., was the wife of Captain Francis Marshall and mother of the late Levi Marshall, and the other the wife of Mr. Naylor Small. The land settled by him is still mostly occupied by his descendants; that of Dominicus Carman, by his grandson, Mr. Tristram Haskell, to whom descended also his grandfather's skill as a cattle-doctor.

MARK HASKELL was the first settler who occupied the lot adjoining that of Mr. Carman on the southeast. He came when quite advanced in years, not far from the year 1768, from what was then known as Sandy Bay, in the town of Rockport, Massachusetts, and some of his sons came at the same time and occupied the premises with him. He was the father of Captain Mark and Deacon Francis Haskell, who came afterward. He resided here several years, but prior to his death he made a contract with Ignatius Haskell, Esq., his grandson, for his support, and in consideration conveyed to him his right as a settler. Not long after he went on a visit to his friends in Massachusetts, where he died, and his right, by virtue of his own occupancy, and that of some of his sons, became, upon a division of the land, the property of his grandson, by whom it was owned at the time of his death. The lot contained two hundred and fifty acres, running about two miles, in a northeast direction from the Northwest Harbor, and a part of it is known as the " Rye Field " lot.

FRANCIS HASKELL, a son of the person before named, was the settler upon the land adjoining on the southeast. He came from Newburyport in 1770 with his family, and but few of his children were born after he came here. When the church was organized, in 1773, he was one of the deacons. The time of his death is unknown to us, but it was prior to the survey of the island, as his lot was assigned to his two sons, Jonathan and Tristram Haskell (two hundred acres). He left four sons, namely: Francis, who removed to South Thomaston and lived on what is known as Ash Point, and died there not far from 1841, over ninety years of age; Jonathan, who lived here till his death; Abijah, before noticed, and Tristram. Of the daughters, one was the wife of Mr. Peter Hardy, Sr.; one, of Mr. William Eaton, Jr.; another married Captain Ephraim Marshall; another was the wife of Deacon Joshua Haskell; another, of Mr. Prescott Powers, and the other, wife of Captain Francis Marshall. His land was owned and occupied by his two sons during their lives, and is now chiefly owned by their descendants.

EZEKIEL MARSHALL was the settler upon the lot of land adjoining that of Mr. Francis Haskell on the southeast. He came about the year 1768. He was a connection of the Haskell family, as I have understood, by marriage. There appears to have been an Ephraim Marshall also (presumably a brother), who came about the same time, but did not remain; and as Mr. Ezekiel Marshall had a two-hundred-acre lot, it is probable that one hundred acres were by virtue of Ephraim's right assigned to him. His lot took in what has since become the most valuable land in that vicinity; in 1772 he sold Mark Haskell, Jr., and his sons, Ignatius and Solomon, what has been since known as Haskell's Point, on which the stores stand at the Northwest Harbor, and which remained the property of Ignatius Haskell till his death. This sale was seventeen years prior to the allotment of the land in the town by the Tylers, till which no individual had a title. The purchase was some years before Messrs. Mark Haskell & Sons removed here and commenced business. Mr. Marshall must have died prior to the survey, as the lot is described as belonging to the "Heirs of Ezekiel Marshall." His sons were Ephraim, Solomon, Joshua, and Francis; and one of the daughters was the wife of Mr. Aaron S. Haskell.

JONATHAN HASKELL, the son of Francis, remained here till his death in 1830, at the age of seventy-five years. His wife was Miss Dorothy Shute, a daughter of the man of that name who settled upon Sandy Point, now in the town of Stockton. She survived him about twenty years, when his real estate was divided among his heirs. Their children were Benjamin S., Jonathan, Jr., known as "Long Metre," Thomas, Francis, and David, and all are now dead. The daughters were the wives of Messrs. Daniel Torrey, John Torrey, Levi Marshall, and Chase Pressey, and they are all dead also. Captain Haskell was for many years an enterprising master-mariner and accumulated considerable property. His sons also followed the sea for many years. His son, the late Captain David Haskell, resided on, and occupied his father's premises till the death of his mother, and after a division of the property retained the buildings and land around them till his death in 1878. They are now occupied by his son and youngest daughter.

TRISTRAM HASKELL, the youngest son of Francis Haskell, remained upon the lot he was entitled to as heir of his father (which was assigned to him), till his death, which took place not far from the year 1860, when he was about ninety years of age. His first wife was Miss Martha Merchant (a daughter of Mr. Anthony Merchant who in 1772, settled Merchant's Island, now within the limits of the town of Isle au Haut), by whom he had six sons and two daughters. The sons were: Francis, who was drowned in Boston Harbor, in 1838, the father of the present Messrs. Tristram and Davis Haskell; Davis, who lived on the road leading from the Northwest Harbor to the steamboat-landing, about two miles from the harbor; Tristram, Jr., who lived on what is known as Beech Hill, about one mile from the harbor; Peter, who lived on Little Deer Isle; John R., the father of the present Captain Sylvanus G. Haskell, and Joshua P., who died in 1880, aged seventy-seven years. The last named was for some time in the British navy, and was present at the battle of Navarino, in 1824, in which a complete victory was obtained by the British fleet over the Turks, in the war which secured the independence of the Greeks. For many years he resided at Liverpool, England. Of the daughters, one was the wife of the late Mr. James Stinson; the other married in Massachusetts. His first wife died in 1803, and Captain Haskell married Miss Betsey Barton, by whom he had four sons and four daughters. The sons were the late Captain William Haskell, George W., John and one who died in childhood. The daughters were the wives of Captain Adam Thompson, Jr., Mr. Frederick S. Pressey, Mr. Frederick Eaton, and Mr. Edwin B. Spofford. Of the above none of the first family are now living, and of the last, Captain John Haskell and the four sisters. After the death of his second wife, in 1835, Captain Haskell married his third wife, a Mrs. Gray, daughter of Mr. Benjamin Weed. He died in, or near, the year 1860, aged about ninety. For many years he was a master-mariner, but, being troubled with deafness, was obliged to abandon the sea.

EPHRAIM MARSHALL was the eldest of the sons of Mr. Ezekiel Marshall, who has been mentioned, and his wife was a daughter of Mr. Francis Haskell. They had two sons, Ephraim and Ezekiel, and four daughters, all of whom are now dead. He lived on the southern side of the road leading toward the Reach, not far from the place occupied by the house — now burnt down — built and occupied by Captain David P. Marshall, who removed from this place a few years ago. Another son of Mr. Ezekiel Marshall, Sr., was Joshua, the father of the present Mr. Ezekiel Marshall, the oldest man now among us, born in 1790. Another was Mr. Solomon Marshall, who lived on the southwest side of the Northwest Harbor, and left one son, Mark Marshall, and two daughters, Mrs. Hanson and Mrs. Murray, all of whom are now dead. Captain Francis Marshall was the youngest son. His first wife, who lived with him but a few years, was, as we have mentioned, a daughter of Mr. Levi Carman. He afterward married Miss Abigail Haskell, the daughter of Deacon Francis Haskell, by whom he had two sons who survived him, Elias D. and the late Francis Marshall, and three daughters, one of whom was the wife of Thomas Lamson, Esq., of Boston. The present Hon. Edwin D. Lamson, of Richmond, Maine, is a son of hers. Another daughter, Hannah, who lived here, remained unmarried, and the other was Mrs. Joy, who resided in Boston. Of the family only one, Elias D. Marshall, is now living.

MARK HASKELL, the second of the name, came here with his family in 1778, having some six years before purchased the land they occupied of Ezekiel Marshall. He was born in 1723, and his wife was Miss Abigail Bray, a sister of the first man of the name who came here. They had quite a large family, some of whom died in childhood. The survivors were Ignatius, Solomon, Joshua, and Edward, and three daughters, one the wife of Mr. Jeremiah Eaton, another, wife of Nathan Haskell, Esq., both of whom have been noticed, and another, wife of Mr. Elijah Dunham, Jr. He was a native of what was then known as Sandy Bay, in the present town of Rockport, Massachusetts, but afterward removed to Newburyport, from which place he came here and commenced business with his two sons. They built a saw and gristmill, which was a great convenience to the inhabitants, and the former of profit to the owners, as there were then logs in abundance to be manufactured into lumber. They also built houses and a store. The saw and gristmills stood until about twenty-five years ago, and were then the property of John P. Johnson, Esq. Mr. Haskell took his two eldest sons, Ignatius and Solomon, into partnership, and the firm was known as "Messrs. Mark Haskell & Sons." They built several vessels, brigs and schooners, and one ship of about four hundred tons, which was a large one for those days. They accumulated, for the times, a large property, owning here at one time more than one thousand acres of land. Solomon, the junior copartner, removed to Newburyport, and did business there many years, in which his father and brother had an interest. After the death of their father, which took place in 1810, the copartnership was dissolved, but Solomon, who remained there till his death, in 1828, had a considerable interest in the real estate here with his brother. At the time of his death he was a deacon in the church, of which the then well-known Rev. Mr. Milton was pastor.

IGNATIUS HASKELL, Esq., after the death of his father, did the business here, in trading and building vessels, for several years, and for the times and locality it was quite extensive. He was a man who had a large share of business capacity, and for a long time was the foremost man in the community, and had great influence, owning a large property, and taking great interest in the affairs of the town and church. He built a meeting-house at his own expense, not far from the year 1800, selling the pews to those who were disposed to purchase. He was one of the earliest justices of the peace here, was often one of the selectmen, and was, in 1819, a delegate to Portland with Asa Green, before named, to the convention which framed the State constitution. He retained his faculties in a remarkable degree till the time of his death, 1842, at the age of ninety-one years. His wife was Miss Mary Stickney, of Newburyport, by whom he had four sons and five daughters. The sons were Aaron S., Mark, Ignatius, Jr., and Solomon, all of whom are still well remembered. The daughters were the wives of Mr. John Foster, Dr. David Angell, Mr. Jonathan L. Stevens, of Castine, Hezekiah Rowell, Esq. (who resided here a long time, then removed to Castine, but after some years returned), and the youngest was the wife of Dr. Theophilus Doe, of Brewer. After the death of his wife, Mr. Haskell married the widow of Moses Gross, whose maiden name was Martha Pritchard, born in Boston, in 1773. At the time of his death he left the largest property of any one in the town, a large portion of which was real estate, and most of which has now passed into other hands. His house, which he built not far from the year 1793, is now the property of his granddaughter, the widow of the late Captain William Haskell.

EZRA HOWARD was the settler upon the lot of land

adjoining that of Mr. Ezekiel Marshall and that purchased of him by Mark Haskell on the southeast. He came early, but the exact year is to us unknown, nor have we ever known from what place he removed here. He had three sons and four daughters, of whom we have had knowledge: one was the Mr. John Howard we have already noticed; another was Mr. Michael Howard, who lived and died at what is known as " Fisk Creek," the father of the late Mr. Samuel and the present Mr. Thomas V. Howard, and one named Benjamin who, in 1812, removed from here to Newburyport where he died. One daughter was the wife of Mr. Chase Pressey; another was the wife of Mr. Paul Pressey; another, that of Mr. Dominicus Carman, and the other, the wife of Mr. James Parker, who once lived here and who was the father of John H. Parker, Esq., a former resident of the town of Mount Desert. After the death of his wife, Mr. Howard married a Mrs. Johnson, whose two daughters by her former husband, were the wives of Deacon Nehemiah Closson and the first wife of Mr. George G. Choate. The year of the death of Mr. Howard is not to us known. His estate passed by purchase from his heirs to Ignatius Haskell, Esq.; and with the exception of a house-lot none of it was owned by his descendants after his death.

AMBROSE COLBY was the occupant of the lot lying on the southeast of that of Mr. Howard. He came from the vicinity of Newburyport not far from 1768, and after he came he married a daughter of Mr. John Pressey. He died about the year 1800; his wife survived him until 1844, and was at the time of her death aged ninety-two years. He built a large house opposite the present Congregational church, upon the site now occupied by the house of Mr. Frederick H. Gross. It was afterward for many years the home of Mr. Amos Gordon, who married a daughter of Mr. Colby. He left two sons, Messrs. Hezekiah and Ambrose Colby, and the daughter already referred to, who was first the wife of Mr. William Torrey, by whom she had two sons, Hezekiah and William Torrey, and a daughter, the first wife of John P. Johnson, Esq. Hezekiah Torrey was, in 1822, the representative of this town to the Legislature, and afterward removed to Belfast, where he died in 1824, much esteemed. The other son, Mr. William Torrey, died on his passage to California, not far from the year 1850, and was at the time of his death over fifty years of age. By her second marriage she had two sons and two daughters who survived her: Mr. Ambrose C. Gordon, who died in 1880, and Captain John Gordon, who died in Bluehill, to which place he had removed. The two daughters were the wives of Mr. Levi Carman and Captain Joseph W. Pressey, and both are now dead. Mr. Gordon, the husband of the daughter of Mr. Colby, came here from Biddeford, Maine, where his relatives still reside. He died several years ago, and none of that name are left in the town.

The lot of land adjoining that of Mr. Colby on the southeast was what is still known as the " parsonage lot." It contained originally four hundred acres, and was granted by the General Court of Massachusetts to the first religious society and the first settled minister. Rev. Peter Powers, the first settled minister, became proprietor of that part of the land, and settled upon the southeastern side of the lot; after his death, in 1800, it passed into the hands of his son, Mr. Prescott Powers, and the farm of Mr. Levi Greenlaw is a part of it. More will be said of the Rev. Mr. Powers in the part of this work in which the religious societies in the town are noticed.

NATHANIEL BRAY and ROBERT NASON were the settlers upon the lot of land containing, according to Peters' plan of the town, over two hundred and fifty acres, which adjoined the parsonage lot on the southeast. They both came here not far from 1768, and were, we believe, connected by marriage; Mr. Bray was also a brother of the wife of Captain Mark Haskell. He settled upon the western part of the lot, and was the father of Nathaniel and William Bray, and his daughters were the wives of Mr. Benjamin Cole, who occupied the lot of land adjoining that of Deacon Joshua Haskell; of Mr. Willaby Nason; of Mr. Edward Howard, of Brooksville; of Mr. Peter Perry, and of Mr. Ezekiel Morey, Jr.

Mr. Nason occupied the eastern part of the lot, which was the farm since owned by Mr. Ezekiel Marshall. Of him but little is known. One of his sons, Mr. Willaby Nason, lived here a number of years, and afterward removed to the town of Knox, in Waldo County, where he died. A daughter of Mr. Nason, Sr., was the wife of Mr. Nathaniel Bray, Jr., and mother of Messrs. Robert, Jonathan, Nathaniel, John N., Daniel, Willaby N., and Isaac Bray, and of three daughters who married Jeremiah and Andrew Gray, and Mr. David Campbell who removed to the British provinces. Mrs. Bray died several years ago, and all her children are now dead. Four of her sons died very suddenly, as have some of her grandchildren.

On the western side of the Northwest Harbor the first settlement was made by Mr. John Pressey, not long after the first made in the town, as early perhaps as 1765. He came from Salisbury, Massachusetts, or some place in that vicinity, as that was the residence of his wife, whose maiden name was Chase — one of the "Chase heirs" about whom much was said not far from the year 1845. He must have been past middle age at the time of his coming, and the time of his death is not to us known. His house was near the shore, and his remains lie not far from the edge of the bank. His sons were John, Jr., Chase, and Paul Pressey. One of his daughters was the Mrs. Colby lately mentioned, and another was the wife of Mr. Nathan Johnson and mother of John P. Johnson, Esq., who is now (1881) eighty-four years of age. The name was originally " Percy," as appeared from what is known as a coat-of-arms which was kept in the family many years.

JOHN PRESSEY, Jr., settled upon the lot of land adjoining that of his father on the southwest, and, we should judge, had a family at the time of his removal. His death was caused by a tree falling upon him while chopping, but the time of its occurrence is not to us known. His son was John Pressey, 3d, the father of Mr. Henry Pressey who was lost in 1849 or 1850, in the schooner *Tamerlane*, Captain John G. Green, master. His daughters were the wives of Mr. John Howard, before noticed; of Mr. Joseph Webster, of North Haven, and of Mr. Michael Howard, the son of Mr. Ezra Howard. Another, named Mercy, was never married. She lived for many years as housekeeper with Mr. Nathan Crockett who, at his death, made provision for her support.

The farm of Mr. John Pressey, Jr., was divided; one part of it is now the property of Mr. Aaron D. Pickering, and the remainder was that of Mr. Jonathan Pressey at the time of his death.

THOMAS SAUNDERS, who came here from Amesbury in the State of Massachusetts, settled upon the lot of land lying westerly of, and adjoining, that of Mr. John Pressey, Jr. His wife was Miss Hephzibah Chase, of Salisbury, Massachusetts, and they were married in Hampton, New Hampshire, in 1755. In 1757 they moved to Amesbury, and came here in 1771. His wife and that of Mr. John Pressey, Sr., were sisters. Mr. Saunders was drowned near the mouth of the Northwest Harbor in June, 1786, while engaged in towing some logs which were to be used in making pumps for the purpose of pumping salt water for the manufacture of salt. He left two sons, Messrs. James and Timothy Saunders, and two daughters, one the wife of Mr. John Dow; another, that of Mr. Thomas Small, Jr. His farm passed into the hands of his sons, who occupied it till they died. It now is the property of their descendants. The wife of Mr. James Saunders was Susan Webb, a daughter of Mr. Seth Webb, one of the early settlers; that of Mr. Timothy Saunders was Ann Staples, the daughter of the person of that name before noticed as having been impressed into the British service during the war of the Revolution.

The sons of Mr. James Saunders were the late Thomas and Captain James Saunders. One of the daughters was the wife of the late Mr. Crowell H. Sylvester. Another was first the wife of Mr. Joseph Whitmore, Jr., and afterwards of Dr. Robert Young who made the treatment of cancers a specialty. After his death she married Mr. Jonah Dodge of Brooklin, Maine, and, lastly, Mr. Sylvester, the husband of her late sister, whom she also survived. Another married Mr. John Averill, of Castine, and afterwards Mr. Josiah B. Woods, of that place. Another married Captain Henry Lufkin, Jr.; another, Captain Joseph R. Lufkin; another, Mr. Benjamin Lufkin, and one, Mary, remained unmarried. All are now dead with the exception of the widow of Captain J. R. Lufkin, who is now (1882) eighty-one years of age.

The sons of Mr. Timothy Saunders were Samuel, John, Asa, and Timothy; the daughters were the wives of Messrs. Thomas, Ezra, and Joshua Pressey, and Captain David Haskell. All the family are now dead.

JONATHAN EATON, a native of Haverhill, Massachusetts, was the settler upon the lot of land adjoining that of Mr. Saunders on the west. He was the youngest brother of Mr. Theophilus Eaton, and was born in 1746. His father dying in his childhood, he was brought up by his eldest brother Theophilus. His wife was Miss Diana Dow, a daughter of Mr. Nathan Dow, with whom he came here in 1767, having previously married; and in the year of his removal his eldest son was born here. He was a man of enterprise and, as has been stated, was engaged in the business of boiling salt. He died in 1805, at the age of fifty-nine years. His children were: Joseph, who lived and died in Sedgwick; Jonathan; John, who was drowned in 1814, while engaged with Mr. Joseph Whitmore, Jr., and a Mr. Brown, of Vinalhaven, in taking a cow across the bay to Vinalhaven in a boat. Their bodies were never found, but that of the cow came ashore on what is called Sellers's Point. Another son was the late Mr. Nathan Eaton, who occupied the homestead of his father. Another was James Eaton, who removed to the town of Prospect, where he lived till his death. The daughters were the wives of Mr. Joseph Weed, Mr. William Weed, and Mr. Samuel Webb. The house built by Mr. Eaton is still standing, and has recently been thoroughly repaired. It is now more than ninety years old, and still occupied by his descendants.

ELIJAH DUNHAM, Sr., with his sons Elijah and Joseph Dunham, occupied the lot westerly of that of Mr. Eaton, on what is still known as Dunham's Point, upon which is located the silver mine which is being operated. Mr. Dunham was twice married. By his first wife he had the two sons mentioned, and a daughter, the wife of Mr. Samuel Pickering and mother of the late Captain Samuel and Mr. Daniel Pickering. Mr. Pickering settled what is known as Pickering's Island, lying northwesterly of Deer Island, which is not included within the territorial limits of the town. By his last wife Mr. Dunham had one son, the late Mr. Elisha H. Dunham, and two daughters. He did not remain long on the lot taken up by him, and it came into the possession of Messrs. Mark Haskell & Sons, and was the property of Ignatius Haskell, Esq., at his death. Mr. Dunham lived upon several other lots of land. He died in this town at an advanced age. His son Elijah Dunham, Jr., was three times married: his first wife was the daughter of Captain Mark Haskell, by whom he had one son and three daughters; his second was the mother of Mr. George G. Choate, and his third was Miss Polly Morey, a daughter of Mr. Elias Morey. He died in 1852, at the age of ninety years.

Mr. Joseph Dunham married the widow of Mr. Charles Chatto, and died not long after the year 1830. The lot taken up by them is now owned principally by Mr. Ebenezer J. Eaton.

CHASE PRESSEY, a son of Mr. John Pressey, Sr., settled the lot of land adjoining that of his father upon the southeast. His wife was the daughter of Mr. Ezra Howard, who was one of the early settlers near the Northwest Harbor. Mr. Pressey died not far from the year 1830, and his widow in 1841. His sons were Thomas, Jonathan, Ezra, Joshua, and Jeremiah. His daughters were the wives of Messrs. Michael Ready, Nathan Eaton, Edward B. Eaton and Michael Howard, Jr. His farm, as also that of his father, is principally owned and occupied by his descendants.

PAUL PRESSEY, a brother of the last-named settler, occupied the lot adjoining on the southeast. It was taken up early by Mr. Lot Curtis, and his right was acquired by Mr. Pressey. His wife was a daughter of Mr. Ezra Howard, and their children were Pearl S., Elbridge G., Calvin, the wife of Mr. David Sawyer, Jr., and a daughter who lived in Boston. His sons remained here, with the exception of Elbridge, who removed to Castine, where he was living a few years since, the sole survivor of the family. His land, which is still known as "the Paul Pressey lot," passed, principally, into the hands of the late Pearl Spofford, Esq., and a large portion of it is now owned by the Hon. C. A. Spofford.

JOHN HOOPER was the settler who occupied the lot adjoining that of Paul Pressey on the southeast, but upon Peters' plan, it stands in the name of William Hooper, who probably acquired a right to the lot through John Hooper. William Hooper, who was known as Captain Hooper, removed to the town of Brooklin, where his descendants still reside, but none of that name remain here. A part of his farm passed into the possession of Mr. Nathan Johnson, who was here prior to 1784, and was the estate occupied by his son, the late Mr. Daniel Johnson, and now by his son and daughter. The other part of the Hooper lot was purchased by Mr. John Whitmore, and by him sold to Captain Richard Greenlaw. It is now owned and occupied by Captain Thomas R. Greenlaw.

NATHAN JOHNSON came here, as stated above, prior to 1784, but there seems to have been no settler's right assigned him, probably because he had not taken up a lot. He was for many years a school-teacher, and was known as "Master Johnson." His wife was the youngest daughter of Mr. John Pressey, Sr. Their sons were Daniel and John P. One of their daughters was the wife of Captain Joseph Raynes; one, the wife of Mr. Ebenezer Greenlaw and formerly of Mr. Abner Babbidge who was lost in the schooner *Shakespeare*, Captain John Green, master, in 1818. Another daughter, Lucy, married quite late in life, and another, Mary, died unmarried. Mr. Johnson died soon after 1800, and his widow survived him not many years.

EZEKIEL MOREY was one of the very early settlers. He came here about 1767, from New Meadows River, in the vicinity of Brunswick, Maine. From what information I have been able to gain, he built the first framed house in the town. Mr. Morey was twice married, and had a large family, thirteen children surviving him. The time of his death I have not learned. After his death the principal part of his farm, a large and valuable one, passed by purchase from his heirs, into the hands of the late Hezekiah Rowell, Esq., who built a house upon it, which was afterward purchased by the late Joseph Sellers, 3d, and is now the estate of his two deceased sons, George W. and Mark H. Sellers, the lot they own containing some six acres. The residue Mr. Rowell sold to various persons, who have built upon their respective lots. His sons who survived him were Elias, Ezekiel, Isaac, Joseph, and James. The daughters were the wives of Mr. Charles Sellers, of this town; a Mr. Calderwood, of Vinalhaven; two were the wives of a Mr. Wooster, of the same place; one of a Mr. Edson; one of a Mr. Sweet; one of a Mr. Day, who resided on the island of Mount Desert, and the youngest of the late Mr. Joseph Noyes, of this town, a native of Atkinson, New Hampshire, who came in 1804, and died not far from 1850. Mrs. Noyes survived her husband a few years. She was a lady held in much respect, a sincere Christian, and beloved by all who knew her. The children of Mr. Noyes, with one exception, have removed from this town, and the land and buildings he occupied are now owned by Mr. William C. Gray. All the above sons and daughters, except Mr. Elias Morey, Mrs. Sellers, and Mrs. Noyes removed from this place; Ezekiel and Isaac to the town of Hope, Maine, and afterward to the State of Ohio; Joseph lived and died in Castine, and James lived in the town of Levant, not far from

Bangor. Mr. Elias Morey died not far from the year 1844; Mrs. Sellers in 1832, aged eighty-three. Mr. Morey, the father, was very tall of stature, being nearly seven feet in height, and a very worthy man.

WILLIAM BABBIDGE was the first settler upon the lot of land adjoining that of Mr. Morey on the east. He came very early — prior to 1770 — and was a brother to Mr. Courtney Babbidge, Sr., who came some years after and resided near the Southeast Harbor. He afterward sold out his right to Mr. Joshua Haskell, a brother of Ignatius Haskell, Esq., and took up another lot of land, on what is known as Babbidge's Neck, which was a few years ago occupied by Mr. Seth Hatch and the late Captain John Greenlaw, but which subsequently became the property of Mr. Hatch's son, the late Captain Jeremiah Hatch. Mr. Babbidge left no son, but had five daughters, who were the wives of Mr. William Greenlaw, Mr. Samuel Stinson, Mr. Joseph Whitmore, Mr. Seth Hatch, and Mr. Samuel Staples. After the death of her husband Mrs. Babbidge became the wife of Mr. Thomas Robbins, Sr.

JOSHUA HASKELL, the resident of the land taken up by Mr. Babbidge, came when a young man not twenty years old with his father, Captain Mark Haskell. His wife was a daughter of Deacon Francis Haskell, before noticed. He was for many years a deacon in the Congregational Church, and was known as "Deacon Joshua." His sons were: Joshua, who for many years tended the gristmill at the Northwest Harbor; Thomas, a master ship-carpenter; Mark, who died when a young man; Edward, who died not far from the year 1862, and Ignatius, the father of the present Captain George C. Haskell. One of his daughters was the wife of Mr. Jonathan Webster who removed to Castine, where she died not far from 1824; another, wife of Mr. Samuel Noyes who was a brother of Mr. Joseph Noyes, and came with him here. He was a noted shipwright for many years, and was well known as " Master Noyes," here and in Castine, where he lived a long time and died. Another was the wife of Mr. Joseph Sellers, 3d, who died here, and the youngest, who is still living, married John Turner, Esq., of Isle au Haut. The others are all now dead. Deacon Haskell, at the time of his death, which took place not long after the year 1830, owned a large and valuable farm, which came into the possession of his heirs. He was a man much respected by all who knew him, being considered an upright man. His widow survived him till 1842.

BENJAMIN COLE was the settler upon the lot of land adjoining that of Joshua Haskell. He came early, between the years 1767 and 1770. About him but little is known, nor do we know from what place he came here. He had one son of the same name, Benjamin, who came with him, and occupied a lot of land that he took up. They both had settlers' rights, one of them being located near Fish Creek, and the farm now occupied by Mr. Joseph S. Greenlaw is a part of it. The remainder is now in the possession of Mr. Benjamin Cole, the great-grandson of the first named. The time of the death of Mr. Cole is not to us known. His daughter was the wife of Mr. Abijah Haskell, a son of Deacon Francis Haskell, and we have no knowledge of any more of the family, if any there were. His son Benjamin married a daughter of Nathaniel Bray, Sr., and their sons were: Benjamin, the father of the present Mr. Enos Cole; Joseph, who lived near the Town House; Willard, who lived at Fish Creek, on the farm now occupied by his son Benjamin; Nathaniel, and one who died many years ago, of the name of Jonathan. The daughters were: one, the wife of the late Captain Samuel Pickering, and another, that of Mr. Willard Bray. Mr.

Benjamin Cole, Jr., was for many years sexton of the first parish church in the town, and after his death Mr. William Morey officiated in that capacity till the time of his death. The farm of Mr. Cole, Sr., is now in part owned by his descendants.

JOSHUA EMERSON, a native of Haverhill, Massachusetts, was the first settler upon the lot of land lying south of that taken up by Elijah Dunham, on what is known as Dunham's Point. He came some time prior to the year 1790, but probably was not here in season to be considered as entitled to a right by settlement, — prior to 1784, — and was one of the class styled " young settlers." He built a sawmill at the outlet of the cove, near the property now occupied by Captain Benjamin J. Sylvester, that is still known as " Emerson's Mill Pond." He resided on the lot taken up by him, which was afterward occupied by the late Mr. Crowell H. Sylvester, and upon which he (Mr. Sylvester) lived till his death in 1863. Mr. Emerson conveyed his property to Major David Coffin, of Newburyport, Massachusetts, who lived several years in Castine, where he died in 1838. In 1807 Mr. Emerson left his farm and moved on to a fifty-acre lot, which, in 1795, he had purchased of Ephraim Packard, of Beverly, Massachusetts (that now occupied by Mr. Samuel Dunham), where he died in 1810. His wife was Hannah, the daughter of Mr. Seth Webb, who will be noticed; she lived upon the farm till her death in 1838. Their children were: Seth, who died in 1827; Joshua, who died in 1842; Samuel, who died not many years ago, in Isleborough, and William, a young man, whose death was caused by lockjaw, about the year 1821. The daughters were the wives of Mr. Daniel Allen, Samuel Allen, Jr., and a Mr. Cummings, of Tyngsborough, Massachusetts, who left her a widow. She afterward married a Mr. Edward Alexander. But one only of the family, the wife of Captain Samuel Allen, is now living.

SAMUEL TRUNDY was the occupant of the lot of land lying on the south side of Emerson's Mill Pond and at the head of the Southwest Harbor. He was a native of Cape Elizabeth, Maine, and came here in 1765,— the first person who made a settlement upon the west side of the island and southwesterly of the Northwest Harbor, except Mr. John Pressey and his son John Pressey, Jr. A former neighbor of his, Mr. Thomas Small, came east intending to settle in the present town of Bluehill, and on his way anchoring in the Northwest Harbor, came over to see him, and was by him persuaded to remain. This was in 1767, and at that time Mr. Pressey had made his settlement. Mr. Trundy's mother came with him and was his housekeeper for a few years, when her other son, Mr. George Trundy, came and removed her to his home. Their father was a native of Holland, and died when a young man, leaving two sons. The wife of Mr. Samuel Trundy was Miss Ann Carey, and they were the parents of fourteen children, and grandparents of one hundred and twenty. Eleven of their children had families. Five of them had twelve children each; two had eleven each; three, ten each; and one, eight. Mr. Trundy died in 1805. His widow became the wife of Mr. James Jordan, who died in 1818; she afterward married Mr. Jeremiah Stover, who outlived her, she dying in 1826. The children of Mr. Trundy were: Daniel, who died in 1835, in Dover, Maine; Samuel, who died in Newburyport; Thomas, who died in 1846, and John, in 1859, in Rockland. The daughters were the wives of Messrs. Peletiah Barter, Abner Lane, David Thurlow, Daniel Crockett, Jonathan Pressey, John Whitmore, and Hon. Richard Warren, all of whom are now dead.

JOHN RAYNES, Sr., and his sons John, Johnson, and William Raynes settled the lot of land lying south of that of Mr. Trundy. They were natives of York, Maine, and came here in 1772, in company with two of the same name, Messrs. Samuel and James Raynes, who were relatives of theirs. Mr. John Raynes, Sr., lived not many years after he came here. His wife was also a native of York, and her name before marriage was Abigail Harmon. Their children were the three sons who came with him and four daughters, — one the wife of Mr. Anthony Merchant, the person who settled what is known as Merchant's Island, now included in the limits of the town of Isle au Haut, who came about the same time. One daughter was Mrs. Mary Kingsley, who remained in York. Another was the wife of Mr. Joshua Staples; another, whose name was Miriam, remained unmarried. The ancestor of Mr. Raynes was Francis Raynes, one of the earliest inhabitants of York, whose name is found in Williamson's *History of Maine* as one of the persons residing there in 1653, when the town was incorporated. His son, John Raynes, Jr., was born in 1753, and was a master-mariner for several years. His wife was Sarah, daughter of Mr. Theophilus Eaton; they lived as husband and wife sixty years to a day, being married December 25, 1777, and he dying the same day in 1837, at the age of eighty-four years. He was at Bagaduce at the time of the attack by the Americans upon the British in 1779. His sons were: William, who died in 1869, at the age of ninety-one years; John, who removed to Newburyport, but returned here a few years before his death in 1862; Joseph, who died in 1859; Benjamin, who died in 1861, and one named Ebenezer who died in 1819, in the West Indies, at the age of twenty-two years. One of the daughters was the wife of Mr. Daniel Lufkin; another married Mr. Stephen

Babbidge, and afterward Mr. Otis Oliver, and there were two who remained unmarried. The wife of Captain John Raynes survived him till 1850, dying at the age of ninety-one years, retaining her mind and memory in a remarkable degree. From her I learned much about the earlier settlers. Two days before she died I saw her, and her health was then very good for a person of her age. Her death took place in the month of February, during very cold weather, which is often fatal in its effect upon persons of great age. At that time she was the oldest member of the Congregational Church in the town.

JOHNSON RAYNES, before mentioned, was never married. His house stood on land now owned by Captain H. T. Lufkin, about thirty rods west of the town road, in the field. His unmarried sister, Miriam, resided with him till her death. He was said to be a man of superior intelligence, was a great reader, and had a good deal of understanding. His brother, William Raynes, married Miriam Robinson (a sister to the mother of the late Captain Henry Lufkin who died very suddenly, in 1868). Their children were Edward and Johnson Raynes, the latter of whom died in 1873. One of the daughters was the wife of Mr. Asa B. Eaton, and the mother of Captain William R. Eaton, formerly of this town, but now of Newburyport. Another was the former wife of Mr. Asa Saunders, and mother of Captain Ebenezer Saunders, of this town. Another was the wife of Mr. William Atherton, of Mt. Desert; another married Mr. Jonathan Pressey, Jr., and another, named Joanna, remained unmarried. Mrs. Atherton is, in 1882, the only one of them living. Mr. William Raynes, some time about the year 1790, sold a part of his land to a Mr. Lufkin, of Gloucester, Massachusetts; upon his death, which occurred soon after the purchase, it came into the possession of his brother, Mr.

Benjamin Lufkin, who removed here from Gloucester with his family, and built a house near that now occupied by Mr. John T. Brown, where he resided till his death. Both himself and his wife were members of the church in Gloucester, of which the celebrated Universalist preacher, John Murray, was pastor, it being the first church of that denomination in New England. The children of Mr. Lufkin were: Benjamin, who lived and died in Sedgwick; Henry, the father of the present Captain Mark H. Lufkin, and Daniel, who died in 1871. The daughters were the wives of Mr. Abraham Babson, who lived near Naskeag Point, now in the town of Brooklin; Mr. Jonah Dodge, of the same town; a Mr. McMullen, of Vinalhaven, and Mr. Edward Raynes, the eldest son of Mr. William Raynes. Mr. Lufkin was by trade a shoemaker, and before he came here, in 1790, had a shop in Gloucester which stood near the site now occupied by the Gloucester House. Those of the same name in that place at present are relatives of his descendants.

SAMUEL RAYNES, a nephew of John Raynes, Sr., settled upon the lot adjoining that of Captain John Raynes on the south. He did not remain many years upon it, but moved back to York. His land passed into the hands of Ignatius Haskell, Esq., by whom it was sold to the late Captain William Raynes, not far from the year 1800, who a few years after built a house upon it, which is still standing, in which he resided till his death. It became the property of his son, the late A. B. Raynes, who died in Norwich, Connecticut, in the year 1881, and from him, went to his son, Mr. Charles H. Raynes, of that place. We have no knowledge of the time of the death of Samuel Raynes, nor of his history after his removal to York.

JAMES RAYNES, a brother of the subject of the preceding sketch, settled upon the lot of land adjoining that of

Samuel Raynes on the south. He died not many years after he came here, and the property fell into the hands of his sister, Anna Raynes, who conveyed it to Mr. Ebenezer Webster, a native of Cape Elizabeth, whose wife was a sister to the wife of Mr. Job Small. They were the parents of Andrew, Joseph, John, and Ebenezer Webster; of Mrs. Anna Small, wife of Captain Ebenezer Small, and a daughter who removed from here. Mr. Andrew Webster lived and died in Brooksville. Joseph lived in North Haven. John was lost at sea in about 1815. He was a master-mariner, and at the time of his death the son of Mr. Nathaniel Bray, noticed before, named Daniel, was one of the crew of the vessel of which Captain Webster was master. Captain Ebenezer Webster, Jr., was an enterprising ship-master, and sailed for many years in the employ of William Bartlett, Esq., of Newburyport, a wealthy ship-owner in the early part of the present century, and after retiring from the sea resided in Cape Elizabeth, where his father lived with him till his death. Mr. Webster sold the land to Mr. Job Small, Jr., and from him it was sold to his brother, Michael Small, Esq., and by him, in 1817, to Mr. Charles Sellers, one of the early settlers, whom we shall notice, who resided upon it till his death; after that it came into the possession of his son, the late Mr. Joseph Sellers, 2d, and is now owned and occupied by his sons and widow.

THOMAS SMALL, who came here in 1767 from Cape Elizabeth, settled upon the lot of land adjoining that of Mr. James Raynes on the south, doing this, as has been stated, at the solicitation of Mr. Trundy, there being no other person in the near vicinity at the time, and as Mr. Small was an old acquaintance, he was the more desirous of having him as a neighbor. A settlement had been attempted upon the lot by a man of the name of Martin, who had abandoned it, or was about to do so. The land taken up by Mr. Small was one of the most valuable lots in the town for farming purposes, there being but very little waste-land upon it. He first settled near the bar which lies across the mouth of what is known as Small's Cove, on the land that is now occupied by his great-grandson, Mr. Enoch Small. He lived upon this place some sixty years, dying in the year 1827, his wife dying at nearly the same time, they having lived in wedlock about sixty-four years. Their eldest child, the late Mrs. Mary Lunt, was in her fourth year at the time of the removal here of her parents, and had a very distinct remembrance of it. She lived until 1859, and died at the great age of ninety-five years, with her mind and memory unimpaired till the last. She was one of those who gave me much information concerning the early settlement of the town, and I never found any other person of her age who, in my opinion, retained the mental faculties so clearly. She was the wife of Mr. Micajah Lunt, of Newburyport, and the mother of the widow of Mr. Avery Fifield, a native of Haverhill, New Hampshire, who came here in 1803, or thereabouts, and who was well known, had many friends, and took a prominent part in business and town affairs. He died in the year 1845; Mrs. Fifield died in 1882, at the age of ninety-six years, having been born February 6, 1786. Mrs. Lunt was an earnest Christian, and in early life united with the church at the Northwest Harbor. The sons of Mr. Small were Thomas, Ebenezer, Benjamin, William, and Joseph; and the daughters, beside Mrs. Lunt, were the wives of Mr. William Sellers, Mr. Joseph Randall, the second son of Mr. George G. Choate, Mr. Simon Smith, and of a Mr. Small in Cape Elizabeth. After the decease of Mr. Small his property was owned by his son Ebenezer and others of the family, and is now in the possession of

Mr. Joseph C. Judkins, Captain H. F. Cole, Enoch Small, a "young settler"; and Captain H. T. Lufkin. His son, Thomas Small, Jr., settled upon the lot adjoining on the south, as a "young settler"; his wife was Miss Anna Saunders, the daughter of Mr. Thomas Saunders, who has been mentioned. Their children were: Thomas, who lived and died in Newburyport; James, who formerly resided on Plum Island, near that place; Reuben who came to his death by burning, in 1827; William, and Joel, who now lives in Islesborough. The daughters were the wives of Mr. Jesse Stinson, Mr. Charles Barbour, Mr. Hale Powers, and Mr. John G. Small who now resides in Belfast. The two last-named daughters, with Joel Small, are now living. Mr. Small, the father, died in 1846, at the age of seventy-eight years.

The second son of Mr. Thomas Small, Sr., was Captain Ebenezer Small, a master-mariner, who died in 1827 or 1828; his wife was Miss Ann Webster, the daughter of Mr. Ebenezer Webster. They were the parents of twelve children, seven of whom were sons: Ebenezer, John W., Edward, Benjamin, Avery, Enoch, and Joseph W. The daughters were the wives of Captain William B. Hatch, formerly of Pembroke, Maine; of Messrs. Edward Richardson; Thomas Tyler who removed to Winterport and died there; William Tyler who removed to the same place and was lost at sea, and one, who was the wife of Mr. Paul Thurlow, is now the only one of the family that remains here. The wife of Captain Small survived him several years.

The third son of the family of Mr. Thomas Small, Sr., was Benjamin Small, who died in 1827, and at the time resided at Burnt Cove, on the place afterward owned by Mr. Avery Fifield, Jr. His wife was Miss Mary Lunt, of Newburyport, to which place she removed with her family after the death of her husband.

The fourth son of the family was William Small, whose wife was Lydia, the daughter of Mr. Joseph Colby, Jr. His death which was caused by a person who represented himself to be a Thompsonian doctor, occurred not far from the year 1814. He was not in good health and consented to put himself under the care of this person, going through the process of steaming to which they subjected their patients, and the succeeding operation of pouring cold water over him to such an extent that he died within an hour. The doctor, finding what was the result of his practice with him, immediately made his escape, and had barely the time to get away from the island, being followed by the two brothers of the deceased, who were so much enraged that they would perhaps have dealt violently with him had they overtaken him. The only child of Mr. Small was Lydia, who was afterwards the wife of Mr. Avery Fifield, Jr. His widow married Mr. Israel Dorr, of Frankfort, and they remained here until 1844, when they removed to Bucksport.

The last son of Mr. Thomas Small's family was Joseph Small who, when a young man, removed to Newburyport, where he followed the sea, married, had one son, and, in 1807, died. His widow afterwards became the wife of Mr. John Howard who has been noticed, and upon his decease she married Mr. Samuel Small, Sr., after whose death she removed to Newburyport.

JOB SMALL, a brother of Mr. Thomas Small, settled in 1768 upon the lot of land on the south side of Small's Cove, not far from the land of his brother. His wife was Miss Mercy Wescott, daughter of the ancestor of all of that name in the towns of Castine, Penobscot, and Bluehill. His name was William, and a son of his of the same name was the grandfather of the present Captain Joseph Wescott now residing in Castine, who was for many years

Town of Deer Isle, Maine. 101

known as a ship-master, and still lives upon the land taken up by his grandfather, who was one of the early settlers there prior to the war of the Revolution. Mr. Small died early in the present century, and his widow died in 1835 at the age of ninety-six years, — the oldest person in the town at the time. There are but two instances of greater longevity among us. The children of Mr. Small were: Andrew, who died in 1828, aged eighty-four; Samuel, who died in 1854, aged eighty-six; Job, who lived and died in the town of Stockton, aged nearly eighty years; Edward, who died in 1864, aged ninety-four years; Naylor, who died in 1863, aged ninety-one years, and Michael, who died in 1837 at the age of fifty-eight years. There was but one daughter in the family, — Alice, who was the wife of Captain John Webster, mentioned before; she died in Portland. The farm of Mr. Small was conveyed by him to his son, Michael Small, and is now the property of his son who resides upon it.

CHARLES SELLERS settled upon the lot of land adjoining that of Mr. Job Small on the west. He was a native of the town of York, Maine, where his father followed the sea and died when a young man. His widow, with two of her sons, Charles and Joseph, came here in 1772. Another brother, William, older than the ones we have mentioned, remained there for some years, when he came, but not in season to be entitled to a lot of land as a settler. Mr. Charles Sellers was born in 1750, and his wife was Jerusha, the eldest daughter of Mr. Ezekiel Morey. He lived upon the farm taken up by him till 1817, when he purchased the one taken up by James Raynes, of Michael Small, Esq., the then owner, who purchased that which Mr. Sellers occupied, it joining his own, and at his death bequeathed it to his two youngest sons. It is now the property of Mr. Thomas S. Powers and of the heirs of the late Charles T. Powers. Mr. Sellers lived upon the place purchased by him till his death in 1834, his wife dying in 1832. Their children were: John, who lived and died in Vinalhaven; Charles, who resided in the Province of New Brunswick, near the St. Croix River between Eastport and Calais, and Joseph the youngest son, who remained with him and lived upon the place during his lifetime, after his removal to it, dying in 1865 at the age of seventy-two years; Martha the wife of Mr. David Torrey, who died in 1879 at the age of ninety-seven years; Susan, the wife of Captain James Torrey, who died in 1875, aged ninety-one years; Sarah, the wife of Mr. Seth Emerson, and two daughters who died unmarried.

JOSEPH SELLERS, the brother of Charles, took up the lot of land adjoining that of his brother on the south. He was born in 1752, and at the time of his removal here he was twenty years of age. His mother lived with him as a housekeeper, till age and infirmity disqualified her; he then married the daughter of Thomas Thompson, when he was forty-eight years of age. They had nine children — three sons: Joseph, known as Joseph Sellers, 3d, who traded at the Northwest Harbor for many years, was interested in navigation, and occupied the house in that vicinity known as the Sellers house, and who died not far from 1850. Another son was Thomas, and another William, both of whom are dead. None of the daughters remained here; the youngest married Captain Thomas D. Toothaker, who removed to Belfast and died at sea. Mr. Sellers died in 1844, at the age of ninety-two years. His farm passed into the hands of his eldest son, by whose heirs it was sold. It was the property of Mr. Charles T. Powers at the time of his death in 1880. Mr. Sellers was for many years one of the board of selectmen, and was one of the first chosen in 1789.

JOSIAH CROCKETT was the settler upon the lot of land adjoining that of Mr. Joseph Sellers on the east, and the body of water which lies on its eastern side is still called Crockett's Cove. He removed here from Portland, then known as Falmouth, or that vicinity, not far from 1768. His wife was a daughter of Mr. Nathan Dow and a sister to the wife of Mr. Jonathan Eaton. He was a singular man, and the date of his death is not to us known. He took up a lot, and when the survey of the town was made, one of two hundred and twelve acres was assigned him. Why he had one so large is not known to us. He had claimed other lots, but no other was run out to him. He sold one hundred acres to Mr. Ephraim Packard, of Beverly, Massachusetts, who, in 1795, as we have stated, sold fifty acres to Mr. Joshua Emerson; the balance is still known "as the Packard lot." It was sold for non-payment of taxes in 1833, and became the property of Mr. Joseph Sellers, 3d, and is now owned by Captain Stephen B. Morey. The land owned by Mr. Crockett at the time of his death came into the possession of his son, Mr. Nathan Crockett, and is now owned by the heirs of the late Mr. Edmund S. Stinson. The children of Mr. Crockett were: Nathan, Ephraim, and Sarah, the last of whom became the wife of Mr. William Webb, and afterward that of Deacon William Stinson before noticed.

CAPTAIN ROBINSON CROCKETT, a brother of the person last noticed, came here in 1785 with a family and remained here till his death. He was not entitled to a lot of land as one of the early settlers, but must have been one of those styled "young settlers." He took up a lot lying east of, and adjoining, the lot of Mr. Samuel Trundy; the homestead of Captain Mark H. Lufkin is a part of it, as is also that of the late Captain James Saunders. The time of his death is unknown to us. His children were: Samuel, who the latter part of his life resided in the town of Prospect, died there, and whose widow was the wife of Mr. Thomas Robbins, Jr., who resided near the bar leading to Stinson's Neck. Another was Mr. Robinson Crockett, Jr., whose wife was a daughter of Mr. Thomas Conary, and who for many years resided on Stinson's Neck, and tended a sawmill, of which he was part owner, afterwards removing to Little Deer Island, thence to Brooksville, where he died not far from 1830, aged over eighty years. Another was Joseph, whose wife was a sister of the wives of Mr. Elias Morey, William Raynes, and Captain Henry Lufkin, and who removed to St. Andrews, in the Province of New Brunswick. Another was Richard, the father of the present Captain L. B. Crockett, who for many years tended a sawmill near what is known as the " Barbour farm," of which he was a part owner. The other son was the late Mr. Ephraim Crockett, who for many years lived on Stinson's Neck, on the farm now owned by Mr. Josiah C. Webb, and who afterward removed to Rockport, Maine, — a part of the town of Camden, — where he died. The daughters were the wives of Messrs. Andrew Small, Samuel Small, David Sawyer, and William Morey, the last the mother of the present Mr. Levi B. Morey. Captain Crockett, the subject of this sketch, was, before he came here, a master-mariner sailing from Falmouth.

JAMES JORDAN came to this town, — but from what place I have been unable to learn, — some time prior to 1790, though not in season to have a settler's lot laid out to him. The place of his birth is not known to us. He was, for many years, in the employment of the Government of Great Britain, on Sable Island which lies east of the Province of Nova Scotia, being there for the purpose of giving aid to the crews of vessels that were wrecked upon the shoals around it. In those days it was considered a dangerous place, as it is a long, low island, not easily discernible on approach, and there are two dangerous bars, one at the eastern, and the other at the western end, upon which a vessel would strike when at considerable distance from the island. It is in the track of vessels bound from Europe to Halifax, and to the ports lying adjacent to the Bay of Fundy. There were huts erected for the accommodation of those who might be wrecked, and horses which could feed upon a sort of grass growing there, were kept upon it. It was his duty while there to ride each day from end to end of the island, to ascertain whether any one needed assistance. For their subsistence it was visited from time to time by persons in the employ of the government, and supplies left there for such as might need them. How long he remained there we do not know, but he removed to some place in this State before he came here. His eldest daughter was the wife of a Mr. Grover, who lived and died in the town of Bowdoinham, in Sagadahoc County. He lived for a long time on what was then known as Sheep, but now as Jordan's, Island, which was a part of the settlers' right of Messrs. James and Timothy Saunders, from whom it was purchased. Later, he removed to a lot which he had bought of Mr. Samuel Trundy, whose widow he afterward married, and there he died of a cancer on his lip, in 1818, at the age of eighty-six years. His sons were Ebenezer Jordan, who died in 1839, and Mr. Samuel Jordan, who lived in Sedgwick. The daughters were the Mrs. Grover above mentioned, and the wives of Messrs. Daniel Trundy, James Eaton, the son of Theophilus Eaton, and Richard Greenlaw. The island occupied by Mr. Jordan was afterward the property of Mr. Ebenezer Jordan, Sr., and after his death it became that of his heirs, but it is now uninhabited, as no one has resided there since the death of the widow of Mr. Ebenezer Jordan, Jr., which took place in 1879.

The wife of Mr. Ebenezer Jordan, Sr., was Olive, the daughter of Mr. William Sellers (a brother of Charles and Joseph Sellers and the father of Mr. William Sellers, father of the present Mr. Amos Sellers). The children of the family were: Benjamin, who went away when a young man and never returned, nor had his parents knowledge of his residence, if he were living; Ebenezer Jordan, Jr., who died in 1852, at the age of forty-seven years; Sarah, the wife of Mr. Thomas Saunders; Hannah, the wife of Mr. John S. Trott, of Castine; Olive, the wife of Mr. Richard Brown who came here from Newburyport; Mehitable, the wife of Captain Richard Greenlaw, and Nancy, wife of Mr. Aaron D. Pickering.

ANDREW SMALL, the eldest son of Mr. Job Small, took up the lot adjoining that of his father on the east, as a " young settler." He was born in 1764, and his wife was Hannah, the daughter of Mr. Robinson Crockett. He was by trade a ship-carpenter, and was a very active, energetic man, and a good citizen. His sons were: the late Mr. Joseph Small, who died a few years ago, over eighty years of age; Captain Benjamin Small, who died when a young man, and Lemuel, who was drowned when a young man. The daughters were: Alice, the wife of Larkin Snow, Esq., of Rockland; Mercy, the wife of Mr. Jeremiah Pressey, who died the same time her husband did, and was buried in the same grave with him; Hannah, the wife of the late Captain John Trundy; Susan, the wife of Mr. David Conary, and Rebecca, the wife of Mr. Joel Whitten who removed to Rockland not far from 1850. The wife of Mr. Small died in 1836, and he afterward married the widow of Mr. James Greenlaw, who survived him. The farm he occupied is now the property of the heirs of the late Mr. Thomas Small.

SAMUEL SMALL settled upon the lot of land lying southeasterly of, and adjoining, that of the subject of the preceding notice, having purchased the right in it which belonged to Mr. Cornelius Brimhall, who claimed to own it by prior settlement. The first wife of Mr. Small was Sarah, the daughter of Captain Robinson Crockett. Their children were the present Mr. Samuel Small, now in his eighty-fifth year, and the wife of Mr. Rufus York who was drowned in 1844, in endeavoring to escape from his vessel which took fire in the night, while lying loaded with wood in Crockett's Cove. Mr. Small's wife died in 1823, and he afterward married the widow of Mr. John Howard, who survived him. He was a very worthy and sensible man who was much respected; and for his advantages he had acquired a good deal of information. For a few years before his death, in 1854, at the age of eighty-six, his mind had been failing him. His land passed into the hands of his son, but is now owned principally by Mr. Josiah C. Stinson.

MICAJAH LUNT, a native of Newburyport, came here not far from the year 1784, but no lot of land was assigned to him, nor have we knowledge that he ever owned one. His wife was the Mrs. Mary Lunt before noticed, and his daughter was the widow of the late Mr. Avery Fifield. Mr. Lunt was in the naval service of the United States during the war of the Revolution, and some years after his death, which took place not far from 1828, his widow received a pension.

The land lying south of what is known as Long Cove was first settled by three brothers named Abraham, John, and Isaac Freeze, no one of whom remained here for many years. The descendants of the last named still reside in the city of Ellsworth and in some of the towns north of it, on the Union River, and now spell their names

Frazier which, perhaps, may have been the name originally. The descendants of Abraham Freeze moved up the Penobscot River; they still reside in the towns north of the city of Bangor, and retain the name of Freeze. The wife of John had no children, and when the late Hon. Richard Warren was, when young, left an orphan (he was a grandson of a brother of her husband), she took care of him till he became able to do something for his own support. After his marriage he took her to his own home and provided for her during her life, showing a commendable gratitude which it is pleasant to remember. The Freeze brothers sold their rights to Messrs. Mark Haskell & Sons, to whom rights as settlers had been allotted adjoining their land, and who, at the time of Peters' survey, had a lot of about five hundred acres therein one body. Of that about ninety acres, those now occupied by Mr. Samuel G. Barbour, were sold to Mr. David Sawyer; about one hundred and fifty acres were set off to Deacon Solomon Haskell, one of the firm, and the remainder, two hundred and sixty acres, was at the time of the death of Ignatius Haskell, Esq., his property, a part of which land is known as the Barbour farm.

NATHANIEL ROBBINS settled the lot of land lying south of, and adjoining, the before-mentioned lot. He came here from Boston with his father about the year 1775. His wife was Miss Betsey Colby, a daughter of Mr. Joseph Colby. Their sons were Tristram T., Thomas, Nathaniel, and James, the last two of whom are still living. One of the daughters was the wife of the late Mr. Nathaniel Thurston, and is still living, aged over ninety years; another, of a Mr. Ackley, of the town of Cutler, and the other is now the widow of the late Mr. Leonard Judkins. The time of the death of Mr. Robbins we do not know. His widow died not far from the year 1850, over eighty years of age. The land he settled upon is still owned and occupied by his descendants.

COURTNEY BABBIDGE, Sr., and his two sons settled the lots adjoining that of Mr. Robbins on the south. They came here from Windham, Maine, in 1773. Mr. Babbidge does not seem to have had a settler's right assigned to him, and it is probable that at the time the survey was made, he was not living, or had removed from here. He was three times married, and was the father of Messrs. Stephen, Courtney, James and William Babbidge. The two former will be noticed. James removed to Vinalhaven, where he lived and died, and William removed to Windham. The daughters were the two wives of Mr. Oliver Lane and the wife of Captain Hezekiah Colby, a son of Mr. Ambrose Colby, Sr. The widow of Mr. Babbidge, whose maiden name was Staples, married Mr. James Joyce who lived here for some time, and afterward removed to Swan's Island, where they died, he being the ancestor of all of the name there and in this town. Mr. Babbidge was a brother of the Mr. William Babbidge who has been noticed.

STEPHEN BABBIDGE, his eldest son, settled upon the southern side of the lot taken up by them, and had his right assigned him there. His wife was Miss Hannah Staples, a daughter of the man who has been mentioned as having been impressed by the British. His sons were: Courtney, who lived for some years near the mouth of Union River, in the city of Ellsworth, and died there; Stephen, the father of the present Mr. William Babbidge; Levi, a master-mariner; John, who died very suddenly, in 1826; Aaron; the late Mr. William Babbidge, 2d, and James, who, in 1833, was drowned, with his wife and child, in passing through the flood-gates into the millpond, at the Southeast Harbor. The daughters were the wives of

Mr. William Barter, of Isle au Haut, and Mr. Nathaniel Robbins, Jr. Mr. Babbidge, who was for many years an invalid, died in 1841, aged eighty-two years. He was much respected; in his day had considerable influence here, and acquired a comfortable property. After the death of his wife he married her sister, Mrs. Saunders, and afterward, in 1835, married the widow of Mr. Stephen Dow, a daughter of Mr. William Sellers.

COURTNEY BABBIDGE, Jr., settled upon the northern part of the lot, where his right was assigned him. He was a soldier in the war of the Revolution, and was, I believe, at the taking of Cornwallis. He was fortunate enough to keep his written discharge from the army, signed by General Knox, which enabled him to prove his claim for a pension. From the difficulty of the proof of service required by the Act of Congress, many who were entitled to pensions were prevented from receiving them. His wife was a daughter of Mr. Hezekiah Lane, and his sons were Courtney, Calvin, Abner, Winthrop, Dudley, Stephen, and Bester, by his first wife; by his second, Walter and Benjamin K. None of them settled here, and all, with the exception of Bester, who resides in Winterport, and Benjamin, residing in New York, — both of whom are master-mariners, — are now dead. The daughters were the wives of Messrs. Thomas, Edward, and Ignatius Haskell, 3d, three brothers, sons of Deacon Joshua Haskell. One was the wife of Mr. William Davis, a master ship-carpenter, who removed to the Province of New Brunswick. They all are dead. After the death of his wife Mr. Babbidge married the widow of Ephraim Stinson, of Vinalhaven, who had been married twice before, and who was formerly well known here. Having sold his farm to his brother Stephen, he removed to an island at the eastern entrance of what is known as Fox Island Thoroughfare, where he lived till his death in 1834, and which is still known as Babbidge's Island. He was a man of very decided political opinions, as was his brother Stephen also, only that in those opinions they differed politically from each other.

GEORGE FREEZE, a brother of the persons noticed of the same name, settled upon the lot east of that of the Messrs. Babbidge. He came about the same time as did the others, which was quite early; where they came from is not known to us; and of him but little is now known. His children removed from here, and nearly all of their descendants reside in the towns north of Bangor, on the river. The only one of his grandchildren who remained was the late Hon. Richard Warren, a son of the Mr. Thomas Warren before mentioned, who was born on what is now known as Freeze's Island, in 1786. Mr. Warren purchased the farm occupied by Mr. Freeze, upon which he resided till his death, and it is now owned and occupied by his son-in-law, Captain Gideon Hatch. He died in 1865, and has been already noticed.

JOSEPH TYLER, Esq., settled upon the lot south of the lands of Messrs. Babbidge and Freeze, which was included within the limits of the "Kent Claim." As the deed to Kent by Greenlaw was made valid by a resolve of the General Court of Massachusetts, Mr. Tyler could not hold it as a settler. He was the son of a Congregational minister in Dedham, Massachusetts; his mother was a niece of Sir William Pepperell, and he was born in 1749. His brothers, Messrs. Belcher and George Tyler, came with him; the year of their coming is not known, but it was prior to 1784. He was a soldier in the Revolutionary army, and his wife was Miss Phebe Fowles. I think I have understood that he contracted to purchase the claim of Mr. Kent. He rebuilt the mills upon it, and was for many years engaged in sawing lumber. He was a man of a good education for those times, and the first, or one of the first, persons holding a commission as justice of the peace in the town, which was in those days considered an office of dignity. He, with his brother George, was appointed a committee to lay out the island into lots to the settlers who were, by a resolve of the General Court, entitled to them. A history of the grant made of the remainder of the land to him and his brother has been given. After a number of years' residence on the land, he left it, and the sawmill became of little value, as the best of the lumber had been cut off in the vicinity. He then moved to the Reach, upon the farm of Mr. Robert Linn, where he remained till his death in 1835, at the age of eighty-six years. His wife survived him, dying in 1857, at the age of ninety-three years. They had twelve children. The sons were: Joseph, Pepperell, Andrew, David, Peter P., James, Thomas and William, all of whom, except James, are now dead. The daughters were: Lydia, the wife of the Captain Joshua C. Howard mentioned before, whose death was in consequence of poison on board a revenue-cutter; Sarah, the first wife of Mr. Richard Brown and mother of Mr. Samuel Brown, now of Newburyport; Phebe, the wife of Mr. John Raymond, then of Boston, who died in Gloucester, and Mary, who died unmarried, when a young woman.

GEORGE TYLER, Esq., came early, and was entitled to a settler's lot if he had complied with the requirements, but I never heard of his occupying one. His residence was with his brother, and he was engaged with him in business. He was also a justice of the peace; was a man of education, and very capable. His occupation before he came here was that of a silversmith; he was the first person who represented the town in the General Court at Boston. He never married. For some years he lived in Castine, being at one time postmaster there, and later removed to Boston, where he died. In his day he was well known here and in the towns around.

CAPTAIN BELCHER TYLER, a brother of the two last-named persons, settled upon the lot lying south of the millpond, which was also within the claim of Mr. Kent. He was a master-mariner, we suppose, as he was styled Captain Tyler. His wife was not a resident here before marriage, and after her death he married Mrs. Elizabeth Toothaker, the person who was noticed as being five times a widow and removed to the farm occupied by her former husband. He resided there till his death, in 1827. Of his family, all the sons removed from this town to the eastern part of the State, where their descendants still reside. Only one of his daughters remained, who was the wife of Captain Jonathan Torrey, and the mother of Messrs. David, William, and Belcher T. Torrey. She died a few years ago at the age of eighty-six years. Another daughter was the wife of Mr. Carr Thurlow, who resided several years on the farm of Mr. Aaron Babbidge, and afterward removed to the town of Cutler, in Washington County. Captain Tyler was a man of information, and, for those times, had a good education.

JOSEPH COLBY, Sr., was the settler upon the lot of land lying south of, and adjoining, that of Captain Tyler. He had a two-hundred-acre lot set off to him, which was within the limits of the Kent Claim, about which mention has been made. In the suit at law referred to in the former part of this work, I have understood that he claimed, in addition to his right as an early settler, that Kent had contracted to sell him the land, and in payment he was to perform a certain amount of labor upon the mill built by Kent and upon the dam, which he had performed; but upon what ground he held the land we do not know. He was a native of Newbury, Massachusetts, or some place in that vicinity, and was born in 1744. When but eighteen years old he entered into an engagement of marriage with Miss Sarah Thurlow, who was eight years his senior; she purchased his "time," as it was called, of his father or master, and they were married. He came here very early — not far from 1766 — and his son Thomas, born in 1768, was the first child born of white parents in that part of the town. Mr. Colby who was a pious and exemplary man, died in 1828, at the age of eighty-four years. His wife survived him till 1833, dying at the age of ninety-seven years. She was the Mrs. Colby before referred to as the one who carried the news of the surrender of Cornwallis to Bagaduce. Their children were: Joseph and Thomas; Eunice, wife of Mr. Thomas Stinson, Jr.; Betsey, wife of Nathaniel Robbins, Sr.; Hannah, wife of Mr. Edward Small, and Sarah, wife of Mr. Leonard Judkins who came here a year or more prior to 1800, from Salisbury, New Hampshire, to which place they removed, but after a few years returned. While at Salisbury, Mrs. Judkins knew the father of Daniel Webster well, and remembered Daniel. The son of Mr. Colby, Captain Thomas Colby, is still remembered by the older persons among us, from his peculiar manner of talking, he having been what is called tongue-tied. He was a master-mariner, and died in 1837, aged sixty-nine years. His first wife was Miss Patience Norton, and after her death he married Miss Betsey Thurlow, of Newbury, and afterward, Mrs. Merchant, widow of Nathaniel Merchant. His children were: Joseph, 3d, Tristram, Thomas J., Anthony, Noah the wife of Mr. Daniel Lufkin, and a Mrs. Deering, now living in Winterport, who is in receipt of a pension for the services of her husband in the War of 1812, and is the only one of the family now living.

The wife of Joseph Colby, Jr., who settled the lot adjoining that of his father on the south, was Miss Eunice Thurlow of Newbury, Massachusetts, a sister of the late Captain David Thurlow who will be noticed. Mr. Colby was what was termed a "young settler." He was a man of large stature and great physical strength, but, like many persons who possess such, often overtaxed it, and was worn out sooner in life than many men much weaker physically, but who, sensible of their deficiency, take better care to preserve what they do have. They were the parents of twelve children. The sons were Abner, David T., Stephen, and William R. The daughters were the wives of the Mr. William Small who died, as before mentioned, under the practice of a Thompsonian doctor; of Mr. Samuel Stinson, Jr., Mr. Nathaniel Ware, Mr. Henry Keller, and Mr. William Thompson. All the family, with the exception of Mr. Stephen Colby are now dead. Mr. Colby died in 1833, and his wife survived him several years.

THOMAS STINSON, Jr., who settled the lot of land adjoining that of Mr. Joseph Colby, Jr., on the south, was a child when he came with his father to Stinson's Neck, in 1765. His wife, as we have stated, was a daughter of Mr. Joseph Colby, Sr.; she was born in 1763. Their children were: Joseph C., known as Esquire Stinson, born in 1782 and died in 1849 or 1850; Thomas, who was for many years a deacon in the Baptist Church; Jesse, who removed to Camden and died there or returned just before his death —the father of the present Mr. Jesse Stinson; Lydia, the wife of Mr. Jedediah Darling, of Bluehill, who lived till 1880, and died aged ninety-two years, and was the mother of those of that name there. Another was the wife of Mr. Gideon Candage, of the same place; another, that of a Mr. Wright, of Machias, and the others were the wives of Mr. Joseph C. Small and Mr. John Judkins of this town.

All of the family are now dead. After the death of his wife, Mr. Stinson married the widow of Mr. Abner Lane, and after her decease he married the widow of Captain Belcher Tyler.

EDWARD SMALL settled the lot lying south of that of Mr. Stinson; he was the son of Mr. Job Small and was born in 1770; his wife was Hannah, the daughter of Mr. Joseph Colby, Sr., with whom he lived in wedlock sixty-six years. She, many years ago practised as midwife, had a great deal of experience, was very successful and quite skillful in many kinds of diseases in those days, when the services of a physician were not so readily obtained as now. She died in 1859, at the age of eighty-seven years, her death being caused by a fall upon the ice near her door. Her husband survived her until 1864, and was, until he lost his sight a few years before his death, able to perform labor upon his farm, retaining his mental faculties remarkably. With but one exception I consider him the most active man, for one of his great age, that I have ever known. He was for some years a member of the board of selectmen of the town, and was a man of excellent judgment. They were the parents of nine sons, — four of whom removed from here; one, Mr. Samuel Small, of Machiasport, is still living; two of the others, Messrs. Ignatius and William Small, reside here; three others, Messrs. Joseph E., Thomas, and George W. Small are now dead, — the latter having been drowned in 1840. There was one daughter, the wife of Mr. Alexander Drew, a resident of Machias, who became a widow and is now dead. The sons of Mr. Small, Ignatius and William, have several times been on the board of selectmen. His property is now owned by the last named, who resides upon it.

SAMUEL WEBB came here with his son, Mr. Seth Webb, from Windham, Maine, not far from 1765. He was born near the city of London in 1695, and his father was a captain in the service of Queen Anne. Being left an orphan when he was quite young, it became necessary for him to seek some permanent employment. When a boy he was apprenticed to a ship-master, as was then the custom there, and while on a voyage to this country, when he was but seventeen years of age, his master died at some place in what is now the State of Rhode Island. He then apprenticed himself to a blacksmith and learned the trade. He was twice married, and was the father of ten sons. Many of that name in that State, and in the vicinity of Salem, Massachusetts, and in the town of Windham, in this State, and other places, are his descendants. He is said to have taught the first school within the limits of the town of Windham. Upon the removal here of Mr. Seth Webb, he and his last wife came with him. For many years previous to his death he was subject to what is known as the "shaking palsy," and died in 1788 at the age of ninety-three years. His remains, with those of his wife, were buried in the graveyard on the land formerly owned by the late Samuel Whitmore, Esq., who some years ago, pointed out to me the place of their burial.

SETH WEBB, the son of the subject of the preceding notice, settled upon what is now known as "Babbidge Neck," on the lot of land afterward the property of Mr. Joseph Whitmore who, when a boy, came here and resided with him. His wife was Miss Hannah Winship, of Windham, a daughter of the man of that name mentioned in Williamson's *History of Maine*, who was, when away from his house, scalped by the Indians, and recovered. He was at the time in company with a man of the name of Brown, who was killed by them, but Mr. Winship escaped death in consequence of the savages becoming alarmed and fleeing, not stopping to strike him upon the head with a tomahawk, as was their practice, fracturing the skull. After the scalping he was for some time insensible, and upon becoming conscious found himself unable to return home. As it happened, he was lying down by the edge of a bog, upon which cranberries grew plentifully, and it was at the time of the year when they are ripe. Fortunately there was no rain while he remained there, so he could creep about upon his hands and knees and procure them to appease his hunger and thirst. As the weather proved moderate he was enabled to recover, and at the end of two weeks, returned to his home, much to the surprise of his family who had given him up for dead. A physician in the neighborhood informed him that cranberries were beneficial to the blood and caused his wound to heal. He lived for many years, and afterward married the widow of the Mr. Brown who was with him.

After Mr. Webb settled upon the first land taken up by him, he gave up his claim to Mr. Whitmore, and took up a lot near what is now known as Webb's Cove; he also, a part of the time, resided upon Kimball's Island, now in the town of Isle au Haut, and was there during the war of the Revolution. When he left Windham he owned considerable property, but having a fondness for hunting, he came East, and was during much of his time engaged in that pursuit with the Indians, with whom he was on good terms, and frequently those with whom he associated, made his house their home when about here. Among others who did so was a noted man among them, a chief named Orono, reputed to be a natural son of one of the sons of the Baron de Castine. Orono lived to a very great age, and was said to be one hundred and ten years old at the time of his death. I have often heard Mr. Webb's last surviving daughter speak of his being at her father's house frequently. Mr. Webb hunted much upon

Union River and its tributaries, and in all probability, the pond near it, now known as Webb's Pond, and the brook leading out of it were named for him. The year before his death he discovered a lead mine on the banks of that river (at a time when the water was so low that he could trace it across), and, as I have understood, not far from its mouth. He brought home a piece weighing several pounds, and at the time of taking it, marked the place with his hatchet so as to enable him to find it on his next visit. He sent a part of it to Boston, where it was pronounced a good specimen of lead ore, in which was some silver. It was probably a continuation of one of the veins of that metal lately discovered in the towns east of the city of Ellsworth. His daughter, before referred to, informed me that the family had the piece for several years, and that it was as large as a man's two fists. His death, caused by accidental shooting, took place in 1785. At the time he was on Kimball's Island and his family on this island, and either in launching his canoe, or in drawing it ashore if it was afloat, his loaded gun was discharged as it lay in the bow of the canoe, killing him instantly, his body being found upon the shore. At the time of his death he was fifty-three years of age. His wife survived him till 1815; she lies buried in what is known as the "old burying-ground," not far from the Town House, and hers is the only gravestone in the yard as now enclosed. Their children were: Mr. Samuel Webb, who died in 1837, much respected, at the age of sixty-five years; and William, who died more than fifty years ago. One of the daughters was the wife of Mr. James Saunders; another, the wife of Mr. Francis Kimball, who removed to Waterville, where his descendants still reside; another was the wife of Mr. Joshua Emerson; another, the last survivor, who died in 1860, was the wife of Mr. John Eaton;

another removed to Portland, remaining unmarried, and another was the wife of Mr. Daniel Moore, of Castine. The wife of Mr. Samuel Webb was Miss Hannah Eaton, and they were the parents of the late Jonathan E. Webb, Esq., the present Mr. William Webb, and Mr. James L. Webb. Mr. Samuel Webb represented this town in the Legislature in 1831, and resided upon the land taken up by his father near Webb's Cove. After the death of Mr. Seth Webb, his widow attempted to procure a title to Kimball's Island, but the agent to whom she intrusted her business did not procure it for her, but did so for himself, as has been stated by the family.

CAPTAIN EDMUND SYLVESTER, a native of Marshfield, Massachusetts, who previous to his removal was a master-mariner, came here in 1788, and settled upon the lot of land lying south of that of Mr. Webb. His wife was Miss Deborah Cushman, a granddaughter of Josiah Winslow who died about 1774, a lineal descendant of Edward Winslow, one of the first governors of the Plymouth Colony, and who was himself, I believe, one of the colonial governors of Massachusetts. He was the owner of a farm at Marshfield that was later acquired by Daniel Webster and upon which he died. Other ancestors of Mrs. Sylvester were among the Pilgrims who came over in the *Mayflower*. After her marriage she persuaded her husband to leave the sea, saying that she was willing to live anywhere if he would but remain at home, and he came here and purchased the land settled upon by him. He was one of the selectmen of the town a few years; was an intelligent and honorable man, very decided in his opinions, and was from the time of the establishment of the Baptist Church here a member till his death in 1828. His wife preceded him about one month. There were many deaths during that year from a distemper not then fully understood, which will be noticed in another place. I have been informed that about sixty persons died of it, few of those attacked recovering. At the time of his death he was sixty-eight, and his wife sixty-four years of age. Their children were the late Mr. Crowell H., Joseph, Mial, Abiel and Edmund, sons; Ruth, the wife of Captain William Raynes, and Salome, the widow of the late Mr. Joseph Sellers, 2d. The two youngest sons removed to Newburyport and died there. Mr. Crowell Sylvester died in 1863, aged seventy-eight years; Joseph in 1847, aged fifty-six; Mrs. Raynes in 1852, aged sixty-three years, and Mrs. Sellers still survives at the present time (1882), aged eighty-one years. The farm of Captain Sylvester was, in 1842, sold to Mr. Robert Knowlton, whose heirs still own it, and most of his children now living reside upon it.

GEORGE GROSS settled a lot of land lying north and east of Webb's Cove, and easterly of the land of Mr. Thomas Stinson. He was not one of the first class of settlers who were here prior to 1784, but must have been one of those styled "young settlers." The place and date of his birth is to us unknown, but he came from the town of Harpswell, in this State, of which place his wife was a native. Her maiden name was Alexander, and she was a sister of the late Mr. Ezekiel Alexander and of the wife of Mr. Solomon Marshall. He was known as "Citizen Gross." The origin of his receiving that appellation was this: He at one time lost his house by fire, and applied to George Tyler, Esq., to write a subscription paper for the purpose of circulation for his relief, and the paper was headed thus: "Whereas, Citizen George Gross, of this town, has lost his house by fire," etc., and ever afterward he was known thus. He died in 1828, and his wife survived him a few years. Their children were: Charles, born in 1782; James and Nathaniel, born in 1789; Betsey, the wife of Mr. David Smith, of Swan's Island, and mother of the present Mr. William Smith, residing in this town; Lucy, the wife of Mr. David Smith, Jr.; Abigail, the first wife of the late Mr. Elisha H. Dunham; Jane and Polly who never married, and Dorothy, the widow of the late Captain Jeremiah Thurlow. We believe she is now the only survivor of the family. Mr. Gross, at the time of his death, was in the receipt of a pension for his Revolutionary services.

THOMAS BUCKMINSTER who came here not far from the year 1790, took up, as a "young settler," a lot of fifty acres lying on the eastern side of Webb's Cove. He was born in the town of Atkinson, New Hampshire, or in that vicinity, and when young lived in the family of the father of Mr. Jonathan Webster who came from that place here in 1804. Mr. Buckminster married Miss Rhoda, the daughter of Mr. Thomas Robbins, and was a very worthy man who left a good name behind him. He lived upon the lot taken up by him till his death, which took place not long after 1850, at the age of over eighty years. Their sons were John, Thomas, Ebenezer, Moody, and William. Their daughters were the wives of Messrs. Robert Knowlton, Swansey Gross, Joseph Knowlton, John Judkins, and Thomas Harvey, and one, named Mary, was never married. Of the family Ebenezer, Moody and Mary now remain. Some of the sons were remarkable for their stature, Thomas being six feet and six and a half inches in height, and John six feet and six inches. The property of Mr. Buckminster is now that of his son, Mr. Ebenezer Buckminster, with whom his sister Mary resides.

THOMAS ROBBINS settled on the lot of land lying easterly of the land of Mr. Buckminster. He came from Boston, or some place in the near vicinity, in 1775, with his family, and in the early years of the town he was a man of considerable influence. He for many years held the office of coroner, and was well known as "Coroner Robbins." He was twice married, his last wife being the widow of the Mr. William Babbidge before noticed, who resided near him. The date of his death is not to us known. Two of his sons who resided here were the Messrs. Nathaniel and Thomas Robbins, Jr., who have been noticed. One of his daughters was the wife of Mr. Buckminster, and the other that of Mr. Thomas Stinson, 3d, known as Deacon Thomas Stinson. The farm of Mr. Robbins came into the possession of Mr. John Buckminster, by whom it was occupied till his death, and now is the property of his son, Mr. William S. Buckminster.

JOSEPH WHITMORE resided upon the northeastern lot on what is known as Babbidge's Neck, which was laid out to him in the survey of the island. On this lot Mr. Seth Webb lived a few years after he came. The birthplace of Mr. Whitmore is not to us known, but as he came when a boy in the family of Mr. Seth Webb from Windham, that was probably his native town. He was born in 1755, and his wife was Abigail, the daughter of Mr. William Babbidge. They went to Bagaduce for the purpose of having the marriage ceremony performed, which was done by the chaplain in the British service there, in 1780, or about that time. Mr. Whitmore was a soldier in the war of the Revolution, for which he received a pension. He died in 1841, at the age of eighty-six years, after having lived in wedlock more than sixty years. His wife survived him nearly ten years. Their sons were: John, who died in the town of Lincolnville; Joseph, who was drowned in 1814; William, who was drowned when going from Isle au Haut to Deer Island; Lemuel, who was drowned in Eggemoggin Reach; Daniel, who lived in the country of Aroostook; Samuel, who lived and died here; James, who lived in the town of Tremont, and Seth, who lived in the town of Trenton, near the shore and near the line of the city of Ellsworth. The daughters were the wives of Mr. Abel Staples, of Swan's Island; Mr. Jonathan Eaton, of Sedgwick, the father of the late Theophilus Eaton, of Searsport, and another was the wife of Mr. George York, of Brooklin. The only one of the family who made this town his permanent residence was the late Samuel Whitmore, Esq., who was engaged in trade, doing quite a large business for many years. Owning considerable navigation, most of which was engaged in the fishing business, he acquired a good property, in addition to the real estate of his father. His place of business is now occupied by C. H. S. Webb, Esq. He was, in 1840, the representative from this town, and for many years prominent in its affairs. Before his death, in 1862 or 1863, he gave up his business to his sons, who for a few years carried it on. At this time but one of his sons, Mr. Seth Whitmore, resides here. His widow, a daughter of Mr. James Joyce, survived him a few years, and the house occupied by them is now the property of Mr. Lemuel Joyce, a son-in-law of theirs.

WILLIAM RICHARDS settled the lot adjoining that of Mr. Whitmore on the west, and it was assigned to him. He came in the early years of the settlement of the town, not far from 1765, from where or for how long is unknown. He removed from here and none of that name remained after him. He sold out his title to the land, and it fell into the possession of Mr. Oliver Lane, who came here with his father in 1784. The wife of Mr. Lane was the eldest daughter of Mr. Courtney Babbidge, Sr., and the sister of Messrs. Stephen and Courtney Babbidge, Jr., and by her he had a family. The sons were: Oliver, the father of the present Mr. Hardy Lane; Stephen B., who removed to Hampden not far from 1845, and Paul T., who remained till his death. One of the daughters was the wife of Mr. Samuel McClintock who came here from Portsmouth, New Hampshire. He was a school-teacher and was styled "Master McClintock." Another was the wife of Captain Abram Colby and afterward of Mr. Timothy Saunders; another was the wife of Mr. Job Small, the son of Mr. Edward Small, who removed to Machias, where he died, and the other married Mr. James Duncan, Jr. All of the family are now dead. After the death of his wife, Mr. Lane married another daughter of Mr. Babbidge by his third wife; he died not far from the year 1840, his wife surviving him.

HEZEKIAH LANE, the father of the subject of the last notice, came here from what was then known as Sandy Bay, now in the town of Rockport, Massachusetts, with his family and took up a lot of land adjoining that of Mr. Richards on the southwest. His other sons were Oliver, John, Abner and Benjamin Lane; the latter was afflicted with insanity for several years. One of his daughters was the wife of Mr. Courtney Babbidge, Jr., and another was the wife of Mr. Robert Douglass, of Isle au Haut. She was killed by being struck with a fragment of a rock that her husband was blasting, further particulars of which will be given in the notice of Mr. Douglass. After the death of his wife, Mr. Lane married the widow of Mr. Abram Thurlow, of Newburyport, the mother of the late Captain David Thurlow and of the wife of Mr. Joseph Colby, Jr.

CAPTAIN BENJAMIN STOCKBRIDGE settled upon the lot of land lying west of that of Mr. Richards, but he was not of the class who were here prior to 1784. He came from Gloucester, Massachusetts, and was a ship-master and in good circumstances. It was said that he commanded the ship which first carried the American flag up the Dardanelles. The exact time of his coming is to us unknown, but it was prior to the survey of the town by John Peters, Jr., as his name appears as the occupant of a lot on his plan. His death took place not far from 1830, at an advanced age. He was a member of the Baptist Church here, and when some difficulty occurred between him and some of his neighbors — members of the same church — and an examination was made before the church, Captain Stockbridge read the thirtieth chapter of the book of Job, beginning with: "But now they that are younger than I have me in derision, whose fathers I would have disdained to have set with the dogs of my flock." His family consisted of two sons, Mr. John Stockbridge, who removed to Swan's Island, and Benjamin, who was lost at sea when a young man. Mr. John Stockbridge died several years ago and was the ancestor of all of that name there. One of his daughters was the wife of Mr. James Duncan, who came here as early as 1800. Another was the wife of Captain John Greenlaw who died in 1870, at the age of eighty-seven years, after having lived with his wife, who survived him, sixty-six years. Another was the wife of Mr. Benjamin Lane before mentioned. Another was the wife of Mr. James Greenlaw, a brother of Captain John Greenlaw. Another was that of Captain William Grover, of Isle au Haut, who removed to Islesborough, and another was the wife of Mr. George Grover. Captain Stockbridge when young was a man of capacity and energy, but had become, before his removal here, somewhat reduced in circumstances.

JOHN THURSTON came here in 1784 from the same place as did Captain Stockbridge, but earlier; they were relatives, but of him little is known, as he died many years ago. His sons were John Thurston, Jr., Amos Thurston, and Solomon Thurston, the latter of whom

Town of Deer Isle, Maine.

removed from here. Mr. Amos Thurston resided here till his death, and his wife, Miss Mary Gott, a sister of the late Captain Isaac Gott, of Tremont, survived him, dying in 1866, at the age of ninety-one years. They were the parents of the present Mr. Ambrose Thurston, the late Mr. Amos Thurston, Jr., the widow of the late Mr. John W. Small and the wife of Mr. Jesse Stinson. The others of the family are now dead. Mr. Solomon Thurston resided while here upon the land now occupied by Mr. Thomas Gross, who inherited it from his father, the late Mr. Swansey Gross, and when he went from here, it was to the town of Vinalhaven. The children of Mr. John Thurston, Jr., were the late Mr. Nathaniel Thurston and the wives of the late Captain Isaac Gott, of Tremont, and of a Mr. Putnam who once resided here, but removed many years ago. A daughter of Mr. John Thurston, Sr., was the wife of Mr. David Smith, of Swan's Island, and was the mother of David, Benjamin, George, and Asa Smith, all of whom resided on Swan's Island. One was the wife of the late Benjamin Stinson, Esq., and the mother of the present Rev. Benjamin F. Stinson. Another of the daughters was the wife of the late Mr. Anthony Merchant, and another was the wife of Mr. Benjamin Kent, and afterward that of Mr. John Beal, who died here not many years since. Another daughter of Mr. John Thurston, Sr., was the wife of a Mr. Gott, and afterwards the wife of Mr. David Harding, of Sedgwick. Another was the wife of a Mr. Hooper and the mother of Captain Jeremiah Hooper, of North Haven.

CAPTAIN SETH HATCH, a native of Marshfield, Massachusetts, settled upon the lot assigned to Mr. William Babbidge, who, as has been stated, took up his settlement first upon the land afterward assigned to Deacon Joshua Haskell, but removed to the neck which was named for him.

On the plan made by John Peters, Jr., the lot on which Captain Hatch settled was laid out to him. Captain Hatch was born not far from 1760 and came here a young man, but not in season to become a proprietor by settlement prior to 1784. He occupied the western part of the one hundred acres laid out to Mr. Babbidge, whose daughter he married, and lived upon the place till his death, in 1844. His wife survived him. Their children were: Captain William B. Hatch, a master-mariner, who resided in Pembroke in Washington County; Seth, who removed to the same place and was in the same vessel with his brother William, who was master, when they were lost at sea, never being heard from. Another son was the late Captain Jeremiah Hatch, and another the present Captain Gideon Hatch who resides upon the farm of the late Hon. Richard Warren. The daughters were the wives of Mr. Tristram T. Robbins, Mr. Simon Stinson, Mr. William Greenlaw, Jr., and of the late Captain William Warren. She still survives, the other sisters being dead. The farm of Captain Hatch became the property of his son Jeremiah, with whom he resided at the time of his death.

SAMUEL STAPLES resided for several years upon the eastern half of the land of Mr. Babbidge, whose daughter he married. Some time not far from the year 1814, he removed to the town of Charleston in the county of Penobscot, or in its vicinity. The cold season of 1816, which was long remembered, obliged him to remove from that place, and in a few years he returned here and took up a lot near Burnt Cove — the one since occupied by the late Captain Joseph Fifield — and built a house upon it which is now occupied by Mr. John Horton. Afterward he removed to a lot of land near the thoroughfare, now occupied by Mr. Paul Thurlow, where he died in 1841, aged seventy-three years. His wife survived him several years, and at the time of her death resided with a daughter, the present Mrs. Walter Greenlaw, a widow. Mr. Staples and wife were the parents of the following children: Samuel who went away when a young man, never returned, and no tidings were had of him; Thomas, who followed the sea for many years, visited many parts of the world, returned in 1845, and died a few years after, and David H., for many years a pilot on one of the steamers running from Bangor to Boston, who died in Belfast. One of the daughters was first the wife of Mr. Joseph Sylvester and afterward the wife of the present Mr. Nathaniel Robbins. She died a few years ago, aged eighty-six years. Another was the wife of Mr. Aaron Stinson. Another was the wife of Captain Walter Greenlaw. Another was the wife of Mr. Joshua Emerson, afterward that of Mr. Elisha H. Dunham. Another was the wife of Mr. William Barbour, of Verona, and the youngest was the wife of Captain Thomas D. Toothaker, who lost his brig in the great gale in 1839, in the harbor of Gloucester, Massachusetts, and Mrs. Toothaker attempting to reach the shore was drowned, while the crew narrowly escaped, the vessel becoming a complete wreck. The members of the family who survive are Mrs. Greenlaw and Mrs. Barbour. The farm Mr. Staples occupied on Babbidge's Neck became the property of the late Capain John Greenlaw, upon which he lived till his death.

BENJAMIN WEED came here among the first settlers not far from the year 1763; but he did not settle upon Great Deer Island and of course had no right to a lot of land upon it when the allotment was made by Joseph and George Tyler, as their authority extended to no other parts of the town than Great Deer and Sheep Islands. Mr. Weed made his settlement upon Little Deer Island and continued to reside there for many years, but afterward exchanged his land for a lot lying near Campbell's

Neck, with Captain Peter Hardy, then the junior of that name. Upon the plan of the island the lot purported to be that of Mr. Hardy. He removed to it and lived there till his death. His wife was the daughter of William Eaton, and his family were Joseph, William, Jeremiah, and John Weed. One of the daughters was the wife of Mr. Josiah Gray; another, the wife of a Mr. Tuttle, after she became a widow, also married Mr. Gray who had lost his wife, and after his death became the third wife of Captain Tristram Haskell. Another daughter was the wife of a Mr. Ferrill, who was a resident of Mount Desert. Mr. Weed has been mentioned as having been engaged in the siege of Louisburg, but what place he came from here is not known. After his death the premises occupied by him became the property of Mr. Josiah Gray, who continued to reside there till his death; and it was afterward that of Mr. Silas H. Gray.

JOSEPH WEED, the son of the subject of the last notice, settled upon the farm adjoining that of Nathan Haskell, Esq., on the east. He was a very industrious and prudent man and a good citizen. He was for many years a collector of taxes. His wife was Miss Judith, daughter of Mr. Jonathan Eaton, and their children were: John, who died when a young man; Joseph, now living; Nathan E., now dead, and who was for many years a collector of taxes, and Caleb who was drowned when a young man in the millpond at the Northwest Harbor. He had shot some seafowl that were in the pond, and in going to pick them up in a small leaky float which either filled or capsized, he sunk before he could reach the shore. The daughters of Mr. Weed were the wives of Mr. Nathan Dow, now living at the age of ninety years, Captain Davis Haskell, Mr. David Dow, Mr. Amos Weed, and Mr. Daniel Weed. One died unmarried. Before the death of Mr.

Weed the town obtained possession of his farm, and the premises were used as a poor-farm until a few years since. Mr. Weed and his wife both lived to be over eighty years of age, living in wedlock more than sixty years.

WILLIAM WEED first settled upon a part of the lot of land taken up by Mr. John Pressey, Jr. In 1822 he exchanged his farm with Ignatius Haskell, Esq., for a tract of land on the south part of the island near what is now known as Green's Landing, which he occupied during the remainder of his life. His wife was Mary, the daughter of Mr. Jonathan Eaton, and their children were Amos, Daniel, and Levi Weed, and a daughter Eunice, who became the wife of Mr. Joseph Weed, Jr. They are all now dead. Mr. Weed died in 1844 at the age of seventy-two years. He was an honest man and a good citizen. His wife lived till about the year 1850, and was respected by all who knew her. None of his descendants now own the real estate left by him, which is the property of Sullivan Green, Esq., and Mr. Stephen B. Barbour. The buildings that were upon it are now taken down.

JEREMIAH WEED settled upon Little Deer Island on a lot of land adjoining that of his father. His wife was Miss Althea Joyce, a daughter of Mr. James Joyce, and they had a large family, the sons being Jeremiah, James J., Ebenezer J., Randolph, who lives in Winterport, and one son who died young; of the above Randolph is now, in 1882, living. The daughters were the wives of Mr. Benjamin H. Eaton, Captain Joseph H. Gray, Mr. Samuel Eaton, Mr. Nelson Haskell, Captain Jonathan Gray and Mr. William Eaton, of Little Deer Isle, and one married in Boston. The four first named are now dead. Mr. Weed died several years before his wife, and she died a few years ago.

JOHN WEED, the youngest brother of the family, was born in 1786, and his wife was Miss Betsey Harris, the daughter of Mr. Joseph Harris. Their children were Henry, James, Davis H., Charles and Dyer D. One of the daughters was the wife of Captain Benjamin Thompson, and two were the wives of Mr. Samuel Torrey. Of the family at this time John and Mrs. Torrey — now Mrs. Manchester, of North Haven — are still living. Mrs. Weed died about the year 1879, and her husband died several years ago.

JOSIAH GRAY, who occupied the premises of Mr. Benjamin Weed, was a native of what is now the town of Brooksville and a brother of the Mr. Christopher Gray who died in that town in 1866 at the age of one hundred and three years. They were grandsons of the person of that name who, in 1760, made the first permanent settlement in what is now Castine, and the ancestors of almost all of that name in the towns in this vicinity. Mr. Gray and his wife were the parents of thirteen children; seven of them were sons, one of whom was Captain James Gray, a shipmaster, who resided in Boston. Another was Mr. Josiah Gray, a master ship-builder, who died in Bluehill. Two removed to Vinalhaven; one went away to sea and never returned; and one resides here — the present Mr. Solomon Gray. Of the daughters, two only remain: one, the late wife of Mr. Silas H. Gray; the other, the widow of Mr. Joshua Pressey, 2d. She was the adopted daughter of the late Captain John Torrey, and came into possession of his homestead, upon which she now resides.

A man named Gray but of another family, lived for many years, and died, here — Mr. Jeremiah Gray — whose wife was Hannah, the daughter of Mr. Nathaniel Bray, Jr., and granddaughter of the first of the name who came here. They were the parents of eleven sons and one daughter who was the wife of Mr. Enos Cole. One of the sons died at sea; another moved to New Brunswick, and another now lives in Gloucester, Massachusetts. The rest remained here, one of whom — Mr. Solomon Gray — died at New Orleans while in the military service of the United States. There are but two remaining here at present. Mr. Gray died several years ago; also his wife, a worthy Christian woman, much respected.

REV. PETER POWERS came here not far from the year 1785, from Newbury, in the State of Vermont — now Hanover, New Hampshire. He was a minister of the Congregational denomination, and was the first settled pastor of the church here, although the church had been established several years. He was a zealous patriot in the Revolutionary times, who for his political opinions incurred the ill will of the Tories in that vicinity, and because of a sermon he preached from the text found in the book of Judges, fifth chapter, twenty-third verse, he was so persecuted by them that he left that place and came here, where he was pastor of the church till his death in 1800, at the age of seventy-two years. He was entitled to a grant of land as the first settled minister here, and his farm was on the eastern side of what is known as the Parsonage Lot of four hundred acres. The town, or parish, built a house upon it, and he resided there during his lifetime. He had several sons, one of whom was the Rev. Jonathan Powers, settled in the year 1796 as the first minister in the town of Penobscot, where he died in 1807. Another son was Hale Powers who built a sawmill in the present town of Brooksville on what is known as Horseshoe Creek. Another was Mr. Prescott Powers who resided here many years, whose wife was a daughter of Deacon Francis Haskell. He came into possession of the land of his father, and after residing upon it for several years, removed to Pond Island, near Swan's Island, and afterward to Bluehill, where he died. Only one of his family remained here

— the wife of the late Mr. Daniel Johnson. Mr. Powers was for several years the clerk of this town and was considered one of the most honorable and upright of men. His wife died not far from 1860, aged about eighty-seven years.

DR. MOODY POWERS was the youngest son of Rev. Peter Powers; he remained here till his death, and was a practising physician. His wife was Miss Betsey Eaton, a daughter of William Eaton, Jr., and they had a large family. The sons were: the present Mr. Hale Powers; Mr. Jonathan Powers, who removed to the State of Vermont; Peter, who removed to Winterport; William E., who resides here, as does his brother, Mr. Samuel E., and the other, Moody, now lives in the State of Kansas. One of the daughters was the wife of Captain Amos Howard; another was the wife of Mr. David Tyler who died very suddenly in 1836, or about that time; she afterward removed to Vermont and married there; another was the wife of John H. Parker, Esq., of Mount Desert, and the other was the first wife of the late Mr. Henry Weed. Dr. Powers died not far from 1850, and his wife in 1871, at the age of ninety-one years.

There were other children in the family of Rev. Peter Powers, but they did not live here, or if they did, they did not remain. The farm he received is now owned and occupied in part by Mr. Levi Greenlaw, but whether the house now upon it was built for Mr. Powers, or not, we do not know; but it probably was, as it is very old — one of the oldest in the town.

SOLOMON BARBOUR for many years occupied the farm lying south of Long Cove, and was ancester of all of the name in the town. He was a native of Massachusetts, and his wife was Deborah Faxon, of Braintree in that State, who, when young, had been for some years in the family of John Adams, President of the United States. She once told me that while she was living with them John Quincy Adams was an infant, and that she had many a time rocked him in his cradle. Mr. Barbour came here not far from 1793 with a family, and with him came Miss Betty Bryant, very well known here sixty years ago and more. She was for many years a school-teacher and lived to a great age. Mr. Barbour did not own the farm, but occupied it under Ignatius Haskell, Esq., the owner, and it is still known as the Barbour Farm. He resided upon it till his death. He was by trade a baker; was a soldier in the Revolutionary War and received a pension till his death, the exact time of which we do not know, but it was a few years prior to 1830. His widow received a pension under the act granting pensions to widows of Revolutionary soldiers, and lived till 1852, dying at the age of ninety-two years. They were the parents of five sons. Mr. John Barbour, born in 1777, who lived on what is known as Beech Hill. His wife was Miss Jane Gibson who died before him, he living to the age of eighty-seven years. He was the father of the late Deacon George Barbour; of the present Mr. Samuel G. Barbour, still residing in this town; of Mr. Solomon Barbour of Swan's Island, and of Mr. John Barbour, Jr., who a few years since removed to Massachusetts. Another of the sons of Mr. Solomon Barbour was Captain Benjamin Barbour, who removed to Newburyport, sailing out of that port for many years. Another was the late Mr. Josiah Barbour; another was Mr. Charles Barbour, and another was Mr. Isaiah Barbour, who removed to Isle au Haut and from there about forty-five years ago removed to Camden, where he died in 1880, or about that time. The daughters were the wives of Mr. Adam Thompson and Deacon Stephen Babbidge, known as Stephen Babbidge, Jr., who after her death married her sister, the widow Thompson.

JAMES GIBSON was another Revolutionary soldier who came here from Massachusetts prior to the year 1800. It seems probable that he might at one time have occupied an island north of, and near, Stinson's Neck, which is still known as Gibson's Island, but he resided for some time on this island, where he died many years ago; but very few now know anything about him. He had two sons, Samuel and James, who died at sea when young men. Two of the daughters married here; one was the wife of Mr. John Barbour; the other, the wife of Captain Nathaniel Bray, Jr., and the mother of the present Captain James G. Bray. Mr. Gibson was engaged in the battle of Bunker Hill, and before they came here he resided not far from Newburyport. I perfectly recollect his widow, who was blind for many years. She once informed me that when General Washington was on his tour North, he and his escort passed them while going from Newburyport to Portsmouth. He was recognized by Mr. Gibson, who had served under him and who spoke to, and saluted, him. The salute was returned and the General, finding that he was one of his soldiers, stopped his company, shook hands, and conversed with him, seeming pleased to have found again a fellow-soldier. She said that General Washington was one of the most noble appearing men she had ever happened to see.

RICHARD GREENLAW was the youngest son of Mr. Jonathan Greenlaw who settled here shortly after William Eaton. He went when a child to New Brunswick with his father in 1783, but returned with his brother William. He was not the owner of any real estate, we think, but resided upon the farm of his son during the later years of his life. His wife was Miss Mary Jordan, a daughter of Mr. James Jordan, and he was by trade a ship-carpenter. Their sons were: Richard, who removed to the town of Kilmarnock,

Maine, which is now called Medford; another was the late Mr. James J. Greenlaw; another was the present Mr. Joseph S. Greenlaw; another was Mr. Samuel J. Greenlaw; another was Mr. William L. Greenlaw, who resides in Newburyport, and another was Mr. John C. J. Greenlaw, who died many years ago. The daughters were the wives of Mr. George Barbour and Mr. Thomas V. Howard; and two live in Massachusetts.

WILLIAM BRAY was the youngest son of Mr. Nathaniel Bray, Sr., and lived on the farm now owned by Mr. Joshua Marshall. He was not one of those who settled prior to 1784, but must have been a " young settler." His wife was the daughter of Mr. Samuel Pickering who lived on Pickering's Island, a sister of the late Captain Samuel Pickering who lived near the Town House. They had two sons, John and Willard; and the daughters were the wives of Mr. Benjamin Cole, father of the present Mr. Enos Cole, and of the late Mr. Joshua Haskell, father of the present Messrs. Mark, Guildford D., and Joshua Haskell. Mr. Bray died not far from the year 1835, and his wife survived him. His real estate passed into the hands of Ignatius Haskell, Esq., and was sold to Mr. Ezekiel Marshall, the father of the present owner.

NATHAN LOW came here from the county of Worcester, Massachusetts, prior to 1800. He became owner of the land laid out to Joshua Staples, and afterward of one of the lots laid out to Mr. Thomas Thompson near Thompson's Cove and other lands in that vicinity. He was by trade a tanner, which business he carried on for many years, and was probably one of the most skillful farmers that ever lived in the town, engaging extensively in that pursuit. His wife was the daughter of Mr. Thomas Thompson. She died in 1836, and he afterward married Hannah, the daughter of Mr. Jonathan Hardy, who was some forty years younger than himself, and who died in a few years after her marriage. By his former wife he had three sons: Mr. Thomas T. Low, now dead; Nathan Low, Jr., who died a few years ago in consequence of the vessel of which he was then master having been run into by a steamer on the easterly route from Portland. Captain Low was thrown into the water, and being then nearly seventy years of age, the exposure caused his death shortly after. He was brought home, but lived only a few days. Another and the sole surviving son is the present Mr. William Low. None of the daughters remained here, and whether any of them are living is not known to us. Mr. Low was a major in the regiment of the militia to which the companies in this town belonged, and was known as Major Low. He was one of the selectmen of the town, and was an influential citizen. He died in 1859, at the age of ninety-four years. A brother of his in Massachusetts lived to be about one hundred years old. He acquired quite a large property, and settled his sons upon farms of which he was owner. He was a large, portly man, and as an officer in militia he must have made a fine appearance. I have been told by one who had seen both that he very much resembled the father of Daniel Webster.

AMASA HOLDEN came here as early as the year 1800, if not before. He was a native of the town of Mendon, Massachusetts, and was born in the year 1775. His wife was Abigail, the daughter of Mr. William Eaton, Jr. She was born in 1783. His profession was school-teaching, which he practised till he was more than seventy years of age, a greater term of years than it was ever practised by any other person in this vicinity. He used to say that he had taught three generations, as he had for scholars during his later years the grandchildren of those who were his pupils in his earlier years. His family consisted of eleven children. The sons were: Prescott P., a blockmaker by trade, now residing in Bangor; William E., now a resident of the town of Tremont; the late Samuel E., for many years a school-teacher; the present Mr. Francis M. Holden, and one son, who died young. One of the daughters was the wife of Mr. Willaby Nason, Jr., who removed to Belfast; one, Hannah, died unmarried; Mary was the wife of Mr. Thomas Howard; Charlotte was the wife of Mr. Stephen K. Howard, and the two others married in Massachusetts. Mr. Holden occupied the farm and house now owned by his son, Mr. Francis M. Holden, the only survivor of the family here. He died in 1853, at the age of seventy-eight years, his wife surviving him.

PETER WILLIAMS, a man of color, came here early. He was born a slave in Virginia, and resided in the family of Mr. Mark Haskell. He married a woman of color who was purchased when an infant by Mrs. Haskell. She was born in 1752, brought up in the family, and treated as one of the children. Her name was Phyllis. Her first husband was a native of the State of Rhode Island, and was named " Newport Rhodeisland." By that marriage she was the mother of one son, named " Reuben Rhodeisland," who was an enterprising man, and acquired considerable property. He was the former owner of the land and house now occupied by Mr. Eben F. Haskell, and died in 1827, unmarried. His mother married Mr. Williams, by whom she had children. They were the owners of the real estate now occupied by Mr. Oliver van Meter, formerly of Bangor, a son of the well-known Mr. Henry van Meter who lived to a very great age. The son of Mrs. Williams, by her last marriage, died when a young man, and her daughter Phyllis, in 1828, married Mr. Sydney Russell whose daughter became the wife of Mr. Van Meter. Mr. Williams died many years ago, and his wife in 1835, aged eighty-four years. All his life Mr. Williams professed great attachment for Old Virginia, the State of his birth.

JOHN FOSTER, a native of Massachusetts, came here prior to the year 1800. The lot of land lying south of that laid out to Jonathan Torrey was once occupied by him, and on the plan of the island it was allotted to him, but he must have purchased it as a " young settler." He was by trade a hatter, and for several years carried on that business at the Northwest Harbor, near the spot occupied by the shop of Mr. Israel B. Higgins. He married Mary, the eldest daughter of Ignatius Haskell, Esq., and they had one son, Mr. Eben B. Foster, who removed to Boston, and was for several years one of the proprietors of *The Boston Courier*. Neither of their two daughters was married, nor did they remain here. Mr. Foster died in Boston when a very old man.

JAMES JOYCE resided for many years on what it still known as the Joyce lot, lying north of the farm of Captain Peter Hardy, Jr., now the property of Mr. John Thompson, but he was probably never its owner, as the lot purports on the plan to be that of Mr. Thomas Thompson. Mr. Joyce came early, removing here from the town of Marshfield, Massachusetts, or that vicinity, and married the widow of Mr. Courtney Babbidge, Sr. By his marriage with Mrs. Babbidge they had seven children. The sons were Messrs. James, Ebenezer, and William Joyce, and the daughters were the wives of Mr. Jeremiah Weed, Captain Levi Torrey, Mr. John Stockbridge, and Captain Samuel Whitmore. Of the family Mrs. Torrey only now survives. The sons removed to Swan's Island, and the two oldest remained there till their deaths; the other removed here in 1848. Of the daughters, Mrs. Weed and Mrs. Whitmore remained here, and Mrs. Stockbridge died on Swan's Island.

JESSE NILES came here from the State of New Hampshire, not far from the year 1800. He was by trade a house-carpenter. His wife was a daughter of Deacon Caleb Haskell, and after the removal of Deacon Haskell, Mr. Niles occupied his farm till a few years prior to his death. After the death of his wife, in 1835, he married Miss Edna, the daughter of Mr. Naylor Small. By his first marriage he had four sons and two daughters, none of whom is now living. One of his sons, Mr. Mark A. H. Niles, was a minister, first a Congregationalist and afterward a Unitarian, and was for a short time pastor of the church of the latter denomination in Belfast, where he died about the year 1840, a short time after he removed there. The other sons were John, Jesse, and Arthur. The daughters married in Massachusetts. None of the family remained here. By his second marriage Mr. Niles had two sons, one now dead; the other went from here. The two daughters remained and married here. After the death of her husband Mrs. Niles became the wife of Mr. Levi Greenlaw.

PEARL SPOFFORD, Esq., came here not long after the year 1800, in company with Mr. Samuel G. Town, with whom he formed a copartnership in trade. He was a native of the town of Pelham, New Hampshire, and his father's residence was not far from the line of the State of Massachusetts. It was his intention when he came East to stop at Fox Island Thoroughfare; but when he came, early in the spring, that passage was closed with ice, and he came to this place, stopping in the Southwest Harbor. Finding that this town might be a profitable place for trade, he concluded to remain. He had his goods carried to the Northwest Harbor, and for some time occupied a part of the house of Aaron S. Haskell as a store, boarding in his family. After some time he dissolved his connection with Mr. Town, who removed from here. He afterward formed a copartnership with his brother, Mr. Frederick Spofford, who was lost in the schooner *Shakespeare*, in 1818. They did an extensive business for the times, built vessels, and at one time owned a good deal of navigation here. After the death of the junior member of the firm, Mr. Spofford continued the business alone for many years, and the last vessel of his building was in the year 1835 — a brig named the *Frederick Pearl*. His wife was Miss Sarah Averill, a native of Massachusetts, a very worthy lady, esteemed by all who knew her. She died in 1858. Their children were: the late Frederick P. Spofford, Esq., who died in 1870; the present Hon. Charles A. Spofford; Edwin B.; George W., who has been for several years a member of the board of selectmen; and William H. H. Spofford, who has been for several years a deputy sheriff. One daughter was Sarah, the wife of Dr. Amos A. Herrick, of Sedgwick, Maine, who practised medicine here. Some years afterward he removed to Sedgwick, where he died, and his widow is now dead. Eliza, the other daughter, was the wife of Dr. William F. Collins, who died in 1858, near the time of the death of Mrs. Spofford. She afterward became the wife of Hon. George Tolman, who resided here. There were other children, who died when young. Mr. Spofford died in 1865, aged about eighty-seven years. He was for many years the most prominent man in the town, filling several town offices, was several times representative to the General Court at Boston, and was the representative, in 1821, to the Legislature of this State, and nearly all his life he took an active part in politics. He was in former times a Federalist, afterward a Whig, and, after that party disbanded, became a Republican. He was postmaster from the first establishment of one here till

1838, when he was removed on political grounds. In 1841 he was reinstated and held the office till 1845. By the loss of the *Shakespeare* he suffered pecuniarily to quite a large amount, as he was the chief owner of the vessel and her cargo, which consisted of merchandise to be used in trade here. At his death he was possessor of considerable property, chiefly in real estate, some of which was quite valuable, and next to Ignatius Haskell, Esq., was the largest owner of that kind of property in the town. He was an educated man and very intelligent, and had a very large share of natural capacity. Had he chosen the law for a profession he would have taken a high rank among others in this part of the State, and for a long time he had a good deal of influence here. He ever took a great interest in education, and was liberal in the support of the gospel, though not a professor of religion. He was one of those men who, whatever matter they may take hold of, do so in earnest. The house he occupied is now owned by two of his sons, Messrs. C. A. and George W. Spofford. The store occupied by him is now taken down; it was standing near the sail-loft of Mr. S. B. Haskell. The chief part, or nearly all, of the estate he left is now the property of his children.

DR. DAVID ANGELL came here as early as 1800, if not a little before. He was a native of the State of Rhode Island, and was born in 1770. His wife was Miss Abigail, the daughter of Ignatius Haskell, Esq., and they had two sons — Amos, who was lost in the schooner *Shakespeare*, and Moses C. Angell, whose wife was a daughter of Mr. Asa Green. She was then the widow of Mr. John R. Haskell, and the mother of the present Sylvanus G. Haskell, Esq. By the second marriage she had several children. The family removed to Hyde Park near Boston several years ago, where he died in 1876. The wife of

Dr. Angell was for many years insane, but quietly so. The loss of her son affected her very much, as it did her husband, for he was a young man of promise. Dr. Angell had for many years quite an extensive practice, in which he was very successful. He had a good education and much natural ability and was a great wit; his observations were often most appropriate. He was also well informed upon almost every subject and capable of imparting a good deal of information, and, when he chose, his conversation would be very instructive and pleasing. In the latter part of his life his practice was more limited, but upon some occasions, when a serious case occurred, his advice and assistance were sought, as he had had a large share of experience. In some cases, no doubt, his aid saved the life of the patient, or at least such was the opinion of those who might be presumed to know. During the administrations of Presidents Jefferson and Madison, he was an officer of the customs here, as his political opinions were those of the then Republican party. In religion he was rather inclined to be skeptical. He died in 1843, aged seventy-three years, and his wife died a short time before him.

HEZEKIAH ROWELL, Esq., a native of Salem, New Hampshire, came here in the spring of 1804, in company with Messrs. Jonathan Webster and Joseph and Samuel Noyes, who were all of that vicinity. Mr. Rowell was by trade a blacksmith, but he did not work at the business here. His wife was Sarah, the daughter of Ignatius Haskell, Esq. She was born in 1789, or about that year. They had two sons, one dying in infancy; the other, Mr. Philip R. Rowell, has for many years resided in Massachusetts. None of the family remained here. Mr. Rowell was for many years a justice of the peace, and was for some time in trade here, occupying as a store the lower part of the house now owned by Mr. Levi Scott. He accumulated considerable property. After the death of Mr. Ezekiel Morey, he purchased his farm, one of the most valuable ones in the town, from his heirs, and built a house upon it which is now the property of the family of the late Mr. Joseph Sellers, 3d. The land was sold to different individuals, and there are upon the lot which was the property of Mr. Morey, more dwelling-houses than upon that of any other of the early settlers. He was a representative to the General Court at Boston at least twice prior to 1820. He removed from this town to Castine, where he resided several years; afterward he returned, remaining till about 1824, when he returned to that place, and for several years was in trade there and was once on the board of selectmen of that town. In about 1844 he returned here, lived a few years, and then removed to Hampden in this State, where he was a member of the family of one of his daughters who resided there, and in that place he died.

AARON S. HASKELL was the eldest son of Ignatius Haskell, Esq., but as in the previous record there was little said of these sons, and as they were men of prominence in their day, it is proper to notice them. The one whose name heads this sketch lived here from the time of the removal of the family here in 1778, when he was but three years of age, till his death in 1864, at the age of eighty-nine years. He was by trade a tanner. The name of his first wife was Hannah Marshall, a daughter of Mr. Ezekiel Marshall, one of the early settlers, whom we have noticed. She had no children and died many years ago. In 1836 he married a widow who came here from the island of Cape Breton. Her place of residence there was the town known as Arachat, not far from Louisburg. She was nearly forty years his junior in age, and they had a family. Only one of her sons by her marriage with Mr. Haskell now remains here, and one by her former marriage — the present Captain Dennis Haskell, as he is called. They are both energetic and capable master-mariners. The house built by Mr. Haskell near the Northwest Harbor is still known as the Aaron Haskell house, and it is now the property of Captain John W. Green. After the death of his father, he had, as a part of his share of his real estate, the land and house formerly occupied by Dr. John Phillips. He resided there with his family after his marriage till his death, his wife dying a few years before him.

MARK HASKELL was the second son in the family, and was born in 1785. His wife was Miss Hannah Beck Cross, of Newburyport. She died in 1882, at the age of ninety-three years, and her bodily and mental powers were very remarkable for one of her extreme age. Mr. Haskell went into trade at Castine, in company with his brother-in-law, Mr. Jonathan L. Stevens, but afterward returned here. While his health permitted, he was in trade here in the store owned by him, opposite the Green House. He was an honest and capable man and was much respected. He had no family, and died not far from the year 1847. His wife came into possession of his property, a part of which was the house owned and occupied by his father, afterward sold to the late Captain William Haskell and now the property of his widow. Some years after the death of her husband, Mrs. Haskell married a Mr. Porter, of Lyme, New Hampshire, now dead. After his death she returned here and resided with Mrs. Eben E. Raynes, a daughter of her sister, Mrs. B. F. Ferguson.

IGNATIUS HASKELL, Jr., the third son of the family, resided at the northern part of the island, first upon the farm afterwards the property of Captain Amos Howard, and later upon that now occupied by his son Mr. Albion K. P.

Haskell. His wife was Sarah, the daughter of Mr. William Eaton, Jr., by whom he had this son and several daughters, one of whom was a deaf-mute. One of them was the wife of the late Mr. A. C. Gordon; the other, that of Captain Oliver Howard, now of Gloucester, Massachusetts, the last of whom only is now living. Mrs. Gordon died in 1878, aged fifty-eight years. Mr. Haskell was, during the War of 1812, in command of a company of the militia; by trade he was a house-carpenter. He died not many years before 1850; his wife died in 1876, aged eighty-four years.

SOLOMON HASKELL, the youngest son of the family, was born in 1794, and was the first child born in the Haskell house, not long after his parents moved into it. His wife was Miss Joanna Carman, the daughter of Mr. John Carman, and sister of the present Mr. Levi Carman. They had four sons and five daughters, the former being Messrs. Hezekiah R., Charles S., Eben F., and the late Philip R. Haskell. One of the daughters was first the wife of Mr. Nathan E. Weed and now the widow of Captain William Haskell. Another was the wife of the late Captain David E. Adams, lost at sea. Another was the wife of Mr. Samuel E. Powers; another, the wife of Mr. William Bell, and one died unmarried. Of the above, Mrs. Powers is not living, and Mrs. Haskell only resides here. Mr. Haskell was twice representative to the State Legislature, — in 1826 and 1848. He was for several years one of the selectmen. He was a prominent man; was in trade many years, formerly in company with the late Benjamin F. Ferguson, Esq., and after a dissolution of the copartnership, was in trade alone. He died in, or about, 1867, and his widow survived him some ten years. His son, Mr. Eben F. Haskell, occupies the house and homestead of his father and is proprietor of the tanyard which was his father's property, in which in former years much more business was done.

JOSEPH NOYES, mentioned as coming in 1804 with Mr. Hezekiah Rowell, resided here till his death in 1850, or about that time. He was a native of Atkinson, New Hampshire, and was by trade a house and ship joiner and a very skillful workman. His wife, as we have stated, was the daughter of Mr. Ezekiel Morey, and survived her husband. Their sons were: Mr. John M. Noyes, who removed to Mount Desert, where he lived many years; Alexander N., who removed to Castine, and thence to Massachusetts; Henry A., who removed to Massachusetts; Joseph, now in Castine; and Albert O., now in the Territory of Arizona. Of the daughters, one only remains here — the wife of Mr. Hezekiah R. Haskell. Another was the wife of Mr. Joshua E. Haskell, a son of Mr. Edward Haskell, who removed to Fairfield in this State, where he was accidentally killed. The others married in other places. Mr. Noyes was a very sensible, capable man, and filled several town offices. His homestead is now the property of Mr. William E. Gray.

REV. JOSEPH BROWN came in 1804, or about that time, and was settled as pastor over the church here as the immediate successor of Rev. Peter Powers. He resided in the house known as the Parsonage, now the property of Rev. Hiram Houston. He was educated by the well-known Lady Huntington at the same place of instruction, and, I think, at about the same time, as Rev. Mr. Milton, of Newburyport, who in his day was quite celebrated as a preacher. He was born in England in 1760, or about that year, and continued here till his death. He was said to have been a preacher of ability and was a man of education. He brought a family, among whom was the late Rev. Charles M. Brown, well known in this vicinity a few years ago, who was settled in Tremont, Maine, and resided there several years, but who for many of his last years, after his wife's death, made this town his home. In his former years he followed the sea, and later became a good preacher, but was a very singular man. Another son was Philemon; another was Americus, and another was Joseph, none of whom remained here permanently. A daughter was a Mrs. Davenport, of Newburyport, and about the family, except Rev. Charles M. Brown, but little is known. In the time of the War of 1812 the sympathies of the Rev. Mr. Brown were very strongly in favor of Great Britain, and he carried them into the pulpit — a practice to be condemned, as it is of no benefit to a cause and productive of much injury to religion. This made him many enemies, and a number in the southern part of the town, members of the church and congregation, dissolved their connection with it and abandoned the place of worship. The result was the formation of a church of the Baptist order, in what is known now as South Deer Isle. This troubled him to a great degree and had an injurious effect upon his mind. At last his church and parish dissolved their connection with him, which so harrowed him that he died shortly after, in 1819. His remains lie in the burying-ground near the Town House, over which a stone was placed, but it was removed by his son several years ago, and where it is now we do not know.

SAMUEL PICKERING settled what is known as Pickering's Island, not included in our territorial limits, but as he was in his day well known here, it seems proper to notice him. Whether he ever resided in the town we do not know, but all his family known to us, with but one exception, did so, and died here. His wife was a daughter of Mr. Elijah Dunham, Sr., and sister to Mr. Elijah Dunham, Jr., who died in 1842. One of his sons was Mr. Daniel Pickering who resided on Greenlaw's Neck near the place now occupied by his son. His wife was Miss Mary Hayden, of a family who then lived here, but of whom nothing is now known. He died not far from 1850, his wife dying a few years earlier. He was the father of the late Mr. Richard Pickering, of the present Mr. Thomas Pickering, and of another son who lived in Orland. The daughters were the wives of Mr. John Bray, son of Mr. William Bray; of the late Mr. Willard Cole, and of Mr. Nathan Ball.

CAPTAIN SAMUEL PICKERING was another son of the family of the subject of this sketch. His wife was a daughter of Mr. Benjamin Cole, the second of the name, upon whose land Captain Pickering settled. His former place of residence is now the property of the widow of the late Mr. Mark H. Bray, and the house occupied by him at the time of his death is now the property of Mr. George W. Bray. It is near the Town House. Captain Pickering was a master-mariner, a very active man, and accumulated property. He died several years ago. His wife survived him for several years, dying in 1860 or about that time. Their family consisted of two sons and seven daughters, the sons being the present Messrs. Aaron D. and Timothy B. Pickering. The latter is a man of business here, owns considerable navigation, and has been in trade many years. The daughters were the wives of Mr. Willaby N. Bray; Mr. William Torrey, before referred to, who died on a passage to California; Mr. Nathan W. Sawyer; Captain Robert Kelsey; a Mr. Wilkinson, of Massachusetts; Mr. David Torrey, 2d, and Captain Dudley Pressey, the latter of whom only now resides here. The others, with the exception of Mrs. Wilkinson, are dead.

The daughters of Mr. Samuel Pickering, Sr., were the wives of Mr. William Bray and of a Mr. Davis. The latter did not reside here. The time of the death of Mr. Pickering we do not know.

DAVID SAWYER came here not far from the year 1800, from some place in the vicinity of Newburyport. He was born on the day of the Declaration of Independence, July 4, 1776, and was by trade a house and ship joiner. In the latter business he had a good deal of practice and was a very good workman. His wife was Miss Rebecca Crockett, the daughter of Mr. Robinson Crockett. Their sons were Nathan W., Admiral G., Mark H., David and Abel Sawyer, the first and last of whom are now dead. David Sawyer, Jr., has for some thirty years resided in Castine, and Abel, before his death, lived in the town of Sedgwick. The daughters were the wives of Mr. Ezekiel Marshall, Mr. Samuel G. Barbour, Captain James G. Bray and the late Mr. Mark H. Bray, all of whom except Mrs. Marshall are now (1882) living. The wife of Mr. Sawyer died not far from the year 1838, and he survived her twenty years or more. By the death of a brother in Groveland, Massachusetts, he came into possession of about ten thousand dollars, which at his death was divided among his children. He was one of the most remarkable men whom I have ever met. He had an extraordinary memory, was a great reader, and, retaining what he read as he did, possessed, of course, a large amount of information. He was a good mechanic, and an honest man whose word was good, for whatever he promised he performed.

AVERY FIFIELD, a native of Haverhill, New Hampshire, came here not long after 1800, and was at the time apprenticed to Mr. Jesse Niles, who has been noticed. For several years after the end of his term as an apprentice he worked at the trade of a house-carpenter. His wife was Miss Sarah, the daughter of Micajah Lunt. She was born February 6, 1786, and is now dead. They had a family of twelve children, all but one of whom lived to manhood and womanhood. The sons were: the late Captain Joseph Fifield, who died in 1874; Avery, who died in 1869; Ebenezer S.; Thomas S.; George, a deaf-mute, and John J. The daughters were the wives of Messrs. William Sweetsir; Thomas Small, a son of Mr. Edward Small; Silvious Simpson; Captain Stephen B. Morey, and Captain Jeremiah H. Greenlaw, all of whom, with the exception of Mrs. Simpson, are now living. Mr. Fifield first lived near Small's Cove, but later purchased a lot of one hundred and sixty acres lying on the south side of Burnt Cove. He removed there not far from 1812, at which time there was not a settlement in that part of the town south of the residence of Mr. Samuel Small. His first house stood not far from the spot upon which the house of Captain Morey now stands. He afterward removed to the place now occupied by Mr. Thomas F. Fifield, upon which he built the house now standing. After a few years he went into the fishing business, owning several vessels, and continued in it till the time of his death, which took place in September, 1845, at the age of sixty-two years. He was a representative to the Legislature in 1836 and 1844, and had a great deal of influence, especially with those of his own political party. He was a warm-hearted man, ready to relieve any one who might be in distress, and was one of those men who mean what they say.

CAPTAIN DAVID THURLOW was a native of Newbury, in the State of Massachusetts. He was born in the year 1775, and could well remember the "dark day" in 1780. While he was still a child, his father, Mr. Abram Thurlow, was suffocated by going into a deep well which had long been covered up and disused. He, with a brother of his wife, a Mr. Boynton, had been soldiers in what is known as the Old French War, and were both at the second attack upon Louisburg. His son, David, came here where he had an aunt who was the wife of Mr. Joseph Colby, Sr.; his sister, also, was here, being the wife of Mr. Joseph Colby, Jr. The latter had settled first for some years upon what is now called Thurlow's Island, where he and Mr. Thurlow built and operated a sawmill. There was an excellent privilege there, and they manufactured much lumber, as there were in that vicinity logs conveniently near as well as in abundance. After a few years Mr. Colby removed, and Captain Thurlow carried on the business alone, purchasing the interest of Mr. Colby in the island and the mill. He built several vessels on the island, — about seventeen in all, I believe: one brig of one hundred and forty tons, two or more coasting-schooners and fishing-vessels, — and at one time owned quite a number. Some of them were of large size for those days and did a good deal of business for the times, employing many men. He accumulated an important property, and at one time was one of the most prosperous men in the town, but in the latter part of his life became somewhat reduced. His wife was Mercy, the daughter of Samuel Trundy, and they were the parents of twelve children. The sons were Jeremiah, Stephen, David, Caleb S., Moody and Paul Thurlow; the last two only are now living. The daughters were the wives of Captain Levi Babbidge, Mr. Aaron Babbidge, Captain Peter P. Tyler, Captain Nathan Raynes (afterward that of Mr. Charles Collier, of Charlestown, Massachusetts), and the present wife of Sullivan Green, Esq. Three of them are now living. He was a captain in the militia at the time that station was considered an honor, and from that circumstance he was always styled Captain Thurlow. He died in 1857, at the age of eighty-two years. He and his wife, who died in 1860, were very charitable, and in the days of their prosperity they remembered the poor, for which their names are still respected. He was a very observing and sensible man, though without early advantages of education, possessed a sound judgment, was one of the selectmen of the town and, in 1829, represented it in the Legislature.

REV. SAMUEL ALLEN came here not far from 1810. He was a native of the town of Columbia, in the county of Washington, and was, we believe, the first or one of the first pastors of the Baptist Church here, continuing in that capacity for several years, often preaching on Isle au Haut and at other places in this vicinity. He was for a time quite popular and had many friends, but for some reason many became dissatisfied, and he ceased to be their pastor, and for many years he did not preach. He was born in 1778. His wife was Miss Lois Look. They had four sons — George, Daniel, Samuel, and William. George died at sea, and Daniel married his widow for his second wife and afterward removed to Levant, near Bangor, where he purchased a farm, and sailed as master of a vessel out of Bangor. Samuel died some ten years ago. William a few years since moved to Portland. The daughters were: Hannah, the wife of Mr. Isaac Crockett, and afterward of Mr. Samuel W. Emerson; Ann, the wife of Mr. Reuben Small, whom we mentioned as being burned to death in 1827, and afterward the wife of Mr. Ward, of Addison, Maine; Louisa, the wife of Mr. Thomas Crockett who moved to St. Andrew's, New Brunswick, and Sarah, the wife of Mr. Levi Scott, only the last of whom resides here. Mr. Allen died in 1833, at Levant, at the age of fifty-five years, his wife surviving him more than thirty years. He was a man of much natural talent, and for many years was a successful preacher, although his education was limited, and if he had had advantages might have taken a comparatively high rank in his profession.

He lived, while here, at what is known as Allen's Cove, near Green's Landing.

JAMES DUNCAN came here as early as 1800, or not long after. He was a native of Massachusetts, and was born in 1779. His wife was the eldest daughter of Captain Benjamin Stockbridge, whom we have noticed, and he settled at what is now known as Green's Landing. There had then but one person lived there, who was named Grover, and who left shortly after Mr. Duncan went there, so that we may consider the latter as its first permanent settler (although Thurlow's Island near there was occupied before that time), and, from the south side of Crockett's Cove by the southern shore of the island as far as Webb's Cove, his was the only dwelling-house for some time. He was engaged for a while in the manufacture of salt from sea-water, the process of which has been described, and also in chopping wood, and probably did more of that than any other man in the town ever did. He took up quite an extensive tract of land, and afterward built another house about two hundred rods from the shore, where he spent nearly all the rest of his life. His wife dying, he, after her death, resided with his children, and died in the family of his son in Rockland, when nearly ninety years of age. The children of the family were: James, the son just referred to, now dead; Mary, the wife of Mr. Robert Barter, who resided on what is known as Wreck Island, within the limits of the town as established in 1868; Elizabeth, the wife of Captain John Barter, of Isle au Haut; Abigail, first the wife of Mr. John Sellers who was lost in Chaleur Bay with Captain David Colby, in the schooner *Georgiana* of Castine, in 1839, and secondly of Mr. Stephen Colby; and Sarah, the wife of Mr. Levi Weed who several years ago removed to Rockland, and later to South Thomaston, where he died not many years ago. All the daughters are living except the wife of Mr. Colby. Mr. Duncan was for several years before his death afflicted with shaking palsy, and was always a hard-working man.

MOSES GROSS came here not long after 1800 from Boston, and was by trade a mason. He was known as Mason Gross, to distinguish him from Mr. George Gross, who, as has been stated, was known as Citizen Gross, but they were not relatives. He at one time did considerable business at his trade in Boston, but becoming somewhat reduced in circumstances, he moved from that place here. He was for much of the time employed at his trade here, doing nearly all the work in his line. He died in 1822, at Castine, while employed upon a block of brick stores there. His wife was a native of Boston, and was born in 1773, about the time of the destruction of the tea in Boston Harbor. She died here in the family of her daughter, Mrs. Pressey, in 1862, at the age of eighty-nine years. After the death of her first husband, she, in 1830, or about that time, became the wife of Ignatius Haskell, Esq. The sons of Mr. Gross were: Samuel P., James, Isaac and the late Mr. Frederick A. Gross. The daughters were: Margaret, the wife of Mr. John Leman, of Boston, who, after her death, married her sister Martha; Mary, the first wife of Captain Jeremiah Thurlow, and Harriet, the wife of Mr. Sylvanus G. Pressey. Another daughter never married. Of the family Mrs. Pressey is the sole survivor. Her son, Mr. Samuel P. Gross, followed the occupation of his father. James was a master-mariner and died after a very short illness in 1828. Mr. Frederick A. Gross died in 1881.

JONATHAN TORREY, Jr. In recording the family of Mr. Jonathan Torrey, I briefly noticed his sons. One of them, who in his lifetime was as well known as any other person in the town, is the subject of this sketch.

He was one with whom I was very well acquainted. He was born here in 1774, and his wife was Miss Prudence, daughter of Captain Belcher Tyler. He followed the sea for many years, and for nineteen consecutive years was master of a vessel employed in the Labrador cod-fishery, the last year being 1824, as the fisheries then had failed to the extent that it was no longer a profitable business. He continued to follow the sea, sometimes in the fishing and sometimes in the coasting business, till 1832 or 1833, when he abandoned it and turned his attention to his farm, which, as we have stated, was the one occupied by Mr. John Billings, adjoining that of William Eaton on the Reach shore. He was a man of integrity and enterprise. The time and cause of his death have been stated in the notice of his father, and his sons mentioned. His widow outlived him about twenty-five years. The real estate owned by him is now in the possession of his heirs.

DAVID TORREY was the eldest brother in the family, and lived for many years near the road leading from the Northwest Harbor toward the Reach. He was a very eccentric man, and died in 1858 at the age of ninety years. His wife was Mrs. Martha Robbins, a daughter of Mr. Charles Sellers, and they had no children. She had three by her former husband, none of whom remained here. She has been noticed in the sketch of the family of her father as dying in 1879, at the great age of ninety-seven years.

CAPTAIN JOHN TORREY was another son of Mr. Jonathan Torrey, Sr., and was for many years a master-mariner, making several voyages in the Labrador fisheries. He was a capable and intelligent man. His wife was Miss Dorothy, a daughter of Captain Jonathan Haskell, and a sister to the wife of his brother Mr. Daniel Torrey. They had no children, but adopted a daughter of Mr.

Josiah Gray when she was very young, who took their name and was afterward the wife of Mr. Joshua Pressey, 2d. She is now a widow, and occupies the homestead of her adopted father. The other members of the family of Mr. Torrey, Sr., have, with the exception of Mrs. Eaton, been dead for several years, and have also been elsewhere noticed. The limits of this work will preclude many such further sketches that I should like to make, and the persons who would be the subjects of them are now remembered by but few of the living.

WILLIAM RAYNES, 2d, the eldest son of Captain John Raynes, was in his day very well known, not only here, but in other places, as he was for many years a master-mariner, and throughout his long life maintained an unblemished reputation which was well known wherever he was acquainted. He was born in September, 1778. His wife was Miss Ruth, the daughter of Captain Edmund Sylvester. He followed the sea until sixty years of age, and resided upon the farm first taken up by Mr. Samuel Raynes, which was purchased by Ignatius Haskell, Esq., from whom it was purchased by Captain Raynes, not long after 1800. Upon the lot, he built a house which is now in a state of decay. The children of the marriage were: William, who died in 1832, aged twenty-three years; Edmund S., whose first wife was Mary A., the daughter of Mr. John Howard, and the second a Miss Small, of Newburyport, in which place he now resides; George who died in 1836, in New York; Abiel who was shipwrecked on Martha's Vineyard, in 1846, being one of the crew of the brig *Lincoln* of this town. He died shortly after reaching the shore, and was there buried. He married Susan, the daughter of Captain Henry Lufkin, Jr., a sister of the present Captain H. T. Lufkin. She afterward became the wife of Mr. Robert Clark, of

Castine, where she is now living. Another son was the late Mr. Aaron B. Raynes, whose wife was Miss Mary M., a daughter of the late Mr. Thomas Sellers, of Bangor, a son of Mr. William, and a brother to the present Mr. Amos Sellers. Mr. A. B. Raynes was formerly one of the selectmen, and represented this town in the year 1871 in the Legislature. In that year he removed from this place to the State of Missouri. He afterward came East and resided in Norwich, Connecticut, where he died in 1881, at the age of fifty-nine years. Another son is the present Captain Eben E. Raynes, whose wife was Miss Elizabeth, daughter of the late Benjamin F. Ferguson, Esq. He is the only member of the family now residing here. The youngest son was Mr. Benjamin Raynes, who went from here in 1854 to California, afterward returning, and who now resides in Gloucester, Massachusetts. The daughters were: Susan, the wife of George L. Hosmer, who died in 1868; Elizabeth, the wife of Mr. Charles S. Torrey, who died in 1853; Caroline, the wife of Mr. Jason Webb, who died in Gloucester, Massachusetts, in 1857. Of the family of twelve children but three are now living. Captain Edmund S. Raynes, the second son, was for years an active master-mariner, making many voyages to the East Indies. The date of the death of Captain Raynes has been stated and also his age. His wife died in 1852.

JOSEPH RAYNES was the third son in the family, and his wife was Betsey, the daughter of Mr. Nathan Johnson. Two of their sons, Captain John J. and Horatio G. Raynes, now reside in Hyde Park, Massachusetts, and one, Nathan Raynes, resides here. One married daughter, Mrs. Lucas, is a resident of Methuen, Massachusetts, and the youngest is the wife of Mr. Bester B. Haskell. One is single, and makes the house of her deceased father her residence in summer, while the rest of the time she lives in Boston. Captain Raynes followed the sea and the fishing business many years. Both he and his wife died within forty-eight hours of each other, in April, 1859, and their remains occupy one grave.

BENJAMIN RAYNES was the youngest son, and his wife was Miss Sabrina, the daughter of Mr. Joseph Whitmore, Jr., who, as has been stated, lost his life in 1814, at the same time with Mr. John Eaton, by drowning. Their only son was the late Captain Edmund Raynes. Their eldest daughter was first the wife of Captain Henry J. Lufkin who was master of the brig *Baron de Castine*, of Castine, and who died on board of her on the coast of Africa, in 1860. She was afterward the wife of Mr. Israel B. Grindle, of Penobscot, and died in May, 1881. Another was the first wife of Mr. Edward P. Haskell. Two now remain; one is the wife of Mr Alvin B. Saunders, and one is unmarried. In 1846 Captain Raynes, then master of the brig *Lincoln* of this town, was wrecked on Martha's Vineyard. The brig being heavily loaded with lumber, with spars on deck, was knocked down, righting after the masts were cut away, and for four days in the latter part of November the crew were on deck without food or water, drenched with sea-water. Two of the crew, William Adams and Richard Brown, died before the vessel went on shore; and soon after she struck, the mate, Mr. Benjamin J. Saunders, in attempting to reach the shore was drowned, leaving three on board, who, when the tide had ebbed, reached the land, one of whom, Mr. Abiel S. Raynes, soon after lay down and died. He had lost his hat when the brig was knocked down and was more drenched than the others with salt water. The two remaining, Captain Raynes and Mr. Charles H. Saunders, attempted to reach a house at about half a mile's distance from the shore, were seen, and assistance was rendered them. The exposure and suffering caused Captain Raynes to become prematurely old, and he died at sea in 1861, at the age of fifty-eight years, his wife dying in 1859. He was for several years engaged in the Banks fishery, and was master of vessels from Castine in that pursuit, but for a number of years prior to his death he was engaged in the coasting business.

CAPTAIN HENRY LUFKIN was a son of the Mr. Benjamin Lufkin mentioned, who came here from Gloucester, and was at the time of the removal about fifteen years of age. He resided here the remainder of his life, and was master of a vessel in the coasting business many years. He purchased a farm of Ignatius Haskell, Esq., which was a part of the land formerly occupied by Mr. Robinson Crockett, upon which he lived till his death. His first wife was Miss Betsey Robinson, and by her he had two sons — the late Captain Henry Lufkin who died in 1868, and Captain Joseph R. Lufkin who died in 1851 — and two daughters. One was the wife of Mr. Timothy Saunders, and the other was the wife of Captain Ebenezer Beardsley, then of Boston, but a native of Damariscotta, Maine. Both of the daughters are now dead. The second wife of Captain Lufkin, the subject of this notice, was Miss Betsey Raynes, and by her he had two sons and two daughters. One son is the present Captain Mark H. Lufkin, and the other died when a young man in the West Indies. One of the daughters was the wife of the late Johnson Raynes; the other died unmarried, and of the family Captain M. H. Lufkin is the sole survivor. The death of Captain Lufkin took place in 1839, at the age of sixty-four years, and that of his wife in 1858, at the age of seventy-eight years. His real estate is now the property of his son, who occupies it.

DANIEL LUFKIN was a brother of the subject of the preceding notice. He was born in 1785. His first wife was Sarah, the daughter of Captain John Raynes. Of their family three now remain: Mr. Benjamin Lufkin who resides here; Mr. Theophilus Lufkin, of Castine; and a daughter, the widow of Mr. Miles Gardiner, of that town. One son, Mr. Daniel Lufkin, Jr., was drowned by stepping off a wharf in Bangor several years ago; he left a family. Two other sons died when young men, unmarried. The wife of Mr. Lufkin died in 1828. For his second wife he married Mrs. Patience Snow, the daughter of Mr. Thomas Colby, by whom he had three sons and one daughter. One son was drowned; another removed from here, and one, the present Mr. Henry F. Lufkin, and the daughter, the wife of Mr. Edwin Tyler, reside here. Mr. Lufkin died in 1871, at the age of eighty-six years. His wife died a year or two after.

EZEKIEL ALEXANDER came here many years ago from Harpswell, Maine. He was well known here. Two of his sisters resided here — one the wife of Mr. George Gross; the other that of Mr Solomon Marshall. The wife of Mr. Alexander was Polly Eaton, a daughter of Mr. Eliakim Eaton, the oldest son of Major William Eaton. She was born in 1776. After her marriage she had two daughters, one of whom married in Massachusetts, and the other is the well-known Avis Alexander. He died in, or about, 1850, and was not far from ninety years of age. His wife was well known as a wandering character, gathering herbs, etc., while she remained able. She afterward became an inmate of the poorhouse, and died in 1869, at the age of ninety-three years.

JOSEPH CLIFTON came here many years ago and was well known. He was born in Medford, Massachusetts, according to his own account, in 1771. His wife was a daughter of Mr. John Scott and the widow of Mr. Ebenezer Ball. By Mr. Clifton she had three daughters: one is the present wife of Mr. Thomas Low; another the wife of Captain William Torrey who died in 1881; the other married in Massachusetts. He was a very singular man, and for many years did not live with his family, preferring to roam about, not remaining long in any one place. He spent considerable time in Winterport and in that vicinity. By trade he was a shoemaker. When, by reason of age, he became incapable of labor, he returned here, where he spent the remainder of his life, dying in 1865, at the age of ninety-four. His wife died not far from 1870, aged eighty-five years.

SIMON SMITH came here not far from 1800. He was the son of Mr. Abiatha Smith, one of the early settlers of Isle au Haut, and was born in Thomaston. His wife was Miss Lydia, the youngest daughter of Mr. Thomas Small, Sr., and they had a family of twelve children. Of the sons the eldest, Simon Smith, died on Isle au Haut, in 1835, of smallpox. The next in age, Captain Benjamin Smith, was lost at sea while master of a vessel belonging in Winterport, at which place he resided. The next in age was the late Mr. Samuel Smith who represented this town in the Legislature in 1854. Another is the present Mr. John Smith. One, Chase Smith, died when a young man. The daughters were the wives of Messrs. William Webb, James Saunders, 2d, Alexander N. Noyes, Henry A. Noyes, Paul T. Lane — all of this town. Another was first the wife of a Mr. Foote and afterward of Joshua Fuller, Esq., of Thomaston. The other was the wife of Mr. James Babbidge, 2d, of North Haven, but now a resident of Falmouth, Maine. Mr. Smith died a few years prior to 1860, and his wife did not long survive him. The farm owned by him was sold by his heirs, and is now the property of Captain H. T. Lufkin.

WILLIAM SELLERS, Jr., was a native of York, Maine, and was born in 1775. He came here early with his father, Mr. William Sellers, a brother of Messrs. Charles and Joseph Sellers, but he did not acquire a settler's right. He, and the rest of the family, with the exception of their father who returned to York and died there, remained here until their deaths. The wife of Mr. Sellers was Miss Abigail, daughter of Mr. Thomas Small, Sr., and their children were: (1) Mr. William Sellers, 3d, who lived not far from Burnt Cove; (2) Mr. David Sellers who lived on Stinson's Neck; (3) Mr. Thomas Sellers who died of the cholera in 1849, in Bangor; (4) Mr. John Sellers who was lost in Chaleur Bay, in 1839, — one of the crew of the schooner *Georgiana* of Castine, Captain David Colby, master; and (5 and 6) the present Messrs. Ebenezer S. and Amos Sellers. Of the two daughters, one was the wife of Mr. John Conary, and the other that of Mr. William Fife who formerly resided on Swan's Island. Of the family two only now are living. The dates of the deaths of Mr. Sellers and his wife were not far from 1850. His property is now owned and occupied by his son, Mr. Amos Sellers. The brother of Mr. Sellers removed to Brooklin, Maine, many years ago. The sisters were the wives of Mr. Thomas Conary, Jr., of Mr. Ebenezer Jordan, of Mr. Stephen Dow and afterward the third wife of Mr. Stephen Babbidge, and another was the first wife of Captain James Torrey.

ELIAS MOREY was the eldest son of Mr. Ezekiel Morey, who came among the earliest settlers. He was born in 1761 and remained here till his death, which took place not far from the year 1845. His wife was a Miss Robinson, and was sister to the wives of William Raynes, senior of the name here, and of Captain Henry Lufkin.

They had a family of thirteen children. The sons were: the late Mr. William Morey, who was the father of the present Mr. Levi B. Morey, and whose wife was a daughter of Mr. Robinson Crockett; another was the late Mr. Elias Morey, Jr., who died on Swan's Island; another was Charles Morey who went away and died when a young man; another was Mr. Ezekiel Morey who died many years ago, and the other was Mr. Joseph Morey, the father of the man of the same name, who now lives here. They all are dead. The daughters were the wives of Mr. Joseph Cole, Hezekiah Robbins, Elijah Dunham, Mark Robbins, and Abram Holbrook — all of this town; and there were others who were married in other places. For some years Mr. Morey resided upon a part of his father's farm, but his right was purchased by Deacon Joshua Haskell. After that he resided the most of the time on Greenlaw's Neck, where he died a few days after his wife's death.

NAYLOR SMALL has been mentioned as one of the sons of Mr. Job Small. He was born in 1772. His wife was the daughter of Mr. Levi Carman, the early settler of that name. Of his family there was one son, the late Mr. Calvin Small. Two daughters were the wives of Captain Tristram Haskell, Jr., and Mr. Charles Walton, of Spruce Head Island, both of whom are now dead; another was the wife of Mr. Jesse Niles, and the present wife of Mr. Levi Greenlaw; another, the wife of the late Mr. Frederick A. Gross, and one died unmarried. Mr. Small died in 1863, at the age of ninety-one years; his wife died a few years before. His property passed into the hands of his son, by whom it was occupied till his death.

MICHAEL SMALL, Esq., was the youngest son of Mr. Job Small. He was born in 1779. His wife was Miss Deborah Perkins, of Castine. They had a large family, most of whom died young. Three of their sons were: the present Mr. Michael Small; the late Mr. Frederick Small, and Mr. Robert P. Small who removed to Gloucester, Massachusetts, and is now dead. Of two daughters, one is the wife of Mr. William Small: the other died, unmarried, not long after the death of her father, which took place in 1837, after a most distressing illness. His wife survived him about twenty years, residing with her son, Mr. Michael Small, who owns and occupies a part of the property left by his father. Mr. Small was for many years a justice of the peace, an enterprising farmer, and accumulated considerable property.

CHARLES CHATTO, MICHAEL READY, and JOHN FINNEY came here about the beginning of the present century. The first was a native of Scotland, the other two of Ireland. They were in the military service of Great Britain, from which they had deserted at the time of their coming here. They were stationed near the river St. Croix, and, either by swimming or in a boat, came alongside a vessel belonging here, the master of which was Captain Ephraim Marshall, who landed them here, where they remained, two of them, and married. Mr. Chatto married a Miss Staples; they were the parents of Mr. Joshua S. Chatto who has resided here and is well known. Mr. Ready married Lydia, the daughter of Mr. Chase Pressey; they were the parents of Messrs. Thomas and Jeremiah Ready, the former of whom resided here until a few years ago, and the latter went to Boston when a young man. Mr. Finney married the daughter of Mr. Moses Staples, of Swan's Island; they were the parents of the late Mr. Moses S. Finney who came here as early as 1838, from that place, and remained till his death, a few years prior to 1860. Mr. Finney, or, as he was generally called, Jack Finney, was a man of small stature, and very excitable. If he deemed himself insulted, he was ever ready for a combat, however great the disadvantages to himself might seem.

GEORGE G. CHOATE came, not far from the beginning of the present century, from some place in the county of Essex, in the State of Massachusetts. By trade he was a house-carpenter. He first married a Miss Johnson, a daughter of the last wife of Mr. Ezra Howard, and by her had three daughters, one of whom was the wife of Mr. Samuel Hall, of this place, but who, many years ago, removed to Long Island in the town of Bluehill. Another married Mr. Thomas Haskell, son of Deacon Joshua Haskell, a master ship-carpenter, who lived here until a few years ago, and then removed to Boston, where he died not long after. He had been married before, and had a family of eight children, his first wife being a daughter of Courtney Babbidge, Jr. The remaining daughter of Mr. Choate by his first marriage was Mary Choate who resides in Boston. The second wife of Mr. Choate was Miss Betsey, daughter of Mr. Thomas Small, Sr. They had two sons. One was the late Mr. Thomas S. Choate who resided here, but died several years ago. The other was Mr. John Choate who, when quite a young man, left this place and went to New Orleans, and before the Rebellion commanded a steamer on the Mississippi River. Of the daughters we know nothing, as they did not remain here. Mr. Choate formerly resided in a house near the Town House, which, after his removal from here, was purchased by Jonathan E. Webb, Esq., and moved to the Northwest Harbor. It is now the property of Captain John W. Green. Not far from 1830 Mr. Choate moved to Bluehill, where he resided till his death, which took place about 1860. He was a great wit, and many examples of it are well remembered both in this place and in Bluehill.

We have given quite an extended sketch, and notices of the settlers and early inhabitants. Among them were many who were not descendants of those first settlers, but who came here and were prominent in their day in that part of the town known as Great Deer Island. We will now notice those persons who were the early settlers of Little Deer Island. As has been stated, the authority of Messrs. Joseph and George Tyler to allot lands to settlers did not extend to Little Deer Island, but was confined to Great Deer and Sheep Islands, or, as the latter is known, Jordan's Island. Whether those persons who were there as settlers prior to 1784 were entitled to their lots of land, or not, we do not know; but as the same rule was observed in Township Number Three (which embraced the present towns of Penobscot, Castine, and a large part of Brooksville), as was on Great Deer Island, we may judge that it was established by resolve of the General Court of Massachusetts, in other towns in this vicinity. The proprietors of that island were residents of Massachusetts. Hon. Thomas L. Winthrop, once lieutenant-governor of the State, was one of the principal proprietors, if not the only one, from whom the titles of occupants were derived. It was surveyed in 1802 by James Peters, of Bluehill, a brother of John Peters, Jr., by whom the second survey of Great Deer Island was made, in 1798. At the time of the survey most of the land was occupied.

ELIAKIM EATON, the oldest son of William Eaton, settled on the lot upon the southeast end of the island. His settlement embraced what is known as Stave Island, now occupied by his grandson, Mr. Benjamin H. Eaton. His wife was Miss Mary Bunker. She was a daughter of a man of that name who, as has been stated, lived to the extraordinary age of one hundred and ten years; but such a statement must be received with a great deal of caution, as there is generally a disposition in such cases to exaggerate. If the statement be correct, there has been but one case in this part of the State of such extraordinary longevity — that of Mr. Laughlin McDonald, who died in Belfast, in 1821, said to be of the same age, and generally believed to be from the statements made by him of persons he had seen, who had been dead more than one hundred years. One of the sons of their marriage who remained here was the late Mr. Solomon Eaton who died about the year 1860, at an advanced age. Another was Mr. Isaac Eaton, who married a daughter of Mr. Peter Hardy, Sr., died when a young man, and whose widow became the wife of Captain Jonathan Haskell who died in 1873. Another son is the present Mr. Peter H. Eaton who is about ninety years of age. Of the daughters, one was the wife of Mr. Ezekiel Alexander, whom we have before noticed. A son of hers, before her marriage with him, who went by the name of Ezekiel A. Clark, was found dead under very suspicious circumstances in Boston, in 1849. As he was known to have had several hundred dollars in money, none of which was found upon his person, it was presumed that he had been robbed and murdered. Another daughter was the wife of Mr. Jeremiah Eaton. She was the mother of the present Mr. Alfred Eaton. After the death of her husband, who was drowned in 1834, she became the wife of Mr. John Gray, in Brooksville. Another daughter was known as Phebe Eaton. She was the mother of the late Captain Rufus Benson, who removed to Camden, and was the master of a bark belonging to that place, which was seized by the Spanish authorities about the year 1850, about which considerable was said at the time, it being the subject of correspondence between the government of this country and that of Spain at the time that Hon. Daniel Webster was Secretary of State. Captain Benson was brought up by Mr. Amos Thurston, of this town, who, when Rufus was a little child, was in his boat fishing near Isle au Haut, and being near a ledge, heard a child crying upon it; he landed there and found him, and he remained in his family till he was twenty-one years of age. After that he removed to Camden and became an active master-mariner. He is now dead. His mother, late in life, became the wife of Mr. Christopher Gray, of Brooksville, the man who lived to be one hundred and three years of age, but we believe she had been married before. Another daughter married in Harpswell, Maine; nothing is known about her. Mr. Eaton died not far from the year 1800. His widow married Mr. Charles Stewart who was well known in Sedgwick and Brooksville. She died between the years 1840 and 1845, at the age of one hundred years, as was supposed. The real estate of Mr. Eaton was afterwards purchased with the exception of the widow's dower, by the late Mr. Abijah Haskell, Jr., who resided upon it till his death, in 1872.

SOLOMON EATON, son of the subject of the preceding notice, lived and died on the island on which he was born, not long after the year 1770. His first wife was a daughter of Mr. Benjamin Howard, of what is now Brooksville, and their sons were: the present Messrs. Benjamin H. and Mark Eaton; the late Solomon Eaton, Jr., of this town, who died in 1849, and Mr. John Eaton, of Sedgwick, now dead. The only daughter who remained here was the wife of Mr. Peter H. Haskell, who is now dead. The second wife of Mr. Eaton was the daughter of Mr. Daniel Billings, who was some twenty-five years younger than himself, and they had three sons who were: Mr. Isaac B. Eaton, of Isle au Haut; Mr. Amos Eaton, and Mr. Hardy Eaton. They all are dead. After the death of his second wife, he married a sister of his first wife,

Mrs. Martha Tibbetts, of Brooksville, and they both died near each other, not far from the year 1860. The settlement of Mr. Eaton was upon the southwest side of the island, and his place afterward became the property of the late Silas L. Hardy, Esq.

JEPHTHA BENSON was the first settler upon the land adjoining that of Mr. Eliakim Eaton on the northwest. He came here not far from the year 1800, from one of the towns in the vicinity of Paris, in the county of Oxford, in this State, and his descendants still reside there. He was a Revolutionary soldier, and was born about the year 1757. He resided several years upon the land he settled, and then removed to Marshall's Island, lying west of Swan's Island. He married a Mrs. Ross who was a daughter of Mr. Thomas Kench who, many years ago, lived near Buck's Harbor, in Brooksville. Mr. Kench was also a Revolutionary soldier, and was one of those who accompanied Benedict Arnold up the Kennebec River and across the wilderness to Quebec in 1775, and was engaged in the attempt to capture that city under General Montgomery. It is said that he was one of the few who reached the top of the wall, but was obliged to jump down to save his life. By his wife Mr. Benson had a family, none of whom ever resided here, but were on Swan's Island a few years ago. He was dispossessed of Marshall's Island, in 1835, by Rufus B. Allyn, of Belfast, and afterward removed to Brooksville, where he died, at the age of ninety-eight years. His land on Little Deer Island afterward became the property of the late Silas L. Hardy, Esq., by whom it was occupied till his death, in 1859. It is now the property of his sons.

JONATHAN HARDY, before noticed, was the occupant of the lot of land lying northwest of that of Mr. Benson, and lived upon it till his death. Some years before that time he sold a part of it to his son, Mr. Jonathan Hardy, Jr., who removed to Winterport, and it was by him sold to Mr. James E. Parker who is now the occupant. The remainder of the lot is the property of the sons of Silas L. Hardy. His second wife, a Miss Susan Jones, of Castine, after his death became the third wife of Mr. Timothy Saunders. She had one daughter after her marriage with Mr. Hardy, who became the wife of Mr. John Hardy, and died in the year 1854, on the voyage with her husband to Washington Territory. Her husband remained there some time, and afterward returned, sometimes residing here and sometimes in other places.

ISAAC GRAY settled the lot of land northwest of that of Mr. Jonathan Hardy, Jr., on which he resided several years, but not till some time after 1800. His wife was the oldest daughter of Mr. Joseph Harris, and they were the parents of the late Mr. Joseph H. Gray and Messrs. Silas H. and Oliver B. Gray. One daughter became the second wife of Mr. George C. Closson, and the other, that of the late Captain Timothy Parker, of Winterport. Mr. Gray removed there several years ago and died in that place. His wife returned and died here in 1876, at the age of eighty-seven years. The real estate of Mr. Gray is now the property of his heirs, and is unoccupied.

JOSEPH HARRIS was a native of the British Provinces, and came here very early. His wife was a daughter of Mr. James Gray, who lived near Walker's Pond, in Brooksville. She was a sister to Mr. Christopher Gray, mentioned before, and to Mr. Josiah Gray who has been noticed. We do not know the exact date of his coming, but as his oldest daughter was born in 1789, if he lived there at that time, he was one of the early settlers. His lot was that adjoining the one taken up by Mr. Isaac Gray on the northwest. They had one son, the present Mr.

Henry Harris. The daughters were the wives of Mr. Isaac Gray; Mr. John Weed; Mr. Samuel Pittee who came here from North Yarmouth, Maine; Mr. John Hutchinson who died here not many years ago; and the youngest was first the wife of Samuel Hutchinson, and afterward that of Mr. Ebenezer Spinney who came here in 1837 from the town of Eliot, Maine. Mrs. Spinney is the only one of the daughters remaining, and is now at the age of eighty years. Mr. Harris died in 1841, at the age of eighty-six years; his wife died in 1854, at the age of eighty-nine years.

DANIEL BILLINGS was the settler upon the lot of land lying northwest of that of Mr. Harris. He was a brother of Mr. Timothy Billings, and was born in this town not far from the year 1768. His wife was Miss Carter, a sister of Rev. Edward Carter, a Baptist elder, who many years ago preached on Cape Rozier, in Brooksville, near what was known as Bakman's Mills. A sister of the family was the wife of Mr. Thomas Wasson, a well-known citizen in Brooksville for many years, who died more than forty years ago, and who was a Revolutionary soldier, and grandfather to Thaddeus Shepardson, Esq., of that town. Mr. Billings and wife had three sons who arrived at manhood, and one who died young. They were Daniel Billings, Esq., who many years lived in Monroe, Waldo County, and practised law. A few years ago he came here and purchased what is known as the " Swain Place." He was afterward appointed a trial justice, for which position he was well qualified. He died not many years since after a short sickness. Another son was the late Mr. Peter H. Billings who also resided in Monroe. He was by trade a millwright, and was a very skillful and ingenious mechanic. He died not far from the year 1850, not quite forty years of age. The other is the present Mr. Edward

C. Billings who occupies and owns the homestead of his father. The daughters were the wives of the late Mr. Peter Hardy, Jr., who died in 1859; Mr. Samuel Howard, of Brooksville; Mr. Solomon Eaton who has been noticed; Mr. Peter H. Eaton; Mr. Samuel Gray, of Sedgwick, and Mr. George Swain. The first four are now dead. Mr. Billings died at an advanced age several years ago, his wife dying before him. He left a good reputation.

SAMUEL HOWARD, one of the family in Brooksville of that name, settled upon the land adjoining the lot of Mr. Billings upon the northwest. His wife was a sister of Mr. Billings. He lived for several years upon it, and afterward removed to the town of Montville. His farm was purchased by Otis Little, Esq., of Castine, who acquired land adjoining it, and had in all about four hundred acres which, a little before 1830, he sold to Captain John Gray, of Sedgwick, who lived upon it about thirty-five years, and then removed to the town of Brooksville, where he died. He had previously sold a part of his land to Mr. Shadrach Black who occupied it from 1836 till his death, not long after 1870. His wife was a daughter of Mrs. Gray by a former husband. Another portion of his land he sold to his son, the present Mr. Jonathan D. Gray who, a few years ago, sold it to Mr. John Douglass who now occupies it. When Captain Gray removed he sold the remainder of his land to his son Jonathan who occupies it at present. Mr. Black's land is now occupied by his son.

TIMOTHY BILLINGS who, as we have stated, was the first child of white parents born in the town, settled the farm on the northwestern end of the island. His wife was a Miss Wells, a relative, doubtless, of those of that name who lived in what is now the town of Brooklin. She died many years before him, leaving a family of three sons, of whom we have had knowledge, and two daughters. Two of the sons were Captain John Billings and Amaziah Billings, who lived in Sedgwick. Of the daughters, one was the wife of Mr. James Gray, of Brooksville, and the other that of Captain Robinson Crockett, Jr., who lived at one time on Stinson's Neck. The other son of Mr. Billings, Jeremiah Billings, who remained here and occupied the farm of his father, died very suddenly, in 1840. After his death his widow married Mr. John L. Lawry, who came here in 1841 from some town in the county of Waldo, and in whose family Mr. Billings, the subject of this notice, resided till his death, after which the farm was sold, and the family removed to Winterport, where Mr. Lawry died. It is now the property of Mr. Michael D. Snowman, who removed there from Brooksville. That which was said of Mr. Daniel Billings, as to character, might be repeated of his brother.

WILLIAM SWAIN was the first settler on the southwest side of the island, upon the lot of land adjoining that of Captain Gray on the southeast. He was a native of Scotland, and came with the British army to Bagaduce in 1779. He was a master-mariner, and in former years a man of enterprise. He was at one time worth a very good property. His wife was a daughter of Mr. Samuel Matthews, of what is now Castine, whose farm, a valuable one, was afterward owned by Mr. Jonathan Hatch, and occupied by him at the time of his death. A cove on the shores of which his place lay is known as Swain's Cove; but the exact time of his coming here is not known. He did not pay for his property, but the proprietors never molested him. After his death his son, Mr. George Swain, made a contract to purchase it, but failed to pay for it, and did not acquire a title. After the removal of Mr. George Swain, Mr. Horatio N. Haskell contracted with the owners for its purchase, but he also failed to meet his payments. Afterward it was purchased by Daniel Billings, Esq., who resided upon it till his death, a few years ago. It is now owned and occupied by his widow. The time of the death of the wife of Mr. Swain is not known, but he died about 1835. In the family there were, to our knowledge, four sons, namely, William, Samuel, Walter, and George Swain. All are now dead. Mr. George Swain removed to Winterport, where his widow and descendants resided till the last of our knowledge of them.

NOAH BLASTER was the first settler upon the land adjoining that of Mr. Swain upon the southeast. Of him but very little is known either of the place he came from or the time of his death. He left one son and one daughter, but of the latter we know nothing. His son was the late Mr. Samuel Blaster, who died in 1860, at the age of eighty-three, having been born in 1777, and whose wife was a daughter of Mr. Christopher Gray, of Brooksville. At the time of her marriage she was the widow of Mr. James Hendrick, by whom she had two sons, Christopher, now dead, and the present Mr. Stillman Hendrick who resides on Little Deer Island; and a daughter, now dead, who was the wife of Mr. Solomon Eaton, Jr., who died in 1849. They were the parents of Mr. Isaiah V. Eaton, who died a soldier in the Union army during the war for the suppression of the Rebellion. Mrs. Blaster died several years before her husband, by her marriage with whom there were a number of daughters, and one son, the present Mr. William Blaster.

RICHARD BANKS settled upon the lot of land lying southeast of that of Mr. Blaster. He came here from the town of Hartford, in Oxford County. He brought a part of his family, and, we believe, married the daughter of Mr. Blaster after he came here. One of his sons whom he left behind was the late well-known Silas Banks, who fell into distress in that town, and, after his father gained a settlement here, this town was holden for his support, and was obliged to provide for and remove him. He was a pauper till his death in 1872, or not far from that year. He was a very witty *non compos* person, and in some things possessed a good deal of shrewdness. None of the other children of Mr. Banks resided here, and in 1835 he removed to the town of Mount Desert, where he died.

The lot on the southern end of the island is the one which was occupied by Mr. Benjamin Weed, whom, with his family, we have noticed. After his exchange with Captain Peter Hardy, the latter moved upon the lot, and resided there several years. It was a valuable farm. When he moved from it, it was occupied by his son, who was known as Peter Hardy, 3d, and after the death of his grandfather, in 1831, as Peter Hardy, Jr. He remained there till his death, in 1859, at the age of sixty-one years. His wife was Miss Joan Billings, the eldest daughter of Mr. Daniel Billings; she died in 1876, at the age of eighty-two years. Before his death Mr. Hardy bequeathed his farm to his son, Mr. George W. Hardy. His mother resided with him till his death, after which she removed to Babbidge's Neck and resided with her daughter, — now the wife of Mr. Hiram Gross, — where she remained till her death. After the death of Mr. George W. Hardy his widow and children occupied the farm a few years; she then married and moved away. It is now the property of Mr. William Blaster.

ABIJAH HASKELL, Jr., has been named as the person occupying the property of Mr. Eliakim Eaton after his death. He was a resident of the island over sixty years. He was a son of Mr. Abijah Haskell who was a son of Deacon Francis Haskell. They both have been noticed.

He was born in 1781. His wife was Miss Susannah Hardy, a daughter of Mr. Peter Hardy, Sr. By their marriage they had one son and three daughters. The son is Mr. Abijah W. Haskell, who now resides in the town of Sedgwick. The daughters were the wives of three brothers of the family of Mr. Jonathan Hardy, — Silas L. who died in 1849 on the island; she is now dead. Another was Mr. Jonathan Hardy, Jr., who removed to Winterport, where he died a few years ago. The other is Mr. Peter Hardy who now resides in that place. Mr. Haskell died in 1872, at the age of ninety-one years, and his wife in 1874, at the age of eighty-five. They lived together in wedlock about sixty-five years.

We have noticed the settlers on Little Deer Island, and will now take up a sketch of the settlements in that part of the town which was set off and incorporated as the town of Isle au Haut, in 1874. The first was made in 1772 on what is known as Merchant's Island. We will state first what is known about the titles of the lands in that town, and the islands lying south of Great Deer Island, now included within the limits of this town. But few of the settlers on the islands acquired titles to the land occupied by them until after the separation of the State of Maine, when both States had a joint ownership in the public lands in this State, and not long after sales of the most of them were made at a very reasonable rate. Thurlow's Island was purchased before the separation by Joseph Colby, Jr., and David Thurlow, and we think that Merchant's Island was bought by the occupant, or his son, Anthony Merchant, Jr. Kimball's Island was purchased not long after the death of Mr. Seth Webb, in 1785, by Mr. Solomon Kimball. We think that many of the settlers on Isle au Haut had also acquired titles. In 1802 a survey was made of the island by Mr. Lathrop Lewis, and the most of it was divided into lots; but a portion of over thirteen hundred acres lying west of the pond on the island was left in one body, and sold after the separation to the late George Kimball, Esq. Another of three hundred and thirty-nine acres, lying near the southwestern point of the island, was purchased by David Thurlow and parties in Castine. We have understood that, before the separation, the late Peletiah Barter was appointed as an agent by the residents who had taken up lots, to go to Boston and take measures for the acquirement of titles, and from the fact that the persons who were in possession of lots at the time of the sales made by the land agents of both States, were not disturbed, we judge that they had acquired titles to their lands. Some of the occupants of islands between Great Deer Island and Isle au Haut neglected to purchase, and others bought them, and after the larger part of them were sold, there remained a number of smaller ones which were sold to the late Hezekiah Rowell, Esq., as also was the island known as Hard Head near Eagle Island. He at one time owned quite an amount of that kind of property, and many of the present owners derived their titles from him or his grantees.

Among others we would name what is now known as Fog Island, which was formerly known as Cutter's Island, lying east of the northern part of Isle au Haut, which was occupied by a man named Cutter who was drowned in attempting to land some cattle from a gundelo some eighty years ago or more. With him were a Mr. Sheldon with his wife, two sons, a daughter, and a colored man named Hall — none of whom escaped. Mr. Sheldon left one daughter who became the wife of Mr. John Pressey, 3d, the son of Mr. John Pressey, Jr., who has been noticed. Her name was Mary, and by the marriage he had one son and one daughter of whom we have had knowledge. The son was Mr. Henry Pressey, who was, in the winter of 1849 and 1850, lost with Captain John G. Green in the schooner *Tamerlane*, bound to this place from Boston. The daughter was the wife of the late Mr. Samuel Howard. After the death of Mr. Pressey his widow married Mr. Nathaniel Merchant who then lived on Camp Island, on the southern side of Deer Island Thoroughfare, upon which he died a few years prior to 1830. After that she became the third wife of Mr. Thomas Colby, who died in 1837, and she then married Mr. Thomas Cooper, of North Haven. When he died she remained here, supported by that town till her death, which was about the year 1859, at the age of eighty-nine years. The island then called Fog Island, by which name it is at present known, was, prior to 1830, occupied by Mr. John Crockett, not a relative of the families of that name here, but a half-brother to the first wife of Mr. John Closson. Not far from the year mentioned, he was drowned between that island and Isle au Haut in the sight of his family. His widow afterward became the wife of Mr. John Gross.

A number of those islands were inhabited. The one known as Saddle Back, over sixty years ago, was occupied by Mr. Edward Howard, whom we have mentioned as a son-in-law of Mr. Theophilus Eaton. Not far from 1820, when he became a very old man, he removed to Brooksville, where he had children who took care of him, and died there. Worthy's Island was occupied for some time by Mr. Charles Gross who failed to pay for it to the owner, H. Rowell, Esq., and in 1839 he removed from it, and it was purchased by Sullivan Green, Esq. Russ Island was the residence, for many years, of Mr. George Harvey, a soldier of the War of 1812. He died there, and the island is now the property of Captain Stephen B.

Morey. Mr. John Coombs occupied what is known as Devil Island, and in 1836 he sold it to Mr. Avery Fifield and moved to the town of Islesborough. Mr. John Harvey, a soldier in the war of the Revolution, occupied Bear Island for some time, and it was afterward the property of Captain David Thurlow who also owned several other islands by purchase from the land agents, and Camp Island, which was sold him by Robert Merchant. On the one known as Round Island, Mr. Hezekiah Robbins resided for several years. Afterward he removed to a small island at the head of Webb's Cove, connected with Deer Island by a bar, upon which he died. It is near the property of Mr. Jack Stinson. Wreck Island was, many years ago, occupied by Mr. Joseph Colby, Jr., for some time, and for the last thirty years or more it has been occupied by Mr. Robert Barter, and by his family since his decease. The island known as Burnt Island, near Isle au Haut, was for several years occupied by Mr. Henry Barter, and York's Island was occupied by Mr. Robert Knowlton, who, in 1842, removed to Deer Island and purchased the Sylvester farm near Webb's Cove. The two latter islands are within the territorial limits of the town of Isle au Haut, and the former ones mentioned are within those of Deer Isle.

Although there were many disadvantages in a residence upon those islands, still there were advantages which were of value to the occupants whose chief business was fishing, digging clam-bait, and in later years the taking of lobsters, — the last of which has been a lucrative employment to those engaged in it. For those pursuits they were very convenient, but social and educational advantages must, of course, be limited. The male inhabitants were skillful in the management of small boats, and they felt as safe in one as others do in carriages upon the mainland It is surprising to one who has not that skill how safely a boat can be managed by a person who has experience in the matter. Those islands were valuable for keeping sheep; if one was present to take care of them, they could be kept the year round with but little expense. The occupant, when but one was on an island, had no necessity for maintaining line fences, which is a serious matter to those that have to meet it, and so such stock can be kept upon them with great profit. The late George Kimball, Esq., at one time had about four hundred on Kimball's Island, and the late Mr. Asa Turner kept about as many upon Isle au Haut. In both cases the expense of wintering was very small, which made it a profitable business. The only drawback was the danger from thieves, who could go to one of the small islands where sheep were kept and upon which no person resided, and obtain both wool and mutton without paying for them. I recollect hearing of an instance where a small vessel from some place up the bay or river, anchored in a little harbor on the southwestern end of Kimball's Island, which lay at some distance from the house, and, undiscovered, those on board drove up, butchered, and carried off several. Upon the islands lying between Deer Isle and Isle au Haut such depredations are often committed upon those having no inhabitants, by a worthless class who have opportunities for plunder. Were it not for that, those islands would be of more value than they now are.

SETTLERS.

ANTHONY MERCHANT, who come from the town of York, Maine, was the first person who settled within the limits of the present town of Isle au Haut, and, as has been understood, he came the same year that his father-in-law did to Deer Island. It must have been in 1772, and the island he settled upon has been ever since known as Merchant's Island. His wife was Miss Abigail Raynes, and was a daughter of Mr. John Raynes, Sr., the father of Messrs. John, Johnson, and William Raynes. Mr. Merchant was a master-mariner and made voyages to the West Indies. They had three sons and five daughters. The sons were: Nathaniel who, as has been stated, resided upon Camp Island; John who removed to Vinalhaven; and Anthony Merchant, Jr., who lived and died upon the island settled by his father. Of the daughters one, Abigail, was the wife of Mr. Joseph Arey, of Vinalhaven. Another, Eleanor, was the wife of Mr. John Smith, of that town, who lived near what is known as Smith's Harbor, on the eastern side of the island, and both her husband and herself lived to a good old age. Another, Miriam, was the wife of Mr. Henry Barter who will be noticed. Another, Martha, was the first wife of Captain Tristram Haskell, of this town, who has been noticed. One, Susan, died unmarried. Mrs. Haskell died not far from the year 1803, but the others, with the exception of Susan, lived to be very old. Mr. Merchant was a very quiet man and a good citizen. The year of his death is not known to us. His wife died not far from 1833, and was at the time considerably over eighty years of age.

NATHANIEL MERCHANT was the eldest son of the family. He married in Portsmouth, New Hampshire, and had two sons and two or more daughters. The sons were the late Mr. Nathaniel Merchant who died, we believe, in 1879, on Isle au Haut, and Mr. Robert Merchant who resided, after the death of his father, on Camp Island, which was for many years the residence of the latter. In 1845 he sold it to the late Captain David Thurlow, and since that time he has been here only a part of the time, as his wife abandoned him. His present place of residence we do not know. One of the daughters of the family was the wife of Mr. John Gott, Jr., who formerly resided on Swan's Island. About the rest of the family we have no knowledge. Mr. Merchant, the subject of this notice, for his second wife, married the widow of Mr. John Pressey, Jr., the daughter of the Mr. Sheldon before referred to, who was drowned near Fog Island. For many years they resided on Camp Island, where he died not far from the year 1830, as before stated. His widow has been noticed.

ANTHONY MERCHANT, Jr., was the youngest son of the family and was born in the year 1790, or about that time. His wife was Miss Eunice Smith, a daughter of Mr. David Smith, of Swan's Island, who was well known here many years ago. He was a soldier in the Revolutionary War. By his first marriage Mr. Merchant had one son, the late Mr. David S. Merchant, and one daughter, who became the wife of Mr. Willard Matthews, who at that time resided upon Merchant's Island, but after his marriage soon removed to Belfast, out of which place he sailed as a master-mariner. After the death of his wife Mr. Merchant married Mrs. Maria Gross, by whom he had a family, of which there now remain two sons. One of the sons, Mr. John Merchant, was drowned a few years since, having been knocked overboard from a small vessel while sailing down the bay. The remaining sons have removed from the town. One of the daughters is the wife of Mr. James Childs who has ever since his marriage lived on the island. The other, the wife of Mr. John Cross, is now dead. Mr. Merchant was for many years a collector of taxes in what was then known as the Isle au Haut collection district, and was a faithful and efficient officer. He died not far from the year 1865. His widow married a Mr. Clark, of the town of Brewer, Maine.

JACOB GROSS was also a resident of Merchant's Island, and lived upon the western end of it. He was a brother of the Mr. George Gross before noticed, but from what place he came, or what year he removed here is not to us known, nor do we know the year of his death. He left a widow, four sons, and one daughter. The sons were Messrs. David, Swansey, John, and James Gross. Mr. David Gross died in 1853; his wife was Miss Parizanda Merithew, and she died in 1880. They were the parents of the present Messrs. David and William Gross. Mr. Swansey Gross married a daughter of Mr. Thomas Buckminster, and they are both dead. They were the parents of Messrs. William B., Hiram, and Thomas B. Gross. The latter resides upon the homestead of his father. Mr. John Gross was the third son of the family, and his first wife, who abandoned him, was a daughter of Mr. James Robertson. He afterward married the widow of the Mr. John Crockett whom we have mentioned as residing on Fog Island and being drowned near there. By that marriage he had two sons. One was Jacob Gross who was one of the crew of the schooner *Sarah* which was lost in 1851 in the great gale in Chaleur Bay with all on board. The other son is the present Mr. Edwin Gross. The fourth son, Mr. James Gross, never married, and for some years before his death was totally blind. The daughter, Mary Gross, was the wife of Mr. William Matthews, who removed to Merchant's Island from the town of Boothbay, Maine. He died in the family of his son, Mr. Stinson Matthews, in this town, his widow surviving him a few years.

The next settlement made in the present town of Isle au Haut was, as has been stated, by Mr. Seth Webb, whom we have noticed, but the exact date is not to us known. It has been said that during the very severe winter of 1780 he went to the top of the mountain on Isle au Haut, and from that eminence could see no water for ice out seaward. If that account be correct, it must have been the most severe winter ever experienced here since the first settlement of the town, as in but few winters within the past fifty years has the ice made to such a degree as to be sufficiently strong to pass over from Deer Island to Isle au Haut. After the death of Mr. Webb, Mr. Solomon Kimball purchased the island now known as Kimball's Island (the one settled by Mr. Webb), and resided upon it. Afterward it came into the possession of his son, the late George Kimball, Esq., who occupied it till his death in 1839. The wife of the latter was Miss Lucretia Amazene, of Newcastle, New Hampshire, and she died not long after 1860. Mr. Kimball was a man who sustained a good reputation, and was active and enterprising. He did considerable business, owning vessels, and was in possession of an extensive property. Besides the island he occupied, he owned over thirteen hundred acres of land in one body on Isle au Haut, lying westerly of the pond on that island. He was, in 1826, representative from this town to the Legislature, and was for many years a justice of the peace. One son in the family was George Kimball, Jr., Esq., who removed to Winterport, and in 1850 removed to California, having organized a company which built a ship of six hundred tons, as we believe, in the town of Cutler, Maine. With a number of others interested in the ship he emigrated, and at the last accounts was living. Another son was Solomon and another William Kimball — both of whom, we believe, went to California at the same time. The latter is now dead. Another son was Mr. Benjamin A. Kimball, who died in 1842, or about that time, at home. The daughters of the family were the wives of Mr. Isaiah Barbour, who removed to Camden; of Mr. Willard Clark, a school-teacher; of the late Captain Benjamin S. Smith, a son of Mr. Simon Smith, who removed to Winterport and was lost at sea. His widow resides at the present time on the homestead of her father with her two sons. The other daughter of the family now living is the second wife of Captain Seth Webb, of this town. Two of the daughters died unmarried.

PELETIAH BARTER was the person by whom the first settlement was made on Great Isle au Haut, and it was in 1792. He was a native of the town of Boothbay, Maine, and resided on what is known as Barter's Island in that town. He was born in the year 1772. His wife was Miss Mary Trundy, the eldest daughter of Mr. Samuel Trundy, of this town, and they were the parents of ten children. Two of the sons grew to manhood, — the late Mr. Peletiah Barter, Jr., and the present Mr. John Barter who now resides there. His wife was a daughter of Mr. James Duncan who has been noticed. One of the daughters was the wife of Mr. David Collins. Another was the wife of Mr. William Dorr, of Winterport. Another was the wife of Mr. John S. Merrill, of the same place. Another was that of Mr. Thomas Littlefield, of Winterport, and after his death she was the wife of a Mr. Raymond, and afterward, of Mr. Benajia Merithew, of Islesborough. The other was first the wife of Mr. Paoli Hews, Jr., of Belfast; second, of Mr. Elijah Toothaker, and third, of the present Mr. Abner Bray. All of the family, with the exception of Mr. John Barter, are now dead. The wife of Mr. Barter died many years ago, and he never remarried. He died not far from the year 1852. He was at one time in possession of quite a large amount of real estate, none of which is now owned by his descendants.

HENRY BARTER came not long after his brother, the subject of the last notice, and settled upon the lot northeast of that occupied by him. His wife was Miss Miriam Merchant, a daughter of Mr. Anthony Merchant. They had one son, the late Mr. Robert Barter, who for some years resided on what is known as Wreck Island. He died there not many years ago. One of the daughters was the wife of the present Mr. Francis Coombs. Another was that of Mr. Peletiah Barter, Jr. One died unmarried. Mr. Barter and his wife lived together for many years, and he had the reputation of being an upright man. He removed from the land first occupied by him to what is known as Burnt Island, now the property of Mr. James Turner, 2d, and both he and his wife died there. After the death of his parents Mr. Robert Barter, their son, sold it to Mr. Turner and removed to Wreck Island, which was included in the purchase made by Hezekiah Rowell, Esq., before referred to.

WILLIAM BARTER, a younger brother of the subjects of the two preceding notices, settled upon the southern part of the land taken up by Mr. Peletiah Barter. His wife was Miss Sarah, the daughter of Mr. Stephen Babbidge, of this town. Their sons were: Mr. William Barter, Jr., who removed to Vinalhaven and died there; the late Stephen Barter, who resided in Isle au Haut; Thomas Barter, who died many years ago, and the present Mr. Amos Barter. The daughters were the wives of Mr. Joab Black, who did not reside there; the late Captain Jonathan Rich; Daniel L. and Ebenezer D. Carlton; Davis Collins; and one married in Winterport. At the present time no one of the family, except Mr. Amos Barter, resides there. Mr. Barter was for many years engaged in trade, owned and built vessels, carried on the fishing business and owned a good deal of property. Both he and his wife died many years ago.

CAPTAIN SAMUEL TURNER was the occupant of the land lying southerly of that of Mr. Barter. He was the son of the wife of Mr. Charles Kempton by a former marriage. He perished at sea in the year 1839, upon the wreck of a vessel of which he was master, which was engaged in the freighting business, an occupation he followed for many years. Of the crew but one, Mr. James Henderson, survived. He was very well and favorably known in this vicinity for many years, and at the time of his death was about fifty-five years of age. He left a widow and a family. The sons were the present Captain James Turner, John K. Turner, and Captain William G. Turner. Two of the daughters resided in Searsport, and one was the wife of the late Captain Ezra Turner, of Isle au Haut.

EBENEZER SAWYER was one of the early settlers there. He came, we believe, from Boothbay or from that vicinity, and was engaged in the fishing business, as were most of the settlers there. Both he and his wife died in the winter of 1839 and 1840, at an advanced age. The land he occupied was that adjoining the lot of Captain Turner on the south. Their sons were: Mr. Paul Sawyer, who removed to what is now the town of North Haven; Nathaniel, a master ship-carpenter, who removed to Islesborough; Ebenezer, who, not long after the year 1840, went to the town of Searsport; and one who died a young man. One of the daughters was the wife of Captain William Yeaton. Another was that of Mr. William Babbidge. Another married Mr. Bickmore, of St. George. The other married Mr. George Allen, and after his death she became the wife of his brother, Mr. Daniel Allen, who removed to Levant, Maine. We believe that all of the family are now dead. The property occupied by Mr. Sawyer is now that of Captain James D. Barter.

WILLIAM YEATON was the occupant of the lot lying south of that of Mr. Sawyer, whose daughter he married. He came here when young, and for some time resided in the family of George Kimball, Esq. He came from Portsmouth, New Hampshire, or that vicinity. He and his wife were the parents of four sons and eight daughters. Of the family but one now resides there, — the wife of Mr. Spencer Robertson. In 1842, or about that time, Mr. Yeaton purchased a farm in Northport, Maine, and removed there, where both he and his wife died. He was by occupation a fisherman, and was very active and successful in his employment.

CHARLES KEMPTON was an early settler, and came from what is the present town of Winterport. He there resided near what is known as Stubb's Point. The maiden name of his wife was Stinson, of a family of that name in what was then the town of Prospect. At the time of his marriage she was a Mrs. Turner, and, as we have stated, was the mother of Captain Samuel Turner. Their son was the late Captain John Kempton, who died on Isle au Haut a few years since. One daughter was the wife of Mr. Ebenezer Sawyer, Jr. Another was that of Captain Theophilus Eaton who is now dead, and their widows now reside in Searsport. Another died unmarried. The lot taken up by Mr. Kempton is near what is now known as Moore's Harbor, named for a Mr. John Moore, of Castine, who was a fisherman and who frequently anchored his vessel there during the time of the Revolution and afterward. Mr. Kempton died not far from the year 1839, and his wife survived him a few years.

CHAUNCEY HOLMES, who was in his day well known, was for many years a resident of the island, near Morse's Harbor. From what place he came, or the time of his coming, is not known to us. His wife was a Mrs. Crockett, whose maiden name was Rendell, of a family who resided in Prospect. Her first husband was Mr. Isaac Crockett, a brother of the Mr. John Crockett mentioned before, and they formerly lived in Vinalhaven. She had a family by her first marriage, but none by that with Mr. Holmes. He was a singular man and had a good share of wit. About the year 1843 they, with others on the island, became converts to Mormonism and removed to Nauvoo, Illinois, and when the Mormons left that place for the Salt Lake, Mr. Holmes and his wife and Mr. Robert Douglass, who will be noticed, went in the company. He, being very old and infirm, perished on the journey from starvation and fatigue.

EBENEZER LELAND, we have understood, was the person who made a settlement on the island next after that of Mr. Peletiah Barter. He came from the town of Eden, Maine, and settled near Duck Harbor, mentioned in the account given of duck-driving. From what I have learned, I am inclined to the opinion that it was used for that purpose by the Indians before the whites settled this part of the country, as it was from them that the settlers here learned of that method of taking ducks. Mr. Leland, not long after the Revolutionary War, lived in what is now the town of Brooksville. Whether he came from that place or not to Isle au Haut is not known, but he was originally an inhabitant of Eden, of which place his father was one of the early settlers. In the war of the Revolution he was a lieutenant in the regular army, and after his discharge happened to be at Bagaduce while the British were there, and was arrested as a spy. Had he not been able to produce his written discharge, he might have suffered death. His wife was a Miss Dyer, of Steuben, near a place known as Dyer's Bay. Of the family, we have knowledge of three sons and three daughters. The sons were: the late Mr. Ebenezer Leland, Jr., who died in this town some twenty-five years ago; Jesse Leland, a *non compos* person; and one who died when a young man One daughter was Ursula, the wife of a Mr. Higgins of Eden, and mother of Captain Eben L. Higgins, of that place, and afterward the wife of a Mr. Salisbury. Another, Nancy Leland, was never married; and another, Hannah, was first the wife of Mr. John Harvey, Jr., a soldier of the War of 1812, and afterward married a Mr. Daniel Getchell. She died, as was supposed, in consequence of violence at his hands, not far from 1868. Mr. Leland died many years ago; his wife died about the year 1837.

ABIATHAR SMITH went to Isle au Haut from the town of Thomaston, Maine, not far from the year 1800. He settled near what is now known as Head Harbor. He had three sons and one daughter, of whom we have had information. The sons were: Mr. George Smith, who will be noticed; Mr. Simon Smith, whom we have mentioned; and another, named Abiathar Smith, who removed from here, and of whom we have no knowledge. The daughter was the wife of Mr. Elisha Holbrook. The property of Mr. Smith is now that of Mr. George Smith, Jr., who is the present occupant. It is one of the most valuable places on the island.

CALVIN TURNER came early with his family, and settled near the northern end of the pond. He formerly resided in what is now the town of Orland. It has been stated that he built the first saw and grist mills in that town, in 1773. The exact time of his coming is not known to us. His wife was a Miss Stinson, a sister of the wife of Mr. Charles Kempton before noticed. The sons of the family were: the late Captain Asa Turner, who lived and died on Isle au Haut; James Turner, who lived in Bucksport; John Turner, who removed to the town of Brooklin, where he died. Another, whose name, we believe, was Calvin, was lost at sea, and was at the time master of the vessel on which he was lost. Of the daughters we know nothing, as none of them remained here. Mr. Turner died in 1838, at the age of ninety years. The land he lived on was afterward occupied by his son, Captain Asa Turner, who was a man much respected. His wife was Miss Abigail Smith, of Prospect, and they had a family of six sons and four daughters. The sons were the present John Turner, Esq., Ezra, James, 2d, and Isaiah B. Turner — all of whom, except Ezra, are now living on the island. One son, Mr. Thomas Turner, was drowned several years ago near the mouth of Union River, and one died when young. The daughters were the wives of Mr. Jacob Wilson, who removed to Massachusetts; of Mr. Patrick Conley; of Mr. John K. Turner, and of Mr. John Doane, of the town of Newburg, Maine. Of the daughters but one, Mrs. Conley, now remains here. A few years ago Captain Turner removed to the western side of the island near the Thoroughfare, and his property on the eastern side of the island is now that of a Mr. Sprowl, formerly of Bucksport, who is now the owner of a large tract of land on that side of the island, which is used for pasturage, and is also the owner of Fog Island. The house of Mr. Turner is now occupied by Mr. Noah Page, formerly of Bucksport, who is in the employ of Mr. Sprowl. In 1843 Mr. Turner represented this town in the Legislature.

ELISHA HOLBROOK was the occupant of the lot of land lying north of that of Captain Turner. He came from Cape Cod not far from 1800, and married a daughter of Mr. Abiathar Smith. Their children were: the present Mr. Abram Holbrook who resides here; one of the name of Simon who went away many years ago; and another, Daniel Holbrook, who removed to Vinalhaven and was killed by falling from a derrick used in hoisting stone, up which he had gone for the purpose of fixing a tackle or something of the kind. The daughters were the wives of Mr. Joseph Morey, and afterward of Mr. Humphrey

Webster; of Mr. Samuel Black; of a Mr. Hall, from some place near Belfast; and another who was brought up in the family of Captain Samuel Turner. What became of her is not to us known. The wife of Mr. Holbrook died nearly sixty years ago, and the family was broken up. During the latter part of his life he was a public charge.

DANIEL GILBERT, a native of Massachusetts, settled upon the lot north of that occupied by Mr. Holbrook, which he afterward purchased. His wife was Miss Sarah Reed, of Boothbay, by whom he had no children. They adopted a child named Francis Merithew, who was drowned about the time of the death of Mrs. Gilbert, in 1839. In 1840 Mr. Gilbert, when fifty-five years of age, married a Miss Lois Ellis, who was then sixteen years of age, by whom he had a family. About the year 1850 he removed to the western side of the island and purchased a lot of land which was formerly the property of Mr. Peletiah Barter, and built a house upon it, residing there till his removal to the town of Bristol, Maine, where he died in 1876, at the age of ninety-one years.

GEORGE SMITH, a son of Mr. Abiathar Smith, settled upon the lot north of that of Mr. Gilbert. He was born in 1780, and his wife was Miss Judith Knowlton, a daughter of Mr. Benjamin Knowlton. One of their sons was the present Mr. George Smith, of Head Harbor, who alone of the family now resides here. Another son was Abiathar Smith, and the other was Joseph Smith — both of whom removed from here many years ago. One daughter was the wife of Mr. George Curtis who went there from the town of Surrey, and afterward returned, where he lived the last we knew of him. Another was the wife of Mr. Samuel Coffin who came here from Kennebec County, or the eastern part of Oxford County, returning after a few years' residence on the island. Another was the wife of Mr. Aaron Merithew, Jr., who went to Vinalhaven. Another was the wife of Mr. Benjamin Merithew, Jr., who removed to Searsport. The youngest was the wife of Mr. Isaac B. Eaton who resided upon the homestead of Mr. Smith. He is now dead, his wife dying before him. Mr. Smith died not far from the year 1860, aged over eighty years, and his wife about ten years after.

THOMAS TYLER, a brother of Messrs. Joseph and George Tyler, settled upon the lot adjoining that of Mr. Smith on the north. He was for many years a school-teacher, and was known as Master Tyler. After he became advanced in years he married Miss Betsey Bagley, of Newburyport. He died not far from the year 1830. Afterward his wife returned to Newburyport, where she had relatives. He formerly lived on Merchant's Island. A matter of dispute arose between Mr. Merchant and Mr. Gross relating to the ownership of a small island near Merchant's Island, and it was referred by them to Master Tyler. He divided it into three equal portions, assigning that on the eastern end to Mr. Merchant, that on the western part to Mr. Gross, reserving the middle part to himself, giving as a reason that it was proper that their lands should not join, and if he had the middle part, it would keep peace between them. Both parties acquiesced in his decision. The lot he occupied on Isle au Haut he had no title to, as he had never purchased it of the State. Afterward it was acquired by Mr. Hiram Small, who resided upon it until his death a few years ago.

ROBERT DOUGLASS was the occupant of the lot adjoining that of Mr. Tyler upon the north. He was an early occupant, but what place he came from, or what time he came, we do not know. He was a brother of Captain James Douglass, who, fifty years ago, or more, was captain of the revenue boat at Belfast. His sisters were the wives of Messrs. Thomas and James Cooper and Benjamin Burrage, Esq., of North Haven. By his first wife Mr. Douglass had two sons: Alexander who removed to some town in Penobscot County, and Robert, a ship-carpenter, who remained on Isle au Haut till about 1850, when he became interested in the ship referred to in the notice of George Kimball, Jr., Esq., and was in the company of emigrants who removed to California. We do not know whether he is now living, but probably he is not, as if he were, he would be a very old man. The lot and buildings he occupied are now the property of Mr. Francis Coombs, who resides upon them. One of the daughters of Mr. Robert Douglass was the wife of Mr. John Rich, and the other was the wife of Mr. Asa Collins who was lost in a gale in 1841, in the schooner *Forest* of Gloucester, of which Captain Stephen Rich was master. After the death of his wife Mr. Douglass married Miss Lydia Lane, a daughter of Mr. Hezekiah Lane, and a sister of Mr. Oliver Lane, by whom he had one son, Mr. Abner Douglass. His last wife was accidentally killed about the year 1832, by being struck on the head with a piece of stone which her husband was blasting. At the time of the Mormon excitement he, with Mr. Holmes and wife, and others from the towns of Vinalhaven and North Haven, joined that sect. As has been stated, he perished upon the journey to the Great Salt Lake. The property owned by Mr. Douglass is now that of his grandson, Mr. Stillman Rich, and it is near what is known as Douglass's Cove. He was a very decided man, and, when his mind was made up, it remained so. A few years after the death of his last wife he journeyed to the Southern and Western States, and on his return expressed the opinion that the people in the Northern States enjoyed life more than those of the other sections of the country, and that, notwithstanding the greater fertility and natural advantages of the other States, still in New England better living was to be found, and more of the real comforts of life.

JOHN RICH occupied the lot of land northerly of that of Mr. Douglass, and his wife, who was of a prepossessing appearance, was the daughter of Mr. Douglass. One son of the family was Captain Stephen Rich, who removed to Gloucester, Massachusetts, out of which place he sailed as master in the fishing business several years. He was an active and enterprising man, and, as has been stated, was lost with all his crew in the year 1841. Another son was Mr. Jonathan Rich who was an invalid for many years, and died not far from the year 1864. Another was Mr. Thomas Rich who was drowned in 1839; and two remaining sons are Mr. Perez Rich, who removed to Islesborough, and the Mr. Stillman Rich named before as the occupant of the property of Mr. Douglass. There was one daughter in the family, who was first the wife of Mr. Josiah Pierce, of Vinalhaven. They became converts to Mormonism and removed to Nauvoo, Illinois, but while there she became disgusted with it and made her escape. With but little means she returned to her friends here and was divorced from her husband, afterward becoming the wife of Mr. Noah Barter, and the mother of one daughter. She died a few years ago. The exact time of Mr. Rich's coming here we do not know, but it was before 1810. He died shortly before 1860, his wife surviving him a few years.

BENJAMIN KNOWLTON was for many years a resident of Isle au Haut. He was a relative of those of that name in the town of Northport and in the county of Waldo, and, we believe, was a native of Massachusetts. When a young man he went to Nova Scotia, and there married a Miss Smith. He was there a part of the time, at least, if not all, of the Revolutionary period, and some time after his return took up his residence on Isle au Haut. His sons were the late Mr. Robert Knowlton, of this town, and Mr. Joseph Knowlton who removed to Islesborough. One daughter was the wife of a Mr. Hamilton. She was the mother of the present Mr. Solomon Hamilton, now nearly ninety years of age. Another was the wife of Mr. George Smith; another was the wife of Mr. Aaron Merithew, and we believe that there was another. Mr. Knowlton died many years ago, but the date is unknown to us; his wife died in 1842, at the age of eighty-nine years. Some years before her death a brother in Nova Scotia, by his will, left her the income of $6,000, which she received till her death, and after that the principal was divided among her children. She resided in the family of her son, Mr. Robert Knowlton, and removed to Deer Isle with him a short time before her death. Mr. Robert Knowlton died in 1876; his wife died a few years before him.

BENJAMIN MERITHEW settled upon a lot of land on the south part of the island, between Duck and Head Harbors. His first wife was Miss Frances Atwood, by whom he had three sons: Mr. Reuben Merithew who removed to Islesborough; Benjamin who removed to Searsport; and Francis, the adopted son of Mr. Daniel Gilbert, who, as has been stated in the notice of him, was drowned. The second wife of Mr. Merithew was a Miss Sarah Coombs, of Vinalhaven, by whom he had a family. At this time one only of the family resides here — the wife of Mr. Stinson Matthews. Mr. Merithew was a son of Mr. Roger Merithew, who many years ago resided upon, and owned, what is now known as Babbidge's Island in the town of North Haven. Both he and his wife are now dead.

AARON MERITHEW made a settlement near Moore's Harbor, where he resided till his death, by drowning, in 1844. None of his family remained here, and his property was afterward purchased by the late Mr. Eli Eaton.

HENRY WILSON, Esq., removed to Isle au Haut from Gloucester, Massachusetts, not far from the year 1820, and was in trade there several years. He was successful in his enterprises, accumulating in them a large property. He built a house, store and wharves, and was for several years an inspector of fish, in which business he was also interested. He was one of the selectmen of the town, and in 1833 was the representative from it in the Legislature. He was a man of ability and intelligence. In 1836 he removed to Ipswich in the State of Massachusetts, with his family, and in a few years removed to Gloucester. His real estate was purchased by John Turner, Esq., by whom it is at present occupied.

JOHN COLLINS was for many years a resident of the place, and his wife was a member of the Lanpher family. Her father, Stephen Lanpher, was one of the early settlers of the town of Bucksport, and his widow died in 1833, at Castine, aged about one hundred years. A daughter, a Mrs. Gross, died in Orland some years ago, at as great an age. The sons of Mr. Collins were: David who died on Isle au Haut, not far from 1863; Asa who was lost, as has been stated, in 1841; James who removed to Bluehill, and afterward to Castine, where he died; John who now lives in Castine, and Otis who moved to Bluehill, with whom his mother resided. Mr. Collins was by trade a tailor and was born on the island of Mount Desert. During the latter part of the last century and the earlier part of the present century he resided in Castine. His death was caused by freezing on a very cold day not long before the year 1830. He was returning to his home from the Thoroughfare, and sitting down to rest on the way, was overcome by the cold and perished.

CAPTAIN JACOB CARLTON, a native of Frankfort, Maine, was for a long time a resident. He was a man of energy, was engaged in trade, and while there built one barque and two large schooners, a gristmill, a large store, and a brick house — the only one in the two towns. In 1838 he was representative to the Legislature. His wife was Miss Elizabeth Dow, a daughter of Mr. John Dow, who has been noticed. Their sons were Messrs. Daniel L. Carlton who was in trade for several years and removed to Rockland; Ebenezer D., and Jacob T. Carlton. There were two daughters, one of whom is now the wife of Captain Bester Babbidge, of Winterport. In 1839 Captain Carlton removed to Winterport and purchased a large and valuable farm on which he lived till his death. At the last accounts his widow was living, but none of the family now reside here.

JAMES ROBERTSON, formerly a resident, went there many years ago. He was a native of Scotland and was, when a young man, in the British navy, being present when the Danish fleet was taken in 1802 we believe, by the British under Lord Nelson, who was the commander there. He came shortly afterward to this country and married a Miss Hopkins, and for some time resided in Castine and afterward went to Isle au Haut. By her he had one son, the present Mr. Spencer Robertson, and two daughters: one the wife of Mr. John Gross, and afterward that of Mr. Anthony Merchant; the other married in Massachusetts. For his second wife he married a sister of Mr. Hezekiah Robbins, now deceased, and had a family, one only of which resides here — the present Mr. James Robertson. Not far from the year 1830 Mr. Robertson

Town of Deer Isle, Maine.

removed from here, and for some time lived in Belfast. In his day he was well known.

JOHN HARVEY resided for some time upon an island between Great Deer Isle and Isle au Haut, but whether he lived on Isle au Haut, or not, is not known to us. He was a Revolutionary soldier, a native of South Carolina, and was born in 1750. In the war he was in the Pennsylvania line under the command of a Colonel Brodhead. After the war he came to this State, and for several years resided in Northport, where he married a Miss Knowlton, in 1789, and afterward came here, but returned. In 1836, when very old and poor, he was chargeable to this town, and was removed here with his wife. He was unable to procure a pension for his services, from the difficulty of proof, as all who were his comrades were probably dead, and he was unable to establish his claim. After his death in 1837, an agent succeeded in procuring it for his heirs; but, as was charged, he kept it himself. Whether the charge were true, or not, we have no knowledge. Mr. Harvey left two sons who have resided here, and one daughter. The sons were the late Mr. George Harvey, who lived on Russ Island, and Mr. John Harvey, who lived at Duck Harbor, where he resided many years, but removed to the State of New York, and after some time returned and died here. Both were soldiers in the War of 1812. The daughter was first the wife of Mr. Daniel Hamilton; second, that of Elisha Grant, Esq., and third, that of Mr. Nathan W. Sawyer, of this town, and died, we believe, in 1879, at the age of seventy years.

ELISHA GRANT, Esq., removed to Isle au Haut not long after 1840, and resided at Head Harbor not far from thirty years. His death was caused by a cancer. For several years he was a deputy sheriff in the county of Penobscot, and was a man of intelligence and capacity. He was three times married, his last wife being Mrs. Nancy Hamilton. By his first marriage he had three sons. One was Mr. Hiram Grant, of Hampden. Another was the present Mr. David Grant, who resides on the premises occupied by his father, and the other was Franklin Grant, who died a young man several years ago. He died about the year 1870, and his remains were by his request taken to Hampden and laid by the side of those of his first wife.

I HAVE now given a sketch of the settlement of the towns of Deer Isle and Isle au Haut, of the earliest settlers, and of those of a later date. It has been written entirely from memory, with the exception of that which relates to the probable discoverers, and of the information that was gained from a list of those who were here prior to 1784, found among the papers of the " Proprietors," which were in the custody of the late Solomon Haskell, Esq., and previously in that of his father, Ignatius Haskell, Esq. Accompanying this list were the dates of their coming and also a copy of a memorial drawn up by a committee of the settlers, setting forth the manner in which a grant of the lands remaining after they had had their lots assigned them, was obtained, which has been already described.

Under the circumstances these records must, of course, be imperfect to a greater or less degree; yet I hope that they may prove of interest, and that it may be a satisfaction to those who will come after, to have even such knowledge respecting them as has been obtained. I have in my lifetime sought to gather whatever information in regard to them, that I could. It has been a matter of fear to me, that, when the task of thus preserving it should be undertaken, my memory might so fail me that I should be able to do so only in part; but I feel confident that what has been written is, in the main, correct, and had it not been attempted by me, perhaps it would have been by no one, and so much of this been lost to posterity. In my notices of individuals I have endeavored to treat the memories of those of whom I have written with candor, not intending to withhold anything to be said in their favor which was justly due, nor to ascribe praise undeserved.

The town, as incorporated in 1789, was of great extent, which was inconvenient to the inhabitants at the extreme parts of its territory, especially those on Isle au Haut, as they lived at a distance from the place where the town meetings and elections were held, and, in order to transact business with the officers of the town, were obliged to cross a distance of five miles by water besides the travel by land from the south part of the island to the center, some six miles. From the northern extreme to the southern was about twenty miles in a direct line. The length of Little Deer Island is about three miles from the southwestern to the southeastern extremities. Great Deer Island is more than nine miles in length in a direct line from the northern end to the southern at the Thoroughfare. Isle au Haut is about five miles in length, besides being five miles from the nearest part of Great Deer Island. The incorporation of Isle au Haut into a town was thus a great convenience to its inhabitants.

After the establishment of the territorial limits of the town in 1868, it contained about twenty-six thousand acres, of which the town of Isle au Haut after its incorporation contained nearly seven thousand acres, leaving now within the limits of this town not far from nineteen thousand. The town of Isle au Haut contains but little land capable of cultivation, and its value consists in its pasturage. It was settled by fishermen because of its convenience for their purpose, as at that time fish were more abundant there than now and could be taken nearer the shores. With them agriculture was not a consideration; had it been, it would never have been settled. The town of Deer Isle contains a large proportion of land that can never be cultivated, especially in the southern part; and most of the early settlers, in that part of the town, depended upon fishing. It has been their chief employment for a large part of the time since, and in past years it has been carried on quite extensively. For the twenty years prior to 1840 Captain David Thurlow was interested in it, employing many men and owning several vessels which he sent out to the Labrador shore and mackerel fisheries. From 1830 till 1845, the late Hon. Richard Warren; from 1830 until 1860, the late Samuel Whitmore, Esq.; and from 1830 until 1844, the late Mr. Avery Fifield were all very considerably engaged in carrying on the various branches of this industry, as were others, also, who followed them, until a later date. The most business carried on in the town at any time was by the Messrs. Warren, and Warren & Tolman, in fitting out vessels, inspecting mackerel, and owning vessels employed in it, also in furnishing employment to a large number of men. It was commenced by them in 1845 and carried on till a few years after 1877. At present most of the mackerel fishing is carried on by the Messrs. Webb, but since 1870 the business has declined to almost nothing, and the many young men who make it an employment sail out of other places — principally out of Gloucester. In 1860 there were owned by inhabitants of this town about ten thousand tons of vessels, a very large part of which were employed in the fisheries.

The northern part of the island is better adapted to agriculture than the southern, as the proportion of land incapable of being cultivated is smaller; but there is still a large share of it which can never be made profitable for the purpose. In former years more attention was paid to that pursuit. The soil originally produced large crops, and had the early settlers been more judicious in the use of fire in clearing their lands, the soil would have retained its fertility much longer. It was by them an object to have the ground as dry as possible when fire was used, so as to clear it up more effectually; but the consequence was that with the wood the vegetable matter upon the top of the soil which was necessary to the durability of its fertility, was destroyed. After the benefit of the ashes was gone, the soil soon became less fertile and required heavy manuring. The same mistake was made elsewhere as well as here, and, had the ground been in such a state as to prevent too deep a burning, our farms would have been far more valuable. I recollect hearing it stated by one that a small farm of a few acres was cleared without burning the wood upon the ground, and its fertility was retained much longer than that of the lands around it. By this we may learn that although fire is necessary for the clearing of lands, its use should be prudent and at suitable times.

The chief products of the farms here were, as in other towns in this vicinity, hay, grain, and potatoes; the latter to quite an extent, especially prior to 1845, when the potato-rot first made its appearance. By the statistics procured by the person who took the census here in 1840, over thirty-six thousand bushels were returned, but since the rot commenced the crop has very much decreased. Now it has another enemy — the potato-bug, which came in 1880. From these two causes the crop will not receive the attention it otherwise would. The crop of grain has fallen short very much in comparison with the yield in former years, from the cause stated in the first part of the work, but should a gristmill be erected and maintained here, it would probably increase.

The chief pursuit of the inhabitants in the northern part of the town is that of following the sea in coasting and on foreign voyages, but comparatively few as fishermen. Although it is profitable as a general thing, yet its effects are visible in the large proportion of widows, many of whom are those of mariners. At this time, March, 1882, there are about one hundred out of a population of about thirty-three hundred. From the nature of their employment many lives are lost at sea. I have annexed a list of what vessels have been lost since 1818, and of the persons on board who have been preserved in my memory.

In 1818 the schooner *Shakespeare*, owned by Messrs. P. & F. Spofford, was lost, bound from Boston to Deer Isle; Captain John Green, master; Frederick Spofford, Esq., passenger; crew, Asa Green, Jr., Abner Babbidge, and Amos Angell.

In 1822, or about that year, schooner *Lingan*, of Castine; Captain Benjamin S. Haskell, master, with his son, and David Perry, of this town.

In 1830 sloop *Huntress*, of Castine, bound from New York to Castine; captain, John Greenlaw, Jr.; Captain William Eaton, pilot; crew, William Buckminster and Joseph Conary.

In 1839 Captain Samuel Turner, of Isle au Haut, and his crew, with the exception of Mr. James Henderson, who survived and was taken off the wreck. The same year in a gale in Chaleur Bay, schooner *Georgiana*, of Castine; David Colby, master; crew, John Sellers, Henry Keller, Thomas J. Colby, Mial Sylvester, Israel Dorr, Jr., and Joseph Dorr.

In 1845 schooner *Commodore Perry*, on Long Ledge, near Mount Desert; William D. Haskell, master; Moses Haskell and Francis Haskell, 2d, who belonged here, and Miss Jane Cole, of this place, a passenger.

In 1846 brig *Lincoln*, with four men, before referred to, from Calais with lumber.

In 1849 schooner *Tamerlane*, of this place; John G. Green, master; crew, Henry Pressey, Ebenezer Ball, Joseph H. Davis, and Joseph Haskell, all belonging here.

In 1851, in Chaleur Bay, schooner *Sarah*, of this place; Captain Levi Knight, master; crew belonging here, William Knight, James Sellers, Amos Babbidge, Stinson Colby, Albion P. York, and Ephraim Crockett.

The same year the schooner *Lion*, of Castine; Captain Enos Pressey, of this town, master; and of the crew belonging here, George Pressey and Henry McClintock lost, Joshua Pressey, 2d, saved.

Also the same year schooner *Mary Moulton;* Captain Joseph Emerson and his brother, Samuel Emerson, both of this place; the crew all lost.

In 1875 schooner *R. S. Warren*, Captain Frederick T. Pickering, master; crew belonging here, George Pickering, Lewis K. Gray, William E. Thompson, Amazene Stinson, John H. Morey, and a son of the captain.

In 1879 Captain William Richardson in a vessel owned by himself; with him were his son and Herbert Greenlaw.

The same year brig *Anna N. Torrey;* Captain John H. Bray, master; James Bray, mate.

In 1881 Captain William C. Emerson and his step-son, when bound to Boston in a vessel loaded with stone.

Several years ago — the exact date to us unknown — there were lost, in attempting to land, on Fire Island near Long Island, New York, four of the crew of a brig commanded by Captain William H. Reed, of this town. They were: Cummings M. Torrey, mate; Alfred Simpson, Warren F. Scott, and Gardiner Weed, seamen.

Of the crew of the schooner *Julietta Tilden*, lost in 1867, in Chaleur Bay, were the captain, Benjamin H. Sylvester, and Everett F. Saunders, residents here. There have been several persons lost sailing out of other ports at different times who belonged here.

We have noticed two of the early physicians who practised here, and it would be proper to extend our notices to those who came after. About the year 1824 Dr. Abiel Reed, a native of Newcastle, Maine, came and remained till his death, which took place not far from the year 1870. He married the widow of Captain Benjamin S. Haskell, and they had two children: the son was Captain William H. Reed, who moved to Portland a few years ago; and the daughter first married a Mr. Austin, of some town near ¦Bangor, and afterward became the wife of Mr. Levi Marshall, Jr. She is now dead. Dr. Reed was a man of education, very well informed, and was said to be well read in his profession; but he did not have much success in his practice.

After him came a Dr. Abbott, who did not remain long; but from what place he came, or went to from here, is not known to us. His leaving town was prior to 1830.

In the year 1830, or about that time, came Dr. John Phillips from the town of Dixmont, Maine. He was a native of Massachusetts and remained about ten years, and while here had considerable practice.

In 1838, or about that time, Dr. Amos A. Herrick, of Sedgwick, came and practised till about the year 1845. He was quite successful in his practice, and married Miss Sarah, daughter of Pearl Spofford, Esq. He removed to his native place and died in a few years after.

In 1845 came Dr. Joel Richardson, a native of the town of Eden, Maine; he remained about four years, then removed to Rockland, where he practised till a few years ago, removing to the State of Wisconsin. He was a diligent student and became skillful in his profession.

In 1849 Dr. William F. Collins succeeded Dr. Richardson and remained till his death in 1858. He had an extensive practice, and all who knew him had a favorable opinion of him as a physician; his death was much regretted here. He married Miss Eliza A. Spofford, the youngest daughter of Pearl Spofford, Esq.

The general health of the inhabitants of this town has been as good as that of other towns in this vicinity. In 1828 a disease prevailed here which was very fatal, and, as has been understood, about sixty persons in the town died of it. What its exact nature was, is now unknown, but, as has been stated, of those who were attacked, every one who was bled (as then was the practice in most diseases) died, and but few recovered.

The longevity in the town will perhaps compare with that in other towns in the county. The number of persons between 90 and 100 years is 3; those over 80 and under 90 years, 23; those over 70 and under 80 years, 84, — in all, 110 over 70 years, or about 1 in 30 persons.

The following is a list of those persons, with their ages, who have since 1833 attained the age of ninety years and upward, and died in this town:

In 1833, Mrs. Colby, widow of Joseph Colby, aged 97.
„ 1835, Mrs. Small, widow of Job Small, aged 96.
„ 1835, Mrs. Carman, widow of Levi Carman, aged 91.
„ 1836, Mrs. Thompson, widow of Thomas Thompson, aged 91.
„ 1838, Mr. Calvin Turner, aged 90.
„ 1842, Ignatius Haskell, Esq., aged 91.
„ 1842, Mr. Elijah Dunham, aged 90.
„ 1844, Mr. Joseph Sellers, aged 92.
„ 1844, Mrs. Colby, widow of Ambrose Colby, aged 92.
„ 1850, Mrs. Raynes, widow of John Raynes, aged 91.
„ 1852, Mrs. Barbour, widow of Solomon Barbour, aged 92.

In 1854, Timothy Billings, aged 90.
,, 1854, John Closson, aged 90.
,, 1857, Mrs. Tyler, widow of Joseph Tyler, Esq., aged 93.
,, 1858, David Torrey, aged 90.
,, 1859, Mrs. Lunt, widow of Micajah Lunt, aged 95.
,, 1859, Major Nathan Low, aged 94.
,, 1860, Francis Marshall, aged 92.
,, 1863, Peter Hardy, aged 93.
,, 1863, Naylor Small, aged 91.
,, 1863, or about that time, Mrs. Closson, widow of John Closson, aged 91.
Mrs. Closson, widow of Nehemiah Closson, aged 91.
,, 1864, Edward Small, aged 94.
,, 1865, Joseph Clifton, aged 94.
,, 1866, Robert Campbell, aged 92.
,, 1866, Mrs. Thurston, widow of Amos Thurston, aged 91.
,, 1869, William Raynes, aged 91.
,, 1869, Mrs. Alexander, widow of Ezekiel Alexander, aged 93.
,, 1871, Mrs. Powers, widow of Dr. Moody Powers, aged 91.
,, 1872, Abijah Haskell, aged 91.
,, 1873, Jonathan Haskell, aged 94.
,, 1875, Mrs. Torrey, widow of James Torrey, aged 91.
,, 1875, Mrs. Carman, wife of Frederick Carman, aged 90.
,, 1879, Mrs. Torrey, widow of David Torrey, aged 97.
,, 1882, Mrs. Porter, widow of William Porter, of Lyme, New Hampshire, aged 93.
,, 1882, Mrs. Sarah Fifield, aged 96.
— In all, thirty-six persons.

Since the above list was compiled:

Mr. Nathaniel Robbins, born according to entry upon the town records, March 13, 1799, died January 27, 1902, at the age of one hundred and two years, ten months and fourteen days, retaining his faculties until the end. He was a son of Nathaniel and Betsey (Colby) Robbins.

Mrs. Salome Sellers who, like Mr. Robbins, has lived in three centuries, is now in her one hundred and sixth year, with no greater indications of being old than are ordinarily shown by any aged person. She was born October 15, 1800, and was the daughter of Captain Edmund and Deborah (Cushman) Sylvester and the wife of the late Mr. Joseph Sellers.

CHAPTER IV.

Municipal and Miscellaneous.

THE act of incorporation was passed January 30, 1789, and was approved by John Hancock, as governor. By the act Gabriel Johonnot, Esq., who then resided in that part of the town of Penobscot now included in the town of Castine, was authorized to issue his warrant to some principal inhabitant, directing him to notify the inhabitants of this town to meet at such time and place as he might appoint, for the choice of town officers; and his warrant was issued March 17, 1789, to George Tyler, Esq., who issued his notice to the inhabitants to meet at the meeting-house — which then stood where the Town House now stands — on Monday, April 6, at nine of the clock in the forenoon, for the choice of town officers, and to act upon such other business as might be necessary, and also to give in their votes for a governor, lieutenant-governor, a state senator, and a registrar of deeds.

Pursuant to said notice the inhabitants met at the time and place appointed and chose Thomas Stinson, Esq., moderator, Rev. Peter Powers, town clerk, and five selectmen, to wit: Thomas Stinson, Esq., Captain Thomas Robbins, Mr. William Foster, Mr. Nathan Haskell, and Mr. Joseph Sellers; and Captain Ignatius Haskell, treasurer, besides other officers. The Rev. Mr. Powers during the year resigned the office of town clerk, and Nathan Haskell, Esq., was chosen, who was elected to said office till the year 1803.

There was the sum of one hundred pounds voted as salary to the minister, according to contract, which contract was made by the inhabitants when the call to Mr. Powers was made, August 23, 1785. There then was an agreement to build him a house thirty-six by twenty feet, of one story, to be finished in the same manner that houses commonly are in country towns.

Also there was the sum of sixty pounds voted to be laid out upon the roads, and for a man's labor the sum of four shillings was to be allowed, and three shillings for oxen per day. George Tyler, Esq., was chosen representative to the General Court.

1790.

The following-named persons were chosen selectmen: Thomas Robbins, William Foster, Joseph Sellers, Theophilus Eaton, and Thomas Stinson. There was also voted the same sum as the year previous, for the support of the minister, and the sum of eighty pounds for the purpose of defraying town charges, and eightpence on the pound as the collector's commission. Also the sum of twelve shillings to Mr. Benjamin Cole for sweeping and taking care of the meeting-house. At a meeting held May 6 it was voted not to choose a representative. In this and the previous year the controversy respecting the lands in the town between the settlers and Messrs. Joseph and George Tyler was often acted upon in the town meetings. This year the town treasurer was instructed to repair the meeting-house, to furnish it with glass so that it might be comfortable, and charge the cost to the town's account.

1791.

This year Messrs. William Foster, Caleb Haskell, and Joseph Sellers were chosen selectmen. It was voted not to choose a representative, and it was also voted to divide

Town of Deer Isle, Maine.   213

the town into five school districts. At the same meeting it was agreed that one school should be kept at the schoolhouse on Webster's land (now occupied by William R. and Albert N. Sellers); one at or near the mill at the Northwest Harbor; one at or near Joseph Colby's at Southeast Harbor; one at or near John Howard's, near the house at present occupied by Mr. William E. Knight, and the other near Jonathan Torrey's, at the corner of the road leading from the Reach to the Northwest Harbor. It was also voted that the inhabitants upon Stinson's Neck should be exempted from taxation for the support of schools, and the sum of thirty-six pounds was raised for the support of schools. If any district should neglect keeping a school for the time according to its proportion of the money raised for one year, such district should forfeit its proportion for the use of the town. The town accepted the house built for the Rev. Mr. Powers, and voted that it be made a town charge.

1792.

Messrs. Caleb Haskell, Joseph Sellers, and William Foster were chosen selectmen, and the sum of forty pounds was voted for the support of schools. It was also voted to raise no money for town charges. At a town meeting held on the seventh day of May, it was voted not to choose a representative, and at the same time it was voted that all future town meetings be warned by posting up three notifications, to wit: one at the meeting-house, one at Haskell's gristmill, and one at Tyler's gristmill. It was also voted to lay out a new burying-ground, and the committee chosen for the purpose were Mr. Ezekiel Morey, Captain John Hooper, and Captain Ignatius Haskell.

1793.

Messrs. William Foster, Caleb Haskell, and Joseph Sellers were elected selectmen, and the sum of fifty pounds was raised for the support of schools. The sum of fifty pounds was raised for repair of highways, and thirty pounds for payment of town charges. In May it was voted not to choose a representative.

1794.

The town chose as selectmen the persons who were elected the previous year, and voted to raise one hundred pounds for the support of schools; also, that Babbidge's Neck be the sixth school district and that Little Deer Island be the seventh. In May it was voted not to choose a representative. At a meeting held September 30, it was voted to give the men who should voluntarily enlist, a sum in addition to their monthly pay, to make up their wages — eight dollars per month — for the time they should be called into actual service, until they were discharged; three shillings per day in case they should be called to form a detachment.

1795.

Messrs. Job Small, Nathan Haskell, and Thomas Thompson were chosen selectmen. The sum of one hundred pounds was raised for the support of schools, the same amount for repair of roads, and the sum of thirty-five pounds to defray town charges. It was also agreed to consider some proper method to build a meeting-house; one hundred pounds was raised to be appropriated for the purpose, and a committee of three, to wit, Messrs. Ignatius Haskell, Thomas Thompson, and Thomas Small, was chosen to expend the said sum in providing suitable timber and other materials for building. No representative was chosen this year.

1796.

Messrs. Edmund Sylvester, Joseph Sellers, and Thomas Thompson were chosen selectmen. It was voted to release the inhabitants of Little Deer Island from working on the highways; also, to build a pound near the Carrying place, and stocks near the meeting-house. The sum of $100 was voted for the purpose; $333.34 was raised for the repairing of highways; also, $166.67 for the support of schools. No representative was chosen this year.

1797.

Messrs. Edmund Sylvester, Joseph Sellers, and Nathan Haskell were chosen selectmen, and there was voted the sum of $100 for town charges; $333.67 for schools, and the same amount for repairing highways. No representative was chosen this year. It was voted that no person not an inhabitant of the town should dig or carry off any clams from any bank or flats within the limits of the town; that the sum of fifty cents for each bushel so taken should be the penalty, one half to the use of the town and the remainder to the prosecutor. A committee of fourteen was chosen to see that the said vote should be put into execution.

1798.

Messrs. Joseph Sellers, Edmund Sylvester, and Nathan Haskell were chosen selectmen, and no money was voted for the support of schools. One hundred pounds was voted for the repairing of highways and $100 for the payment of town charges. This year Captain Ignatius Haskell was chosen representative to the General Court. In November a town meeting was held for the purpose of agreeing upon some suitable method of supplying the preaching for the coming winter, as the Rev. Mr. Powers was unable to fill the pulpit through infirmity and sickness. A committee was chosen, and it was instructed to apply to Mr. Ebenezer Eaton, if he could be obtained.

1799.

At the annual meeting in April the persons who were elected the previous year were chosen selectmen. The sum of three hundred dollars was raised for the support of preaching. A committee was chosen for the purpose of providing for the pulpit, and a committee of one from each school district to provide teachers for the several school districts. Three hundred dollars was raised for repair of highways, one hundred dollars for the payment of town charges, and the same sum for the purchase of military stores. At the meeting in May it was voted not to send a representative, which vote was reconsidered at a meeting on the twenty-seventh day of the month. The town agreed to send one on the condition: " That he should bring no additional expense on the town, and procure two bondsmen for that purpose." Messrs. Joseph Tyler and Peter Hardy offered themselves as such for any person whom the town should chose, and were accepted by the town. George Tyler, Esq , was elected representative.

This year there was a controversy between the town and Mr. Josiah Crockett, who claimed a lot of land sold by the town to Mr. Ebenezer Webster, for the support of a pauper. Mr. Crockett had recovered the land at an action-in-law, and after considerable expense the matter was settled with the occupant of the land under Mr. Webster, of whom he had purchased it. The sum paid by the town was six hundred dollars.

1800.

This year Messrs. Joseph Tyler, Prescott Powers, and Edmund Sylvester were chosen selectmen. It was also voted that when any vote which was of importance should be called for, it should be by written ballot, and after such a vote should be declared, it should not be disputed. This was to apply to all future meetings. The committee formerly chosen to supply the pulpit was instructed to engage the Rev. Mr. Page, if he could be obtained. The sum of $333 was raised for the support of preaching, $250 for the support of schools, $333.33 for repairing highways; and $100 for the payment of town charges was voted. The selectmen were directed to take measures to prevent the setting of fires in dry times and the carrying firebrands about so as to expose the property of individuals, by drafting some orders; to annex fines and penalties for the breach thereof, and to procure the approbation of the Court of Sessions to the same, that it might become a town law. In May it was voted not to send a representative; there being 17 votes in favor of, and 36 against, sending one.

1801.

This year Messrs. Joseph Tyler, Jonathan Haskell, and Prescott Powers were chosen selectmen. The following sums were voted: $300 for the support of preaching, and $100 to pay town expenses. There appears not to have been any sum raised for the repair of highways, only the town was to furnish two thousand feet of two and one-half inch plank for the use of the bridge over Tyler's Millstream. It was also voted that each district should raise its own money to keep its schools and pay its teachers; also, that a new valuation be taken, and that "no person should use firelight in taking fish within the limits of the town, under the penalty of thirty dollars for each barrel so taken." Joseph Tyler, Esq., was this year chosen representative. At the same meeting, which was held in May, the sum of two hundred pounds was voted for the purpose of repairing the highways. In December a meeting was held, and it was voted that the treasurer should call on Mr. George Tyler's bondsmen to refund the money which said Mr. George Tyler took out of the treasury at Boston, with which the town was taxed as "representative's pay," agreeably to a vote of that meeting at which he was chosen. By reference to the doings of the meeting in May, 1799, the matter will be understood.

1802.

This year Messrs. William Foster, Jonathan Eaton, and Ignatius Haskell were chosen selectmen, and Messrs. Edmund Sylvester, Caleb Haskell, and David Angell, assessors. The following sums were voted: $330 for the support of preaching, $330 for the support of schools, $150 to defray town charges, $600.67 for repairs of highways; that one half of these sums should be paid in six months, and the remainder in one year. At the meeting in May it was voted not to choose a representative.

1803.

This year Messrs. Joseph Tyler, Chase Pressey, and Jonathan Haskell were chosen selectmen, and Mr. Prescott Powers, town clerk. The following sums were raised: $333.33 for the support of schools, $666.66 for repairs of highways. At the meeting in May it was voted not to send a representative. At the same time the sum of $100 " was raised for the support of the gospel, $200 for town use, and $150 to provide a town stock of powder, lead, flints, kettles, etc.," and it was voted that no man should carry a firebrand off his own land between sunset and sunrise, on penalty of five dollars. In July of the same year the sum of $100 was raised for the support of the gospel, and $50 in addition for contingent expenses. The sum of $50 was taken from that which had previously been raised to procure a stock of powder. At a meeting held in October it was voted to give Rev. Joseph Brown a call to settle over them in the ministry and to pay him $400 yearly as salary. He was to have the use of the parsonage lot, and the expenses of moving his family and furniture were to be paid, also to furnish him a residence until a parsonage house was built. In November it was voted to build a parsonage house and a barn of the dimensions of thirty by forty feet, said building to be finished by the first day of November, 1804.

1804.

This year Messrs. Jonathan Haskell, Chase Pressey, and Joseph Tyler were chosen selectmen. Fifty dollars was raised for the support of the poor, $300 for town charges, $421 to pay the salary of the Rev. Mr. Brown and arrearages, $1,000 for the purpose of building the parsonage house and barn, $600 for repair of highways; and that each district vote and raise its own school-money. At the meeting in May it was voted not to send a representative. In November the sum of $300 was raised for the purpose of repairing Long Cove Bridge. On August 14, Rev. Joseph Brown was installed over the church here.

1805.

This year Messrs. Jonathan Haskell, Chase Pressey, and Prescott Powers were chosen selectmen. The following sums were raised: $700 for town charges, $200 for support of schools, $50 for payment of frame of the parish barn, and $600 for repairs of highways and bridges. In May, $160 was raised for the purpose of finishing the parsonage barn, and $75 for digging a well near the house on the parsonage lot. A new valuation was voted to be taken by one of the assessors. It was voted not to send a representative to the General Court.

1806.

This year Messrs. Jonathan Haskell, Nathan Haskell, and Chase Pressey were chosen selectmen. There were voted, in addition to the sum raised for the salary of the Rev. Mr. Brown, the following sums: $250 to pay up arrearages, $100 to lay out on the parsonage house, $300 for town charges, $400 for schools, and $600 for repairs of highways; and, although the warrant contained an article for the choice of a representative, nothing is shown by the records that action was taken upon the subject.

1807.

Messrs. Jonathan Haskell, Nathan Haskell, and David Angell were chosen selectmen. It was voted that there should be but one constable and that William Young be constable. The following sums were raised: $400 for the salary of the Rev. Mr. Brown, $150 for town charges, $400 for support of schools, and the vote upon the sum to be raised for repairs of highways was postponed till the meeting in May; $80 was raised for the support of the poor. At the meeting in May it was voted not to send a representative, and it was voted to give a bounty to destroy crows; the sum of $700 was raised for the purpose of repairs of highways and bridges. At a subsequent meeting, held on the twenty-eighth of the same month, the sum of $300 was voted, in addition to the sum before raised, for repairs of highways, and also $50 additional for town charges.

1808.

This year Messrs. Jonathan Haskell, Nathan Haskell, and Pearl Spofford were chosen selectmen. Besides the salary of the Rev. Mr. Brown, the following sums were raised: $50 for the support of the poor, $200 for the support of schools, $800 for highways and bridges, and $250 for town charges. It was voted that the taxes be paid into the treasury in quarterly payments; also, to pass over the petition of James Eaton and others, praying to be excused from paying the minister's salary. In May it was voted not to send a representative. This year Messrs. Hezekiah Lane, James Eaton, and others petitioned the General Court that they might be incorporated into a religious society, by the name of the First Baptist Society of Deer Isle; and at a meeting held on the twenty-sixth of December the town voted to remonstrate to the General Court against it, and a committee of three was appointed to draft the remonstrance.

1809.

On January 17 it was voted at a town meeting that the town disapproves the embargo laws then in force, and a petition was voted to be made to the General Court for relief under the said law, for the distressed and embarrassed situation of the people here. At the annual meeting Messrs. Nathan Haskell, Pearl Spofford, and David Thurlow were chosen selectmen. It was voted to release James Eaton and fifteen others from paying their money toward a minister tax. The usual sum was raised for the salary of the Rev. Mr. Brown, $200 for town charges, $250 for schools, and $800 for highways and bridges. This year Captain Pearl Spofford was chosen representative.

1810.

This year Messrs. Nathan Haskell, Pearl Spofford, and Chase Pressey were chosen selectmen. The salary of the Rev. Mr. Brown was raised, $300 for support of schools, $100 for arrearages on account of poor, $76 for expense on the account of poor for this year, $60 to purchase a stock of powder, $110 due Captain Ignatius Haskell on account of interest money, $100 for town expenses, and $500 for highways and bridge. It was also voted to tax the Baptists with others for minister tax, and allow those who belonged to that society to receive their part of the same, to appropriate to their own religious use. Pearl Spofford, Esq., was chosen representative at the meeting in May.

1811.

Messrs. Jonathan Haskell, Nathan Haskell, and Pearl Spofford were chosen selectmen this year. The following sums were raised: $420 for salary of the Rev. Mr. Brown and the Baptist brethren, $500 for highways, $130 for support of the poor, $400 for schools, $200 for town charges, and $40 to complete the town's military magazine and to replace ammunition that might be drawn out on muster days. In May two representatives were chosen, namely, Captain Ignatius Haskell and Pearl Spofford, Esq., and an additional sum of $276 was raised toward defraying town charges. A vote was at the same time passed adverse to setting off the District of Maine into a separate State. The representatives from this town were instructed to oppose it.

1812.

This year Messrs. Nathan Haskell, Pearl Spofford, and Joshua Haskell were chosen selectmen. In addition to the salary of the Rev. Mr. Brown, the following sums were raised: $400 for schools, $500 for highways and bridges, $200 for a bridge over Tyler's Millpond. The other votes relative to the raising of money were deferred till another meeting, at which the sum of $250 was voted to defray the expense of the poor and town charges. Pearl Spofford and Prescott Powers, Esquires, were chosen representatives. At a meeting held on the eighteenth of July, it was voted that the selectmen be authorized to petition the government of the United States, or some suitable officer of the United States Army, for one or more companies of United States soldiers, to be stationed on Deer Isle for defence of the same. Also that the selectmen be authorized to petition the Governor and Council of this Commonwealth for the loan of sixty muskets and four four-pound guns for the defence of the town, and that the late detachment from the militia may not be taken away from the town. This same year at a town meeting held on the fifteenth day of August, resolutions were passed reflecting strongly upon the then present administration, and the declaration of war; but at that time party feelings ran high and led to acts of indiscretion and violence of language.

1813.

The board of selectmen elected the former year was re-elected, and $500 was raised for the repair of highways and bridges, $400 for support of schools, and the usual sum as salary of the Rev. Mr. Brown. At a meeting in April several amounts were voted for town purposes. Messrs. Prescott Powers and Pearl Spofford were chosen representatives, and the vote raising $400 for support of schools was reconsidered, and no sum was raised for the purpose at the meeting. A remonstrance was voted against removing the courts from Castine to Buckstown, now Bucksport.

1814.

At a meeting held on the thirty-first of January, resolutions were passed relative to the late embargo law, and it was then voted that they be presented to the General Court. At the annual meeting the board of selectmen for 1813 was re-elected, and the following sums were voted: $400 for minister's salary, and the same amount for support of schools. At a meeting on the fourth of April the sum of $100 was voted for town expenses, and it was voted to build a pound. In May Nathan Haskell and Frederick Spofford, Esquires, were elected representatives. In November a meeting was held, and it was then voted to make a new assessment of all town taxes before assessed, leaving out the state tax; also to indemnify the assessors and collector from all costs and damages that might hereafter arise on account of not assessing the county tax and not collecting the state and county taxes. The town ordered the assessors not to assess the county tax for 1814.

In August, this year, the United States frigate *Adams* ran upon a ledge near Isle au Haut and the guns on board with other articles were landed. A tent was erected for the accommodation of some of her crew who were sick of the scurvy. She had several prisoners-of-war on board. Her captain employed the late Mr. Robert Knowlton and his brother, who had a small vessel that was employed in fishing, to carry their prisoners to Thomaston, the part of which is now Rockland. While on their passage there they made an attempt to take the vessel, but

Mr. Knowlton and his brother were very resolute and gave them to understand that it would not be safe for them to undertake it. They then became quiet and were carried to their place of destination. The ship was got off the ledge and went up the river to Hampden, where, a short time after, she was blown up by her captain — Morris — in order to prevent her falling into the hands of the British, who took possession of Castine shortly after she was taken up the river.

During the latter part of this year, or in the earlier part of 1815, an English brig loaded with beef, pork, and salmon, with a deckload of lumber, sailed from Castine for the West Indies. Her mate was a resident of this town. While sailing down the bay she was intercepted by an American privateer who gave chase to and fired upon her. Finding escape impossible the brig ran into Small's Cove, and went aground upon the bar at its mouth, the privateer following and continuing firing which was answered by the brig. After the brig grounded, the privateer anchored as near as was safe and, by firing, disabled her. The noise of the guns attracted many people to the spot, and soon quite a large crowd was gathered. One of their number, having a gun, fired at the lieutenant of the privateer, who had gone aloft to look out. The brig was taken possession of by the officers of the privateer; they gave the inhabitants permission to take the lumber or other articles of which her load was composed, and a prize-master was put on board. During the night a number of persons assembled with the intention of retaking the brig and carrying her back to Castine. The prize-master escaped to the shore and was lost in the woods, and in the morning went to the house of an inhabitant who did not sympathize with the enemy, and was carried to a place of safety. The lieutenant of the privateer was on board the brig and would have fired into the mob, as it certainly was, had not some one of the inhabitants taken what powder there was to be found on board her. She had guns on board, which, if loaded and discharged into the crowd, might have done much damage, and at the time it was fortunate that the powder was carried off. He heard the names of the persons assembled called over, and learned by whom they were headed, but the attempt to retake her was unsuccessful. The next day the brig was taken off. The captain of the privateer, armed, came on shore and took the mate who was among others assembled there, and by threats compelled him to go with him on board the privateer which took the prize to Wiscasset, where she was condemned. Not long after the prizemaster was taken over to Thomaston, but the inhabitants here were cautious, for fear that what they did might be the cause of trouble to them from the enemy. The British at Castine did not thank their sympathizers here for what they did, as they said " they were able to fight their own battles." It was said that the captain of the privateer intended to retaliate upon the persons in the company whose names he heard called over, by raising a company of persons engaged in the business of privateering, and coming here and doing to the individuals whatever damage he was able, but as peace was soon proclaimed, it was not done. With all the charity we have, we can see no excuse for the act of attempt to retake. It was one of the cases in which political feelings vent themselves in acts not to be justified, as the practice of privateering was allowed by all nations at the time. If it had been attempted in the case of a prize taken by a United States armed vessel, it must, of course, have been treason, as it would have fallen within the limits of its definition given in the Constitution. The act was long remembered to the prejudice of those engaged in it. Thirty years afterward one of their number was a candidate for an office of respectability, when the charge was brought up. He was interrogated about it in the public town meeting and admitted it, while his competitor was one of those who enlisted and served through the War of 1812, and was honorably discharged. This shows us that if any one comes before the people as a candidate for their suffrages, there is always some one who remembers his wrongdoings.

1815.

The board of selectmen for 1814 was re-elected. It was then voted that the state and county taxes for the year 1814 be assessed and committed forthwith. By the records of that year we find they were not assessed, and we are at a loss to discover why. Six hundred dollars were raised for the highways and to complete the town pound, $400 for the Rev. Mr. Brown, and the same amount for schools. It was also voted that " no swine should be allowed to go at large upon the commons or highways in the town with or without yokes and rings." In May Messrs. Nathan Haskell and Pearl Spofford, Esquires, were elected representatives. At a meeting on the third day of April the sum of $300 additional was voted for the support of the poor and for town charges. At a meeting on the tenth of June it was voted to choose sixteen men as a committee to assist the tithingmen of the town to enforce the due observance of the Sabbath, and for the suppression of intemperance in said town. The committee was: Messrs. Deacon Joshua Haskell, William Foster, Benjamin Cole, John Howard, James Jordan, Chase Pressey, Courtney Babbidge, Nathan Low, Peter Hardy, Jr., William Greenlaw, William Stinson, John Scott, Peletiah Barter, Elijah Dunham, Thomas Robbins, and Joseph Whitmore.

1816.

This year the previous board of selectmen was chosen. The sum of $300 was voted to defray town charges and support the poor, $400 for repair of highways and to finish the pound, $400 for support of schools. In May Messrs. Pearl Spofford and Prescott Powers, Esquires, were elected representatives. For a choice of a delegate to attend a convention to be held in Brunswick in the month of September, a meeting was held in August, and Pearl Spofford was chosen. On the question of a separation of the District of Maine from Massachusetts there were given: for the separation, none; against it, one hundred and sixty votes. This year there appears to have been no salary for the Rev. Mr. Brown.

1817.

This year Messrs. Ignatius Haskell, Jonathan Haskell, and Frederick Spofford were elected selectmen. It was voted " that the overseers expose for sale at public auction the poor of the town to the lowest bidder on the day of the next annual April meeting." Four hundred dollars was voted for highways and bridges, and $600 for support of schools. In May Messrs. Frederick Spofford and Nathan Haskell, Esquires, were elected representatives, and the sum of $500 was voted to pay town charges and support the poor. The vote for the sale of the poor was amended so as to allow the overseers to dispose of them, and apply town moneys for their support at their own discretion.

1818.

This year the board of selectmen for the previous year was elected. Three hundred dollars were voted for repairs of highways and bridges, and $400 for schools. At a meeting in April the sum of $400 was raised for town charges and for the poor. In May Messrs. Pearl Spofford and Hezekiah Rowell, Esquires, were elected representatives, and the latter was chosen to fill the vacancy in the board of selectmen occasioned by the death of Frederick Spofford, Esq. Mr. Benjamin Cole was chosen sexton.

1819.

This year Messrs. Ignatius Haskell, Jonathan Haskell, and Joseph Noyes were elected selectmen. The sum of $400 was raised for the support of schools, and $600 for repair of highways and bridges. In May the sum of $900 was voted for town expenses and support of poor, $200 to pay the Rev. Mr. Brown for betterments on the parsonage, and the article for raising money for the support of the gospel was passed over. Messrs. Pearl Spofford and Hezekiah Rowell, Esquires, were elected representatives. In July the question of a separation of Maine from Massachusetts was acted upon, and there were given in the affirmative twenty, and in the negative eighty-eight votes. In September a meeting was held for the choice of delegates to attend the convention for the purpose of forming a State Constitution. Messrs. Ignatius Haskell and Asa Green were chosen, and the Constitution was voted upon at a meeting in December. The number of votes in favor was twenty-two, and in the negative one.

1820.

This year Messrs. Ignatius Haskell, Nathan Haskell, and Joseph Noyes were chosen selectmen. The sum of $400 was voted for the support of schools, $600 for highways, and $400 for the support of the poor and the payment of town charges. At the meeting a committee was chosen "to prevent non-residents from digging clams in the town." It was also voted that the selectmen and clerk prepare and forward a petition to the First Legislature praying in behalf of the town, "that the Circuit Courts of Common Pleas may be abolished, and such courts established as a substitute in each town, and such extension of power given to justices of the peace as the Legislature shall think fit and proper." Pearl Spofford, Esq., was elected representative to the Legislature of Maine, and the votes were as follows: For Pearl Spofford, 92 votes; for Asa Green, 70; Ignatius Haskell, 7; and Samuel Allen, 6.

1821.

This year Messrs. Pearl Spofford, Stephen Babbidge, and Richard Warren were elected selectmen. The sum of $200 was raised for town charges and $600 for the same purpose for the year previous, $400 for the support of the poor, $300 for support of schools, and $500 for repair of highways and bridges. It was also voted to sell the poor, at auction, and there follows a list of such unfortunate persons as were disposed of under this vote. At the annual election in September Hezekiah Torrey was elected representative, having 60 votes, to 54 for Asa Green, 2 for Solomon Haskell, and 1 for Hezekiah Rowell, Esq., and in the February following five persons were licensed as retailers of spirits under the law then in force.

1822.

The board of selectmen for the year previous was chosen. The sum of $450 was voted for town expenses and support of poor, $736.80 for schools, and $800 for highways and bridges. For representative, Richard Warren was elected, having 68 votes. Ignatius Haskell, Esq., had 65 votes, and Mark Haskell 1.

1823.

This year Messrs. Pearl Spofford, Richard Warren, and George Kimball, Esquires, were chosen selectmen. The sum of $750 was raised to defray town charges, $736.80 for schools, and $1,000 for highways and bridges. At the annual election in September, Solomon Haskell, Esq., was chosen representative, having 96 votes to 51 for Hezekiah Torrey, Esq.

1824.

This year Messrs. Solomon Haskell, Stephen Babbidge, and Peter Hardy, Jr., were chosen selectmen. The sum of $350 was voted for town charges, $736.80 for schools, and $1,000 for highways and bridges. It was voted that the expense of assessing and collecting taxes, together with the fees of the treasurer, be taken out of the school-money. It was also voted to defend the law case of the town with the town of St. George on account of the Welch family. At the election in September Deacon William Stinson was elected representative, having 69 votes to 40 for Stephen Babbidge, 16 for George Kimball, Esq., 2 for John Foster, and 1 for Asa Green.

1825.

This year Messrs. Solomon Haskell, Peter Hardy, Jr., and Samuel Webb were chosen selectmen. The sum of $400 was voted for town charges, $736.80 for schools, and $1,000 for highways and bridges. It was voted to provide rations for soldiers on the days of inspection and review. George Kimball, Esq., was elected representative, having

106 votes. No other person was voted for, as appears by the records.

1826.

This year Messrs. Solomon Haskell, Samuel Webb, and Joseph C. Stinson were chosen selectmen. The sum of $550 was voted for town charges and support of the poor, $736.80 for schools, and $1,000 for highways and bridges. It was voted to pay each soldier twenty cents in cash instead of rations otherwise provided by law. At the election in September William Webb was elected representative, having 55 votes to 32 for David Thurlow, 7 for Stephen Babbidge, and 2 for Edward Haskell.

1827.

This year Messrs. Joseph C. Stinson, Jonathan E. Webb, and Stephen Babbidge, Jr., were chosen selectmen. The following sums were voted: $736.80 for schools, $750 for town charges and support of poor, and $1,000 for highways and bridges. It was voted not to impose a tax on dogs, and twenty cents to soldiers on duty once a year. At the election in September Rev. Abijah Wines was elected representative, having 62 votes to 11 for Joseph C. Stinson, 7 for Stephen Babbidge, 7 for David Thurlow, and 1 each for Stephen Babbidge, Jr., and Peter Hardy, Jr. There was an article in the warrant for a town meeting on the same day, to see if the town would pay a bounty on foxes, but it did not pass.

1828.

This year Messrs. Solomon Haskell, Stephen Babbidge, and Nathan Low were chosen selectmen. The sum of $700 was voted for town charges and support of poor, $1,000 for highways and bridges, and $736.80

for schools. Captain David Thurlow was elected representative, having 54 votes to 4 for Nathan Low and 2 for Stephen Babbidge.

1829.

This year Messrs. Nathan Low, Daniel Johnson, and William Babbidge were chosen selectmen, and the following sums were voted: $500 for town charges and support of the poor, $1,000 for highways and bridges, $736.80 for schools. It was voted to pass over the article respecting militia rations, and to have the town orders on interest taken up by the treasurer. At the annual election in September John P. Johnson, Esq., was elected representative upon the fourth ballot, having 53 votes to 44 for Michael Small.

1830.

This year the board of selectmen for the previous year was re-elected, and it was voted that the treasurer issue warrants against all collectors of taxes prior to 1829, from whom there were any moneys due, after giving them sixty days' notice. The collectors for 1829 were to have three months after they were ordered by the assessors to pay it in, after which the treasurer was instructed to issue his warrant for the payment of what was then due, and that of the tax for this year one half was to be paid in six months and the remainder in one year from the date of the bills. The sum of $600 was raised for town charges, $1,000 for highways, $736.80 for schools, and it was voted that the overseers of the poor sell the poor at auction if they see fit. Mr. Samuel Webb was elected representative, having 120 votes to 50 for Mr. Joseph Noyes, 37 for Solomon Haskell, 7 for Jonathan Pressey, and 3 for other persons who were ineligible.

1831.

This year Messrs. Stephen Babbidge, Jr., William Babbidge, and Asa Turner were chosen selectmen. The following sums were voted: $1,300 for town charges and support of the poor, $2,000 for highways and bridges, and $900 for schools. It was voted that the selectmen do not draw any orders until first knowing that the money was collected by the collectors and in the treasury, and that the collectors pay in one fourth of their collection in three months, one half in six months, and the remainder on or before the next April; if not, a warrant was to be issued by the treasurer. Mr. Stephen Babbidge, Jr., was chosen representative, having 84 votes; Mr. Joseph Noyes, 35; Avery Fifield, 22; Peter Hardy, 10; and Edward Haskell and Mark Haskell 1 vote each. It was voted that the annual meetings be held on the first Monday in March after that time.

This year the celebrated riot took place at the Northwest Harbor, and it is proper that a history of its cause and consequences should be given. For some two years previous there had been in progress a radical reform in the minds of a large part of the community all over the country with regard to the use of ardent spirits, as it had grown to be an alarming evil. To persons who do not remember those days it would now seem very surprising that the habit was then so prevalent, involving consequences so serious. Almost every man at that time made use of spirituous liquors; drinking was the rule, abstinence the exception. The evils so often portrayed respecting the degradation, poverty, crime, and distress caused by it have not been exaggerated, and we all know that it has been a most fruitful theme. In 1829 public opinion had become so thoroughly awakened with regard to it that a movement was begun for its suppression.

Societies for the promotion of temperance were formed all over the country, and the members were by their opponents styled " cold water men." No one who used liquor would admit that he made an immoderate use; neither was he a drunkard, but only a " moderate drinker," and so freely was it then used on almost all occasions, that, had the liquor then been so injurious as it now is, a great addition would have been made to the number of deaths in the community yearly. The practice was indulged in by the clergy as well as the people, and no class was exempt from it. No doubt a great deal of misdirected zeal was put into the work, but it was of such proportions that it called for the efforts of every one who had the welfare of the community at heart. Many who had been in the habit of its use abandoned it and became temperance people for a while at least, and although some returned to its practice, many held out ever after. Comparing the state of public opinion at the present day with that of those times, a great change has been wrought, as is visible to any whose recollection enables them to have a knowledge of those days. Previous to that time the laws of this State empowered the selectmen, clerks, and treasurers of towns, to grant licenses to such persons as they judged proper for the retailing of liquor. The sum paid for such licenses was put into the town treasury. The selectmen also had power, if in their judgment any person was intemperate, to make out a list of such and post it up in the shops of all persons engaged in retailing liquor, forbidding the sale of it to the persons named. If the order was disregarded, the seller laid himself liable to a fine, and his license to be taken from him. The practice was styled " posting," and it was considered by those subjected to it a great disgrace. Within my own recollection I have seen several of these lists put up in such places. After the change in public opinion the law of licenses was repealed, and many abandoned the traffic, but some still kept on, and it was several years before it ceased entirely in this town. This year a complaint was made to a justice of the peace against two persons for illegal sale, a warrant was granted and arrests made in each case, and when the day of trial came, a large crowd of those whose sympathies were upon the side of liquor, gathered. A drum was beaten and a swivel was fired during the time of the trial which resulted in the conviction of the persons complained of, who paid their fines with the costs accrued. After the close of the trial the complainant and his friends left the place where it was held (the store of Pearl Spofford, Esq.), and when he went into the street he was knocked down by one of the rioters, but his friends surrounded him and conveyed him to a place of safety, where he remained till night, when he was escorted home. A warrant was afterward procured for the arrest of three persons, including one of the persons convicted of illegal sales, for a participation in the riot, and they were carried to Castine, where an examination was had. They were bound over to the court, but at its term the grand jury failed to find a bill, which might not have been the case had the occurrence happened a few years later. For many years the complainant, who was a very worthy man, was the subject of a very strong prejudice on the part of those who were not friendly to temperance.

1832.

This year a meeting was held on the sixth day of February, at which a committee was chosen to remonstrate to the Legislature against the removal of the courts from Castine to Ellsworth, and John P. Johnson, David Angell, and Solomon Haskell were chosen, by whom a remonstrance was drafted. At the annual meeting Messrs. William Webb, Robert Campbell, and Asa Turner were chosen selectmen. The following sums were voted: $1,300 for town charges, $1,000 for highways and bridges, and $900 for support of schools; and a vote was passed, authorizing the selectmen to grant licenses for the sale of liquors, and also one for the limits of the company commanded by Captain Ignatius Haskell, 3d. At the election in September, on the third ballot, Henry Wilson, Esq., was elected representative, having 63 votes to 49 for Robert Campbell and 7 for Asa Turner.

1833.

This year Messrs. William Webb, Peter Hardy, and Henry Wilson were chosen selectmen. The following sums were raised: $600 for town charges and support of the poor, $900 for support of schools, and $1,000 for repairs of highways and bridges. At the election in September Captain Peter Hardy was elected representative, having 76 votes to 54 for Jonathan Pressey and 5 for H. Wilson.

1834.

The board of selectmen for the previous year was elected; $1,000 was the sum voted for town charges and support of poor, $900 for support of schools, and $1,000 for highways and bridges. At the election in September, on the fifth ballot, Richard Warren, Esq., was elected representative, having 105 votes to 45 for Mr. Andrew Small.

1835.

This year Messrs. William Webb, Joshua Pressey, and Edward Small were chosen selectmen, and $1,000 was voted for payment of town charges and support of poor, $900 for schools, and $1,000 for highways and bridges. Avery Fifield, Esq., was elected representative, having 76 votes to 48 for Richard Warren, Esq., 6 for Jonathan E. Webb, Esq., 2 for John Turner, Esq., and 1 for Mr. Samuel Small, Jr.

1836.

The board of selectmen for the previous year was chosen; $1,000 was the sum voted for town charges and support of poor, $900 for schools, and $1,500 for highways and bridges. The town voted against the sale of ardent spirits. Joseph C. Stinson, Esq., was chosen representative, having 84 votes; William S. Green, 40; Samuel Small, Jr., 13; Jonathan E. Webb, Esq., 16; Peter Hardy, 2, and J. Sellers, 3d, 1 vote. Upon the question of the shire town which was before the meeting, there were given for Castine 145 votes, and for Bluehill 1.

1837.

This year Messrs. Solomon Haskell, Peter Hardy, and Richard Warren were chosen selectmen. The following sums were voted: $800 for town charges, $900 for schools, and $1,000 for highways and bridges. This year the surplus revenue was divided among the towns in the State by the Legislature, and it was voted to receive this town's share. Captain Peter Hardy was chosen to receive it from the treasurer of the State, and to conform to all the requirements of the act which shall be obligatory upon the town; and he was also required to give bonds for the faithful discharge of his trust. It was also voted to choose five trustees to manage the said money, and Messrs. Edward Small, Avery Fifield, Stephen Babbidge, Pearl Spofford, and Robert Campbell were chosen, who were not to loan more than the sum of $300 to any one person; and the town was authorized to borrow a sum not over $1,000 nor less than $700 to be applied for the payment of the debts of the town, and pay interest on same, and the interest on said moneys was to be appropriated for the support of schools. In May two persons were chosen trustees in the places of Messrs. Stephen Babbidge and Robert Campbell, who had declined, and Messrs. Peter Hardy and Samuel Whitmore were chosen. At the election in September, upon the third ballot, Captain Jacob Carlton was elected representative, having 130 votes to 98 for Jonathan E. Webb, Esq., and 16 for Mr. William S. Green.

1838.

This year Messrs. John P. Johnson, Joseph C. Stinson, and John Turner, 2d, were chosen selectmen, and $500 was voted for town charges and support of poor, $900 for schools, and $1,000 for highways and bridges; also the sum of $872.76 for the money borrowed from the surplus fund, and said fund was voted " to be divided among the inhabitants of the town *per capita*." At the annual election Captain Peter Hardy was elected representative, having 200 votes to 186 for Solomon Haskell, Esq., and 4 for Jonathan E. Webb, Esq.; and at a town meeting held upon the same day, on the proposition to set off what is now the town of Isle au Haut into a separate town, it was passed by a unanimous vote.

1839.

This year Messrs. Solomon Haskell, Richard Warren, and Joshua Pressey were chosen selectmen, and the sum of $800 was voted for town charges and support of poor, $900 for schools, and $1,400 for highways and bridges.

Samuel Whitmore, Esq., was elected representative upon the second ballot, having 158 votes to 137 for Jonathan E. Webb, Esq.

1840.

This year the board of selectmen for the previous year was elected, and $800 was voted for town charges and support of the poor, $900 for schools, and $1,000 for highways and bridges. It was voted to pass a by-law to prevent any persons from playing ball in the highways. It was was also voted to hold the persons who took the census for the distribution of the surplus fund accountable for all omissions in their respective lists. At the election in September, Captain William Webb was elected representative, having 235 votes to 198 for Captain David Haskell.

1841.

This year Messrs. William Webb, William Babbidge, and George L. Hosmer were elected selectmen; the sum of $1,250 was voted for town charges, $1,100 for schools, and $1,000 for highways and bridges. At the election in September, William S. Green, Esq., was elected representative, having 173 votes to 128 for S. G. Pressey, David Haskell, 20, A. A. Herrick, 4, and Samuel Small, 1. Upon the question of reducing the number of representatives to 151, it was voted, Yes. At a town meeting upon the same day, it was voted that the town meetings should be held at the meeting-house near the house of Richard Warren, Esq., by 138 in the affirmative to 103 in the negative.

1842.

This year Messrs. Ignatius Small, George L. Hosmer, and Charles Eaton were chosen selectmen. It was voted that the selectmen might hire a suitable man to assess the taxes. The sum of $1,200 was voted for town charges and support of the poor, $1,140 for schools, and $2,500 for highways, etc. It was also voted that the overseers of the poor be instructed to contract with some suitable person, or persons, for the maintenance of the poor, for a reasonable compensation for any term of years not exceeding five, and require bonds for the same. In conformity with the said vote, said overseers made a contract with Mr. Edward Small for said support for five years, for the sum of $485 yearly, he paying no expense of paupers out of the town and none until their delivery to him. This year an attempt was made, in consequence of some alleged mistake in the copy of the warrant for the meeting, to choose the officers that were by law required to be chosen at the annual meeting, in the place of such as had been chosen at the said meeting. A number of persons assembled at the time and place named for the purpose, under a warrant from a justice of the peace, the selectmen having refused to call said meeting. Officers were then and there chosen, but said officers did not attempt to act. At the election in September Captain Asa Turner was elected representative, having 162 votes to 83 for Jonathan E. Webb, Esq.; Joseph Weed, Jr., 3; John Turner, 1; William S. Green, 2; James Saunders, 2, and 3 were blanks.

1843.

This year Messrs. Richard Warren, William Webb, and George L. Hosmer were elected selectmen, and $1,140 was the sum voted for schools, $1,000 for town expenses, $350 for payment of surplus fund, and $1,400 for highways. Avery Fifield was elected representative, having 91 votes, besides 29 on Isle au Haut, which was organized so to have the privilege of voting separately for state and county officers and members of Congress. Samuel Small, Jr., had 34; David Haskell, 38; Michael H. Pressey, 2, and Crowell H. Sylvester, 1 vote.

1844.

This year Messrs. Joseph Sellers, 3d, Amos A. Herrick, and Abijah Haskell were elected selectmen; $1,140 was voted for schools, $1,000 for current expenses, $264 for payment of money borrowed of the surplus-revenue fund; and $1,000 for highways and bridges. It was also voted that the future meetings be held at the Northwest Harbor. In April a town meeting was held for the purpose of taking into consideration the building of a Town House. It was voted to build one, and the sum of $400 was raised toward the purpose. The next annual election was held in said house. In September Captain John Gray was elected representative, having 257 votes to 190 for John Torrey.

This year Messrs. Peter Hardy, Jr., Levi Weed, and George L. Hosmer were elected selectmen; $1,140 was raised for schools, $1,200 for town expenses, and $1,200 for highways, $75 to be used for the repair of the bridge over Tyler's Milldam. Mr William Babbidge was elected representative, having 119 votes; 83 for Mr. Joseph Sellers, 2d; Hale Powers, 11; and Peter Hardy, Jr., and M. H. Pressey, 1 each.

1846.

This year Messrs. Henry A. Noyes, Michael H. Pressey, and George L. Hosmer were elected selectmen; $1,140 was the sum voted for schools, $1,200 for current expenses, $1,500 for highways and bridges, and $150 for the Town House. Mr. Samuel Small, Jr., was elected representative, he having upon the fourth balloting 133 votes to 50 for Franklin Closson, Esq.; 42 for William Haskell; 9 for Ambrose C. Gordon; 5 for William Stinson, Jr., and 1 for William S. Green. At a town meeting on the same day it was voted to choose a new board of trustees for the surplus-revenue fund, and George L. Hosmer, Samuel Whitmore, Benjamin F. Ferguson, Edward Small, and Michael H. Pressey were chosen.

1847.

This year Messrs. George L. Hosmer, Benjamin F. Ferguson, and Ignatius Small were chosen selectmen; $1,140 was the sum voted for schools, $1,300 for current expenses, $1,500 for highways and bridges, and $100 to be expended upon the Town House. William S. Green was chosen as a member of the board of trustees of the surplus-revenue fund in place of Michael H. Pressey, who declined. Solomon Haskell, Esq., was elected representative, having 83 votes to 79 for John Thompson and 3 for William E. Powers.

1848.

This year Messrs. Samuel Small, Jr., Benjamin F. Ferguson, and Gideon Hatch were elected selectmen; $1,500 was raised for town charges and support of the poor, the same amount for highways and bridges, and $1,140 for schools. In September Charles A. Spofford, Esq., was elected representative, having 136 votes to 113 for Benjamin Raynes and 15 for Hale Powers. At a meeting held the same day a committee of three, to wit, Messrs. Thomas Saunders, Solomon Haskell, and Pearl Spofford, Esq., was chosen to settle with John P. Johnson for a right of way through his sawmill, and that the town make all necessary repairs in order to make said way safe for travel.

1849.

This year Messrs. Solomon Haskell, Levi Babbidge, and Franklin Closson were chosen selectmen; $1,600 was voted for current expenses, $1,140 for schools, and $1,200 for highways and bridges. The wages of men for labor on the roads was fixed at 12½ cents per hour; for boys in proportion, according to what it was worth; for oxen from 8 to 12 cents, and plows from 33 cents to $1 per day. The selectmen were to designate the several school districts by numbers, as they had before been known by local names, and the selectmen were authorized to sell lands that had become forfeited to the town for non-payment of taxes. John Turner, Esq., was elected representative, having 115 votes; Henry Lufkin, 90; Samuel E. Powers, 21, and N. W. Sawyer, 2. On the question of changing the time of meeting of the Legislature from May to January, there were 134 votes in the affirmative to 39 in the negative.

1850.

This year Messrs. Franklin Closson, George L. Hosmer, and Ignatius Small were chosen selectmen. The sum of $2,000 was voted for current expenses, $1,140 for schools, and $1,200 for highways and bridges. Henry A. Noyes, Esq., was elected representative, having 114 votes to 82 for John Thompson; Samuel E. Powers, 9; William S. Green, 4; and Albion Haskell, Ignatius Haskell, William H. H. Spofford, and Nathan W. Sawyer, 1 each.

1851.

This year Messrs. Samuel Small, Franklin Closson, and Aaron B. Raynes were chosen selectmen. The sum of $1,700 was voted for current expenses, $1,221 for schools, and $1,200 for highways and bridges. It was voted to give the surveyors of highways warrants of distress, and the selectmen were instructed to prosecute, in behalf of the inhabitants of the town, for the sale of intoxicating liquors contrary to law. This year no representative was elected, as no election was held in September.

1852.

This year Messrs. William Webb, F. P. Spofford, and Aaron B. Raynes were chosen selectmen. The sum of $1,700 was voted for current expenses, $1,215 for schools, and $1,000 for highways, which last sum was to be separately assessed, and in case any person did not work out or pay his tax during the municipal year the same was to be committed to the collector. It was also voted to instruct the assessors to tax personal property that had been conveyed as collateral security and held in other towns, namely, owners of interests in vessels who have the control and earnings of the same, although they have no bill of sale. William Webb was elected representative, having 113 votes to 63 for F. A. S. Colby, 17 for William E. Powers, 14 for A. C. Gordon, 2 for Franklin Closson, and 1 each for Thomas Dow and John Thompson.

1853.

This year Messrs. F. P. Spofford, A. B. Raynes, and Seth Whitmore were chosen selectmen. The sum of $1,215 was voted for schools, $1,700 for current expenses, and $1,000 for highways and bridges. Samuel Smith was elected representative, having 79 votes; William F. Collins, 74; Thomas T. Low, 32; William Stinson, 14; William Babbidge, 1. At a town meeting held on the same day of the annual election, an article was acted upon relative to the vote passed the year previous in regard to vessel property, but the town instructed the assessors to adhere to the vote of the previous year.

1854.

This year Messrs. William Webb, F. P. Spofford, and Aaron Babbidge were chosen selectmen. The sum of $1,700 was raised for current expenses, $1,525 for the support of schools, and $1,500 for highways and bridges. It was voted that the selectmen contract with some person to vaccinate the inhabitants of the town for the purpose of protection from the smallpox, and the sum of $25 was voted for the purpose. Captain Benjamin Raynes was elected representative, having 131 votes to 92 for Benjamin S. Wood, and 31 for Nathan Low, Jr.

1855.

This year Messrs. Henry A. Noyes, Jeremiah Hatch, Jr., and Amos Howard were chosen selectmen. The sum of $1,700 was raised for current expenses, $1,525 for the support of schools, and $1,000 for repairs of highways and bridges. It was voted that the poor be kept in the house on the Weed Farm, now owned by the town, and that the overseers of the poor be vested with the requisite authority to carry the same into effect. Benjamin F. Stinson, of Swan's Island, was elected representative, having 162 votes to 134 for Solomon Barbour, and 1 for David Pressey.

1856.

This year Messrs. William Webb, Frederick P. Spofford, and Ignatius Small were chosen selectmen. The sum of $1,525 was voted for schools, $2,800 for current expenses and support of the poor, and $1,200 for repairs of highways and bridges. It was voted that if any damage should happen on the highway in consequence of the negligence of the surveyors, the selectmen were instructed to proceed with them according to law. It was also voted to instruct the overseers of the poor to make sufficient accommodations at the poorhouse for the paupers, and to bind out all paupers that they have a chance to. Charles A. Spofford, Esq., was elected representative, having 207 votes to 176 for James Turner, 2d, and 17 for Joshua H. Sellers.

1857.

This year Messrs. Franklin Closson, Thomas Warren, and Benjamin S. Wood were chosen selectmen. The following sums were voted: $2,500 for current expenses, $1,525 for schools, $1,200 for repairs of highways and bridges, and $100 of the sum raised for current expenses was to be appropriated for the road leading to Babbidge's Neck, which road was changed to its present location. Mr. William Babbidge was elected representative, but the records do not show how many votes were cast for the several candidates.

1858.

The board of selectmen for the previous year was re-elected. The following sums were voted: $1,809 for support of schools, $2,500 for current expenses, and $1,200 for highways and bridges. It was voted to finish a room in the Town House for the use of the selectmen, etc. In June there was a meeting to act upon the license law of 1856. In its favor were 11, and against it 51 votes. At the election in September William S. Green, Esq., was elected representative, having 225 votes to 171 for T. B. Pickering.

1859.

This year Messrs. George L. Hosmer, Levi B. Crockett,

and George C. Hardy were chosen selectmen. The following sums were voted: $1,809 for schools, $2,500 for current expenses, and $1,200 for highways and bridges, besides $50 in cash to be expended upon the road from near the house of William E. Knight to Nathan Low's house, and $100 for the road leading from land of Samuel Small toward Green's Landing. At the election in September, Mr. Ebenezer Joyce, of Swan's Island, was elected representative, having 135 votes to 134 for Franklin Closson, Esq. It was voted to accept the bridge leading on to Babbidge's Neck, which had been built about thirteen years ago by individuals, the greater part by Samuel Whitmore, Esq., as a public way, and the sum of $125 was voted for repairs of same.

1860.

The board of selectmen for the previous year was chosen. The following sums were voted: $2,500 for current expenses, $1,820 for schools, $1,200 for highways and bridges, $100 for the purchase of two iron safes for the use of the selectmen and treasurer, and $25 in cash for repair of a road. The use of the town landing on Isle au Haut was granted to Captain John Kempton. It was also voted that no abatement of taxes be made to any person who might neglect to bring in a list of his property to the assessors according to law, unless he was unable to do so by absence. Mr. Ignatius Small was elected representative, having 243 votes to 176 for F. M. Holden, and 37 for A. C. Gordon.

1861.

This year Messrs. Henry A. Noyes, Ambrose C. Gordon, and David T. Warren were elected selectmen. The sum of $2,154 was voted for schools, $2,500 for current expenses, and $1,500 for highways and bridges. On the eighteenth of May a meeting was held, at which it was voted that the selectmen and treasurer be instructed to furnish reasonable and necessary assistance to the families of such of the volunteers from the town in the service of the United States as may need it; that they be authorized to borrow, upon the credit of the town, a sum necessary for the purpose, not exceeding $2,000, and that a sum not exceeding $2.50 per month be allowed for each member of the families, to commence at the date of the enlistment. In September Thomas Warren, Esq., was elected representative, having 227 votes to 3 for other persons.

1862.

This year Messrs. George L. Hosmer, Ambrose C. Gordon, and John Robbins were elected selectmen. The following sums were voted: $2,500 for current expenses, $1,500 for schools, and $1,000 for highways and bridges. It was voted that the vote of the previous year respecting aid to families of volunteers, to furnish aid to such as, in the judgment of the selectmen, needed the same, be passed, and that the sum so furnished to any one family should not exceed $10 per month. It was provided further that the volunteer whose family applies for assistance shall, when practicable, send to his family the sum of $10 monthly, and that the town orders for such aid be payable in eight months from their dates. At a meeting held July 26, it was voted to pay a bounty of $100 to each volunteer who might be accepted by the United States, and that the treasurer be instructed to borrow, upon the credit of the town, a sum sufficient for such purpose and interest; that any person who might loan money for the purpose, if such sum should exceed his tax, the excess should be paid with interest, and a receipt from the treasurer should be evidence of the sum loaned. On the 30th of August the town voted that the sum of $100 be paid to each person who entered the service as a drafted person, or as a substitute for any person drafted. The selectmen were instructed to borrow, upon the credit of the town, a sum sufficient, with interest, for the purpose; and a committee of three, namely: Charles A. Spofford, Thomas Warren, and F. M. Holden, was chosen to negotiate for, and provide, volunteers; also, that the selectmen be instructed to provide them with means for the purpose. This year William S. Green, Esq., was elected representative, having 132 votes to 81 for Seth Webb, and 1 vote each for William Webb and Henry A. Noyes. At a town meeting on the day of the September election, the sum of $1,000 was voted for the payment of expenses incurred for support of families of volunteers up to the 18th of March, 1862, and that all orders drawn for said support after said date be made payable in six months, interest after. The sum of $2,000 was voted for payment of supplies of the latter class; also, that the said sums be assessed and committed to the collectors of taxes and to be paid before the first day of March, 1863.

1863.

This year Messrs. William Webb, A. C. Gordon, and Ignatius Small were chosen selectmen. The following sums were voted: $2,500 for current expenses, $2,156 for schools, $2,000 for the support of families of volunteers, $2,000 for the purpose of payment of bounties to volunteers and substitutes. The selectmen were instructed to borrow of citizens of the town a sum in addition, to pay the money due, borrowed out of town, with interest, and one year's interest of what was borrowed in the town; that the sum now raised be assessed as a tax separate from the state, county, and town taxes. The sum of $1,000 was raised for highways and bridges. At the election in September Sullivan Green, Esq., was elected representative, having 322 votes to 147 for Daniel L. Carlton. At a town meeting it was voted to pay $100 to every drafted man who might be accepted by the United States. On the 28th of November a vote was passed to pay a bounty to each volunteer or drafted man who might procure a substitute, who should be credited to the town, or those who might enter the naval service and be so credited; that the selectmen be authorized to borrow, upon the credit of the town, on the most favorable terms that they might be able; that said bounty be paid when the person receiving it entered the service and was placed to the credit of the town. The selectmen were instructed to call a meeting when they should ascertain what the exigencies of the case might require. At a town meeting by request of the citizens of the town, on the thirtieth day of December, it was voted to instruct the treasurer of the town to borrow, on the most favorable terms as to time of payment and interest, the sum necessary to pay the bounties referred to in the vote at the last town meeting, on the same conditions of entering the service and being placed to the credit of the town. The number was not to exceed the number required of the town under the last call. A committee of three was chosen, to wit, Messrs. Sylvanus G. Haskell, town treasurer, A. C. Gordon, and F. M. Holden, to procure volunteers or substitutes, and the last named were instructed to borrow money (in case the treasurer should neglect to do so) in order to carry out the instructions given said treasurer, and that the town be bound to abide by their doings in the matter. Also the sum of $50 was voted to each person not an inhabitant of the town who shall enlist and be credited to this town. A vote was passed giving each drafted man, or his substitute, or volunteer, under the last call for three hundred thousand men, who should be placed to the quota of the town either in the land or naval service, the sum of $300, not to exceed the number of said quota. The treasurer was instructed to borrow a sum sufficient for the purpose. At a meeting in January, 1864, the milldam was purchased of John P. Johnson, as a town road, for the sum of $475. It was voted to build a bridge across the place where the mill formerly stood. The committee for the purpose was Messrs. M. H. Lufkin, David Haskell, Nathan Low, H. T. Lufkin, and A. J. Beck. They were to make a plan of a permanent bridge, to let the job out to some responsible person, or persons, by contract, and in the meantime to cause a temporary bridge to be put up.

1864.

This year Messrs. George L. Hosmer, Charles A. Spofford, and William Torrey were elected selectmen. The following sums were voted: $2,800 for current expenses, $2,156 for schools, $1,500 for aid to families of volunteers and drafted men, $2,500 for interest and for payment of the town debt, and $1,000 for highways and bridges. A new valuation was directed to be taken, and there was a vote directing the selectmen to sell the mill privilege, remove the stone, and sell the building at auction. A vote was also passed forbidding the sale of firecrackers, and for the payment to Daniel W. Low and Mark T. Low of $100 each as compensation for having put each a substitute into the army for three years, the same being credited to the quota of the town. On the twentieth day of August a meeting was held; it was voted to pay $25 for the expense of recruiting each person entering the land or naval

Town of Deer Isle, Maine. 253

service and placed to the credit of the town, or for each volunteer so entering. The selectmen were to act as agents in filling the quota, and, if necessary, to appoint assistants. Benjamin F. Ferguson, Esq., was elected representative, having 218 votes to 121 for M. H. Lufkin. On the sixth day of October a town meeting was held. It was voted to pay to each person entering the service of the United States, toward filling the quota of the town under the last call of the President for troops, the sum of $300, and that notes for said sum be issued by the selectmen, payable in one year with interest. On the eighth day of November, it was voted to instruct the treasurer to hire such a sum of money as might be necessary to pay the notes that had become due, upon demand of the holders, upon the most favorable terms as to time and interest. It was also voted to instruct the selectmen not to give any person a note for a larger sum than was paid for a substitute.

1865.

The board of selectmen for the previous year was chosen; $3,600 was the sum raised for current expenses, $2,157 for schools, $1,000 for highways and bridges, and $750 for payment of enlisting fees; $100 was voted to Joel H. Powers and the same to Charles H. Martin for entering the service as drafted men in 1863. It was voted to instruct the selectmen and treasurer to issue bonds for the sum of $300 to each person entitled to the same, with interest redeemable in fifteen years, with coupons for interest semi-annually at six per cent. Said bonds were issued in sums of $300 and $100 for those persons who entered the service under the call in July, 1864, for five hundred thousand men, and the call in December for three hundred thousand men. In conformity with said vote the selectmen and treasurer issued bonds to the amount of $30,000, which were paid to the persons entitled to receive them. The treasurer "was instructed to borrow a sufficient sum to pay the notes given to those entering service by themselves as volunteers, or drafted men, or by their substitutes," which notes were given up by the holders upon the receipt of the bonds in exchange.

This year closed the war. The total expense of the town for war purposes was $59,128, or about one fifth of the value of the property as by the valuation of the assessors, and one sixth as fixed by the state valuation; perhaps nearly as much more was paid by private individuals for substitutes; in some cases under the last calls $600 was paid. It left us with a heavy debt in proportion to our valuation, which was small in proportion to our population. By the census of 1860 the population was 3,592 — a much larger proportion, compared with our property, than most other towns in the county. Quite a large proportion of the debt was paid by exchange of state for town bonds. The amount received from the State was $22,400. The whole number of men credited to the town was 314, at a cost of $208 for each recruit. The following-named persons, residents here, were either killed or died in the service:

John S. Gray.
Charles Gray.
Solomon Gray.
George Spaulding.
Alva Emerson.
Harlan P. Powers.
Albion P. Stinson.
Solomon Stinson.
Alfred M. Robbins.
Hezekiah H. Robbins.

John L. Harris.
Caleb Harris.
Isaiah V. Eaton.
William S. Toothaker.
Farnham Haskell.
Nathaniel Robbins, 2d.
Otis S. Greenlaw.
Alexander Henderson.
John Henderson.

In all, nineteen persons. Several others returned with constitutions seriously impaired.

At a meeting, April 12, an additional sum of $539 was voted for support of schools, and at one held June 18 it was voted to issue bonds to such persons as procured substitutes up to March 5. Another matter was acted upon which it is proper here to explain. During the early part of the present year some persons contributed the sum of $28 each to raise a fund to procure substitutes, and among them were some who did not pass examination with the surgeon, while others went into the service or put in substitutes. Those who were rejected by the surgeon applied to the town for repayment on that ground, and the town at said meeting voted to pay said sum to such persons as put into the service substitutes or volunteers and had not received back the sum they paid. Thus they rejected the claims of those who did not pass examination, as it was not in conformity with any vote of the town that the sum was raised by the persons, but was, on their part, a voluntary act. Any one was fortunate who escaped with no greater loss; but as usual in such cases, the persons who were thus relieved of liability to service could not view it in such a light. At the election in September Mr. Ambrose C. Gordon was elected representative, having 139 votes to 91 for H. T. Carman, and at a meeting on the same day the sum of $1,800 was raised for payment of interest on bonds.

1866.

This year Messrs. William Webb, Thomas S. Fifield, and John Thompson were chosen selectmen. The sum by law required was voted for schools, being seventy-five cents per inhabitant; $6,000 was voted for current expenses and interest on bonds, $1,700 was raised for the drafted men who furnished substitutes or entered the service themselves, the sum of $25 each to those persons who had not received such sum under a former vote for enlistment expenses, provided that each person had received a town note for $300, and it was not to be paid until said note was exchanged for a town bond. The same was voted to pay such persons as had paid commutation money, and $775 was raised for the purpose. At the election in September Captain Levi B. Crockett was elected representative, having 182 votes to 114 votes for Joseph Saunders.

1867.

This year Messrs. George L. Hosmer, Ignatius Small, and John Thompson were chosen selectmen. The following sums were voted: $8,000 for current expenses and interest, $2,696 for schools, for the repair of highways and bridges the sum of $1,500 in labor and $500 in cash. At a meeting on June 3, a vote was had upon the act for the suppression of "drinking-houses and tippling-shops." Thirty-nine votes were in favor and two in the negative. Mr. John Stockbridge, of Swan's Island, was elected representative, having 152 votes to 74 for William H. Reed.

1868.

This year Messrs. George L. Hosmer, Ignatius Small, and A. C. Gordon were chosen selectmen. The following sums were voted: $4,500 for current expenses, $1,000 toward the town debt, $2,000 for interest, $1,500 in labor on highways, $100 for purchase of material for bridges, and $2,696 for schools, and to all persons who paid their tax before the first day of August, six per cent. discount, but nothing after that date. George L. Hosmer was elected representative, having 351 votes to 184 for Stephen D. Higgins. Upon the amendment to the Constitution authorizing " a limited reimbursement of war expenses by loaning the credit of the State," there were 536 votes in the affirmative to none in the negative.

1869.

This year Messrs. William Webb, Henry A. Noyes, and Richard Warren were chosen selectmen. The sum of $4,000 was voted for support of the poor and payment of town charges, $2,000 for interest, $3,595 for schools, $1,500 for highways and bridges, also $1,000 toward payment of the town debt. It was also voted to purchase the Town Hall in the Masonic Building for a town house and selectmen's office, and sell in exchange, as far as it would go, the present Town House, provided the same could be done on fair and equitable terms. This vote was not carried into effect. At the election in September Mr. Samuel W. Campbell was elected representative, having 140 votes to 52 for James Turner, 2d, 63 for Stephen D. Higgins, and 20 for Jonathan Eaton. At a meeting upon the day of the annual election, the vote respecting the purchase of a part of the Masonic Hall was before it, and was passed over.

1870.

This year Messrs. George W. Spofford, William Small, and George C. Hardy were chosen selectmen. The following sums were voted: $5,000 for current expenses, $3,592 for schools, $1,200 for interest, $1,000 to be paid upon the town debt, $200 in cash on a road from Aaron Babbidge's to William Dunham's, $175 for shingling the Town House, and $1,500 for highways, but to such persons as might work out their taxes before July 4, it should be credited on the tax, and the balance was to be paid in money. The treasurer was instructed to obtain the state bonds and exchange them, according to a previous vote. Mr. Aaron B. Raynes was elected representative, having 168 votes to 98 for F. M. Holden, 16 for John Smith, 2 for Oliver van Meter, and 1 for C. H. S. Webb.

1871.

This year the board of selectmen for 1870 was chosen. The sum of $3,500 was voted for current expenses, $3,417 for schools, $1,500 in cash for highways, to be expended under the supervision of commissioners to be appointed by the selectmen, and $500 for interest; besides, there was the sum of $200 voted to pay damage to Mr. Aaron Babbidge, William Dunham, and Serena M. Thurston, for the road leading from Burnt Cove over their lands to the Southeast Harbor, and $25 for road damage to Clara A. Williams at Green's Landing. Mr. Ebenezer S. Fifield was elected representative, having 165 votes to 84 for Captain Caleb W. Haskell.

1872.

This year Messrs. George W. Spofford, A. C. Gordon, and Samuel Judkins were chosen selectmen. The following sums were voted: $4,000 for current expenses, $4,000 for schools, $1,000 for interest, and $1,500 for highways, to be expended by the following-named persons as commissioners: William P. Scott, Andrew S. Trundy, and Eben Eaton. It was voted to tax dogs one dollar per head. Mr. John Robbins was elected representative, having 290 votes to 153 for Mr. William Stinson.

1873.

This year Messrs. William Small, Joseph C. Judkins, and F. B. Ferguson were chosen selectmen. The sum of

$3,000 was voted for current expenses, and the sum required by law for support of schools, $1,000 for interest, and $1,500 in labor on the highways. It was voted to empower the selectmen to investigate the sales of lands belonging to the town and see if any conveyance had been fraudulently made. The sum of $200 was raised to be expended on the new road from the granite quarry of R. Warren & Company to the main road, and $50 to be expended in filling up the channel on the bar leading to Little Deer Island. Mr. William Babbidge was elected representative, having 111 votes to 54 for Mr. Hardy Lane.

1874.

This year Messrs. Joseph Saunders, Levi B. Crockett, and John Robbins were chosen selectmen. Mr. Saunders afterward resigned, and his place was filled by Mr. George W. Spofford. The sum of $2,000 was voted for current expenses, $2,800 for schools, $1,000 for interest, and $3,000 in labor for highways, $500 to be reserved for clearing them of snow, and $50 for a road leading from near the house of John McDonald to the house of Job Goss, 2d. On the question of building a new jail at Ellsworth the vote was: Yes, 0; No, 148. It was also voted to establish two high schools, and the sum of $500 was raised for the purpose. George Tolman, Esq., was elected representative, having 226 votes to 61 for Samuel Smith, and 26 for George L. Hosmer.

1875.

This year Messrs. Levi B. Crockett, John Robbins, and George L. Hosmer were chosen selectmen. The sum of $3,000 was voted for current expenses, $2,550 for schools, $500 for high schools, $3,000 in labor on highways, and the same sum as the previous year reserved for clearing the roads of snow, $1,000 for interest, $25 for a road near Mr. Samuel W. Campbell's, and $50 for filling up the channel on the bar leading to Little Deer Island. Sylvanus G. Haskell, Esq., was elected representative, having 296 votes to 81 for David T. Warren, Esq.

1876.

This year Messrs. William Torrey, William Small, and Martin V. B. Green were chosen selectmen. The sum of $3,000 was raised for current expenses, $2,500 for schools, $500 for a high school, $1,200 for interest, and $1,800 for highways and bridges, and the sums remaining due on the first day of November were to be committed to the collectors of taxes to be collected the present year. It was voted to exempt the wharf owned by the Bangor Machias Steamboat Company from taxation for ten years. Mr. Martin V. Babbidge, of Swan's Island, was elected representative, having 268 votes to 173 for A. O. Gross.

1877.

This year the board of selectmen for the previous year was elected. The following sums were voted: $2,000 for current expenses, $2,500 for schools, $1,300 for interest, and $1,800 for highways, and for men's labor twenty cents per hour was voted. It was also voted to allow the deaf-mutes to draw their school-money for their benefit, to be educated at Hartford, Connecticut. Captain Seth Webb was elected representative, having 178 votes to 121 for George M. Warren and 29 for Charles S. Torrey. Upon the amendment to the Constitution providing that no person should vote unless he had paid a tax within two years preceding the election in which he proposes to vote, the vote stood: Yes, 36; No, 111; and with regard to the provision limiting municipal debts the vote was: Yes, 147.

1878.

This year Messrs. Martin V. B. Green, A. C. Gordon, and Moses S. Joyce were chosen selectmen. The following sums were voted: $1,000 for current expenses, $2,500 for schools, $1,500 for interest, $1,500 in labor on highways and bridges. Charles A. Russ, Esq., was elected representative, having 168 votes to 157 for Captain Benjamin G. Barbour.

1879.

This year the selectmen for the previous year were chosen. The following sums were voted: $2,500, or what the law requires, for schools, $1,500 for current expenses, $1,200 for interest, and $1,500 for labor on highways. It was voted to instruct the treasurer to ascertain on what terms he might be able to fund the town debt and report at a meeting in September; also, what part of the same would be taken in this town. One hundred and fifty dollars were voted as compensation to Mrs. Thomas Small for injuries received upon the highway; that in taking the valuation for the present year, all persons were to be put under oath. Charles H. S. Webb, Esq., was elected representative, having 221 votes to 169 for Rodney K. Witherspoon. Upon the question of biennial sessions of the Legislature the vote stood 93 yeas to 4 nays.

1880.

This year Messrs. George W. Spofford, Edwin P. Cole, and A. C. Gordon were elected selectmen. The sum of $2,000 was raised for current expenses, $2,500 for schools, $1,000 toward payment of the town debt, $1,200 for interest, and $2,000 in labor on the highways and bridges. Upon the question of the debt of the town, as the time for the payment of the principal upon the bonds issued in

1865 had arrived, it was voted to issue new bonds with coupons, payable semi-annually, not to exceed five per cent. for interest. Said bonds were to be of the denomination of one hundred dollars, payable in ten years from March 6, 1880, and were to be exchanged for those outstanding; or, if sold, not to be under their par value. The sum of $100 was voted to be expended upon the Oceanville bridge; it was also voted to enact a code of by-laws concerning truants and children between the ages of six and seventeen years not attending school; also, $50 was voted to be expended toward filling up the channel at the northern end of the bar leading on to Little Deer Island. Captain Seth Webb was elected representative, having 343 votes to 193 for Moses S. Joyce and one for Martin V. Warren. Upon the question of the election of governor by a plurality vote, there were in the affirmative 125, to 184 in the negative. Upon the amendment changing the terms of office of senators and representatives, there were 129 in the affirmative to 168 in the negative.

1881.

This year Messrs. George W. Spofford, George H. Howard, and George W. Redman were chosen selectmen. The sum of $2,500 was voted for current expenses, $2,613 for schools, $1,300 for interest, $200 for repair of the Oceanville (or Babbidge's Neck) bridge, and $30 for repairs of the road on Greenlaw's Neck. This year no election was held in September, as the Constitution had been changed.

1882.

This year Messrs. George W. Spofford, George H. Howard, and W. B. Thurlow were chosen selectmen. The sum of $2,000 was voted for current expenses, $2,613 for schools, $900 for interest, $140 for damages and expenses of building a road laid out by the county commissioners at Green's Landing, $29 to compensate Roswell P. Davis for damage to his horse by a defect in the town road, and $2,000 in labor on highways. It was also voted to exempt Preston J. Tarr from taxation upon a gristmill, to be built by him at the Northwest Harbor, for ten years. Said Tarr had the previous year purchased the mill privilege and dam on condition of the erection and maintenance of a gristmill, the town retaining the right of way and the liability of keeping it in repair for such purpose.

ECCLESIASTICAL.

Many of the early settlers here were religious people, and several were members of churches in the places whence they came. They felt the deprivation of their accustomed privileges very sensibly, and as soon as a sufficient number could be gathered together, measures were taken for the organization of a church. In 1773, upon the first day of August, according to the early records of the church, it was gathered by Rev. Oliver Noble. The church then chose Mr. Thomas Stinson to be their moderator to call the church together and preside till another be chosen by the brethren. This record was attested by Oliver Noble, moderator.

At a church meeting August 20, 1773, it was unanimously voted that Francis Haskell and Thomas Stinson should serve as deacons in the newly erected church on Deer Island as occasion shall serve. Nothing more is stated in the records with regard to the doings of the church, nor have we any knowledge whether they had a pastor or not, until 1785, when a call was given to Rev. Peter Powers, dated August 23 of the said year. According to a vote of the church, the said call and answer thereto were recorded in the records of the town. The vote referred to was passed October 20, 1791, and the call was as follows:

"We, the inhabitants of Deer Island, in the county of Lincoln and Commonwealth of Massachusetts, having been a number of years destitute of the ordinary means of grace, are sensible of the supineness, ignorance, etc., which prevail among us, and would therefore view it our indispensable duty to God, ourselves, and our children, cheerfully and willingly to contribute toward the settlement and support of a gospel minister among us. And as we are well satisfied with the qualifications of the Rev. Peter Powers, his wisdom, prudence, etc., we, therefore, the said inhabitants, do earnestly call and invite him to settle with us in the office of the ministry; to take upon him the care of our souls; to be our guide in the way of the gospel truth; and to be our pastor and teacher in the Lord. And in consequence promise that honor and obedience enjoined us in the gospel to them who are set over us in the Lord. And as it is consistent with the divine institution that those who labor in the gospel should live of it, we, therefore, the said inhabitants, hereby covenant and agree with the Rev. Peter Powers, on his accepting this our call, and becoming our teacher, then to give to him, his heirs, and assigns forever one hundred acres of land on said island, beginning at the easterly line of that land called the 'parsonage' and running across half the front; then running back in concurrence with the other lines until one hundred acres be included. Also, to build him a dwelling-house twenty by thirty-four feet, one-story, and finish the same in such manner as such buildings are commonly finished in country towns. And for yearly salary one hundred pounds, namely, eighty pounds in specie at the market price of this place and twenty pounds in cash. In witness whereof we have hereunto set our hands this twenty-third day of August, in the year of our Lord one thousand seven hundred and eighty-five.

Francis Haskell.
Thomas Stinson.
Mark Haskell.
George Frees.
John Frees.
Belcher Tyler.
Job Small.
John Pressey.
John Hooper.
Nathaniel Robbins.
John Frees, Jr.
Joseph Colby.
John Pressey, Jr.
Hezekiah Lane.
Stephen Babbidge.
Ignatius Haskell.
Seth Webb.
Thomas Warren.
Elijah Dunham.
Benjamin Cole.
Thomas Haskell.
Joshua Haskell.
Jeremiah Eaton.
Andrew Small.
Benjamin Small.
Job Small, Jr.
Samuel Stinson.
William Stinson.
Thomas Small.
Thomas Small, Jr.
Joseph Whitmore.
Joseph Dunham.
Tristram Haskell.
Ambrose Colby.

Benjamin Rea.
John Closson.
William Raynes.
Josiah Closson.
Johnson Raynes.
John Raynes.
William Babbidge.
Joseph Colby, Jr.
Thomas Colby.
Ezekiel Marshall.
Ezekiel Marshall, Jr.
Solomon Marshall.
Joshua Marshall.
Ezra Howard.
Joseph Cole.
Edward Haskell.
Timothy Saunders.
Nathaniel Merchant.
Rolf Annis.
Benjamin Annis.
Simon Annis.
Samuel Trundy.
Nathaniel Hamblen.
William Eaton.
John Thurston.
Nathan Closson.
Charles Sellers.
Lot Curtis.
Micajah Lunt.
William Whitmore.
John Howard.
Samuel Pickering.
Abijah Haskell.
Courtney Babbidge.

William Greenlaw.
Elijah Dunham, Jr.
Peter Hardy.
James Saunders.

Francis Haskell, Jr.
Jonathan Haskell.
Ephraim Marshall.
Nathan Haskell.

[ANSWER.]

DEER ISLAND, September 17, 1785.

To the Church of Christ, on Deer Island:

DEARLY BELOVED IN OUR LORD JESUS CHRIST, — You have invited and called me to the pastoral oversight of you in the Lord, and it appearing to be of God, after mature deliberation and prayer, I now publicly return you my answer in the affirmative. I ask a daily interest in your prayers for the gracious fulfillment of that great promise: " Lo, I am with you even to the end of the world." Amen.

To the inhabitants and good people who have concurred with the church in the call and liberally offered for my support, I thankfully accept it, and promise through the grace of God to serve you all, the poor as well as the rich, according to my poor ability. You will, I trust, strive together with me in your prayers to God for me that I may be enabled to be faithful unto the death, and present you and your dear children faultless before the presence of our Lord Jesus Christ, at his coming, with unspeakable joy. Finally, brethren, be perfect, be of good comfort, be of one mind, live in peace, and the God of love and peace shall be with you. So prays your pastor-elect,

PETER POWERS.

The land described in the foregoing offer became the property of the Rev. Mr. Powers, who occupied it until his death, when it passed to his son, Mr. Prescott Powers. Part of it is now the property of Mr. Levi Greenlaw who lives in the house built for Rev. Mr. Powers, probably the oldest entire one now standing in the town.

A church covenant and confession of faith were drawn up and subscribed to by the members of the church. It shows that a large proportion of the adult population were members.

May 18, 1786. It was voted that a tax of one shilling on each communicant be paid for support of the Lord's table, and that the sacrament of the Supper be on the third Sabbaths in March, May, July, September, and November.

October 20, 1791. It was voted that there be a number of persons chosen as elders to assist the pastor and church in church-watch for one year. At a meeting on the third day of November, Deacon Francis Haskell, Deacon Thomas Stinson, and brethren James Jordan, Ezekiel Marshall, Thomas Small, George Frees, John Frees, and Nathan Haskell were chosen. At the same time Messrs. Caleb Haskell and Nathan Haskell were chosen deacons.

January 8, 1793. At a meeting of the church the following-named persons were chosen as elders: Thomas Stinson, Caleb Haskell, Nathan Haskell, Ezekiel Marshall, George Freeze, James Jordan, Joshua Haskell, and Thomas Thompson. It was also voted that Caleb Haskell should assist the pastor in keeping the church records.

Previous to this time there had been difficulties in the church respecting the immoral conduct of members, and but little satisfaction was obtained from the persons implicated after the church had done its duty toward them, which shows us that then, even as now, the practice of members was not always consistent with their profession. Several pages of the records are occupied with the history of the dealings of the church toward them, from which we incline to the opinion that the church and pastor faithfully performed their duties upon the several occasions. We do not deem it advisable to go into a further examination of the matter, as it would at this day be productive of no good, but would be a cause of sorrow to the descendants of the persons dealt with. It may serve as an admonition to all to endeavor to walk worthily, as far as we may be able, so as to bring no scandal upon the profession.

November 25, 1794. It was voted that the church would not receive any members to communion from other churches without examination, except such churches as were known to be sound in the faith. On the tenth of June, 1795, it was voted to hold their members bound to attend public worship in ordinary cases when there was no preaching. At the same time it was voted that this church do not allow its members to go to law one with another until their case is laid before the church and brought to judgment in the church. It was also voted to assist in gathering a church in Penobscot, and that the Rev. Mr. Powers assist; and Messrs. Joshua Haskell and Nathan Haskell were chosen delegates.

November 22, 1798. At a town meeting it was in consideration to see if the town would agree upon some suitable method for supplying the town with preaching the ensuing winter, as the Rev. Mr. Powers was unable to supply the desk through infirmity and sickness. It was voted to hire some person for sixteen Sabbaths. A committee of three was chosen which was instructed to apply to Mr. Ebenezer Eaton, if he could be obtained for the above term, and as reasonably as it could. Messrs. Thomas Stinson, Ignatius Haskell, and Edmund Sylvester were the members of said committee.

In April, 1799, at the annual meeting, the sum of $300 was voted for supplying the pulpit for the ensuing year. A committee was chosen for the purpose, to wit: Messrs. Thomas Stinson, Joseph Tyler, and Caleb Haskell. At a meeting held on the fourth of November, said committee was instructed to apply to Mr. Ebenezer Eaton to preach through the winter season, unless it could obtain some other gentleman who may be as agreeable to the unanimous wish of the people. It was also voted to choose a committee of three to wait upon the Rev. Mr. Powers and inform him of the wishes of the town, and see if the same would be agreeable to his desires, that, if Mr. Eaton may be obtained, he may minister to the people and be on amicable terms with Mr. Powers and not be a means of disagreement in the association. The committee were Messrs. Joseph Colby, Courtney Babbidge, and Nathan Haskell.

In 1800 the Rev. Mr. Powers died. A notice of him has already been given in a former part of this work. From what we can learn he was a faithful minister, and, for those days, liberal in his views and charitable toward others whose opinions were not in exact unison with his own.

During the preceding years the place of public worship was in the old meeting-house, as it was called, but at what time and by whom it was built we have not been able to learn. It was standing at the time of the incorporation of the town in 1789, as the first town meeting was held there. It was used for that purpose for many years, or until the one was built which occupied the site of the present one. Neither the town nor church records throw any light upon the matter, and but very few people now among us can remember it. It stood upon the spot now occupied by the Town House and was sometimes used as a schoolhouse. It was for several years in contemplation to build another, and at a meeting held on the second Monday of May, it was voted that a new one be built as near the present one as shall be convenient. At a meeting held March 16, 1793, the former vote respecting the site of the house was reconsidered, and it was voted that it should be built on Mr. Ambrose Colby's hill, which was the spot occupied by it till its destruction by fire. At a town meeting held April 6, 1795, it was voted to consider some proper method to build the house, and the sum of one hundred pounds was voted for the purpose, and a committee of three, to wit, Messrs. Ignatius Haskell, Thomas Thompson, and Thomas Small, was chosen to expend the above-named sum in providing suitable timber and other materials for building. At a meeting held October 8, the same year, the building committee laid a plan before it, providing that the dimensions of the house should be fifty-four by forty-eight feet, which was accepted, and Messrs. Thomas Robbins and Jonathan Eaton were added to the committee. As the location formerly agreed upon was not satisfactory to some of the people, the matter was acted upon, and there was a majority in favor of adhering to the vote of March 16, 1793. At the annual meeting in March, 1796, it was voted that the committee be renewed and empowered to go on with the building.

In August of the same year it was voted to accept the proceedings of the committee procuring the frame and raising it. It was also voted to give the frame, as it then stood, to any one who had or might subscribe to finish the same. The records of the town show us no further in the matter. It was built chiefly by Ignatius Haskell, Esq. He was the grantor in the deeds by which the pews were conveyed to purchasers, one of which is on record in the town records, dated April 18, 1803. He was a large proprietor, and at his death, in 1841, owned several pews.

After the death of the Rev. Mr. Powers the church had no settled pastor for several years, and at a town meeting held February 4, 1800, it was voted that the committee for supplying the pulpit wait on the Rev. Mr. Page and present the thanks of the town for his past services, and request that he preach five Sabbaths more, as it seems that he had been employed instead of Mr. Eaton. At a town meeting held on April 6, 1801, it was voted to raise money for the support of preaching. It seems that a Mr. Johnson had been preaching to them, and in May, at another meeting, it was voted that the committee should apply to him to preach a few Sabbaths more, or until they could procure another candidate. At the annual meeting held on April 5, 1802, it was voted to give the Rev. Phineas Randall a call to settle with them in the ministry, and a committee was chosen to make out one and to present it to him. The committee were Messrs. Caleb, Joshua, and Nathan Haskell, and instructions were given them to insert in the call an offer to pay $600 for settlement, to be paid in two years, and a salary of $330 yearly, with the use of the parsonage land as long as he should continue to be their minister, in which call the church united.

At a meeting of the church, May 10, 1802, it was voted to follow the rules of discipline laid down by Christ in Matthew xviii : 15, 16, and 17, and that they understood said passage as expounded by the Apostle Paul in I Corrinthians v: 11, namely, to keep no company with the excommunicated persons, so much as to eat at common table with them. It was also voted to observe the rules laid down in II Thessalonians iii: 14, that if any brother refuse to observe the rules as laid down in the sixth verse, in not complying with the rules of the church, to note that brother and keep no company with him. According to the record, those votes were unanimous, but it seems that at a meeting on the twentieth of October, 1803, the two votes referred to were recalled. At the same meeting it was voted that the church invite the Rev. Joseph Brown to settle with them in the ministry. The deacons were instructed to make out a call. On the thirty-first of the same month the town voted to give him a call, and to give him a yearly salary of $400 while he supplied the pulpit, payable quarterly, namely,

$100 at the end of every three months. He was also to have the use of the parsonage lot during said term, to be provided with a comfortable house or part of one till the town should build a parsonage house and barn, and to defray the charges of bringing his family and furniture to the town. Messrs. Thomas Stinson, Caleb Haskell, and Nathan Haskell constituted a committee for the purpose of waiting upon him and obtaining an answer. The committee for the supply of the pulpit was to provide a place of residence until a parsonage house was built, which was not long after.

The Rev. Mr. Brown appears to have been earnest and industrious in his calling; but from causes named in the sketch noticing him, there seems to have been much dissatisfaction on the part of several members of the church — particularly in the southern part of the town — whose political views did not correspond with those he advocated, as was charged, in the pulpit. Upon one occasion one of the members of the church was brought before the church for "accusing the minister of not preaching the gospel," which he acknowledged; but not showing repentance for the assertion, he was suspended. Afterward he was restored. In 1812 two members, one of whom was the person suspended, were excommunicated for signing a paper purporting a withdrawal from the church with intention to form another society in the town. This was the first step taken with a view to the formation of a Baptist Church in the town.

In 1818 Mr. William Stinson was elected a deacon of the church, which office he retained till his death, in 1848. In 1819 the death of the Rev. Mr. Brown took place, and the family removed from the town.

After the death of the Rev. Mr. Brown the pulpit was supplied by Rev. Abijah Wines for several years. The first notice of him, in the records of the church, is June 3, 1824, when he, with his wife, was received into the church by letters; but probably he had preached here some time before. In 1829 the question of temperance began to be agitated, and Mr. Wines took a very active part. In November of that year the matter was brought up at a meeting of the church, with the obligations of members in respect to joining the societies organized for the suppression of intemperance. Not long after, Mr. Wines' connection with the church as pastor was dissolved, as his mind had become impaired in consequence of his earnestness in the movement, and he removed from town. His death took place not long after. He was a man of learning, and we believe at one time a professor in the theological seminary at Bangor.

In 1832, Rev. Jonathan Adams, a native of Boothbay, Maine, moved here from the town of Woolwich, Maine, and became pastor of the church. He continued as such about twenty years, at a salary of four hundred dollars and the use of the parsonage farm. In 1838 an extensive revival of religion took place, and on August 12 fifty-seven persons were admitted to the church; on September 9 twenty-eight were added, and on November 4 twenty-seven were added. On November 18 twenty-nine also were added — in all, one hundred and forty-one persons. On February 10, 1839, complaints were made against three members for imbibing sentiments different from those of the church and for refusing to make application to the church for counsel. Having been cited to appear before the church, they did so on the twentieth of the same month, and, as their remarks were not satisfactory to the church, they were suspended for six months. They afterward united with the Methodist Church which was organized a few years after.

In 1852 the Rev. Mr. Adams ceased to be pastor of the church, and removed to Boothbay, where he preached for some time. Before his death, which took place a few years after he removed from that place, we believe he resided with his son, Rev. Jonathan E. Adams, now secretary of the Maine Missionary Society. The year of his death is unknown to us. He was an able preacher and had many friends here. Of his sons only one now remains, the one alluded to above. In 1846 his son William perished at sea on board the brig *Lincoln*. Two others, Captain David E. Adams and Charles Adams, were lost at sea together in one vessel, and another — Samuel — died at some place in the Western States. The first three died several years before their father, and, we believe, the latter a few years after them.

Mr. Adams was succeeded in the pastoral office by Rev. William V. Jordan, who did not long remain. After him Rev. William A. Merrill supplied the pulpit for a few years. During his ministry the present house of worship was built and dedicated, in 1858, the one built about 1800 having been lately burned. Mr. Merrill afterward removed to North Deer Isle and was the first pastor of the church there, where he remained for several years, and built for his own use the house now owned by Mr. George W. Holden. The last knowledge we had of him he resided in the town of Sherman, in the county of Aroostook. After Mr. Merrill, Rev. Simeon Waters came here from Iowa, and preached two years or more. The next pastor of the church was Rev. Samuel S. Drake, who preached here till 1867. He, also, was pastor of the church at North Deer Isle about one year, and afterward removed to Kittery, Maine.

In 1868 Rev. Hiram Houston became pastor of the church. He had previously preached in Stockton and in

Orland, and continued as pastor here till 1881, and later as a resident. He purchased the house and land set off to the Rev. Mr. Drake on execution in an action against the parish, and made extensive repairs on the house which was the one occupied by Mr. Brown and those who succeeded him as pastors of the church. It was built not long after Mr. Brown became pastor. The church has now no settled minister, nor do we know the number of its members. It was formerly one of the largest in point of membership in the county. Since the revival mentioned in 1838 there have been two, one in 1858 and one in 1867, in both of which numerous additions were made to the church.

THE BAPTIST CHURCH.

Allusion has been made to the dissatisfaction felt toward the Rev. Mr. Brown. As a result many members left the Congregational Church, and some time not far from the year 1813 a Baptist Church was organized, a branch of which extended to Isle au Haut. We think that Rev. Samuel Allen was its first pastor, or became so shortly after its establishment. There was at one time, not long after, a revival, and an addition was made to its members. We have no records of the church, nor do we know of any, nor in whose custody they may be, if any there are. Mr. Allen preached several years, both here and at Isle au Haut; but dissatisfaction was felt toward him on moral grounds, which was, if any cause really existed, in part due to exaggeration, as is usual in such cases. While he was pastor quite an extensive reformation took place, and many became church members. After some years his connection as pastor was dissolved, and he ceased to preach. A Mr. Bedell preached for some time, principally on Isle au Haut, and after him, Elder Samuel

Macomber. As the church and society were small, a sufficient support could not be procured for the preacher, and for several years there was no preaching, except occasionally, until about 1844, when Rev. Leonard Mayo became the pastor. He was pastor for some two or three years, when he removed from this town. At the last accounts he was residing in the town of Hodgdon, in Aroostook County. The deacons of the church were Messrs. Stephen Babbidge, Jr., and Thomas Stinson. A house of worship was commenced but not finished, which stood near the site of the present Methodist Church. Some years after, a house of worship was built on Babbidge's Neck (now Oceanville), a large proportion of the cost of which was borne by the late Samuel Whitmore, Esq. Occasionally the pulpit is supplied, but at present the church has few members.

METHODIST CHURCH.

The Methodist Society and Church were established in 1842. That year Rev. Hezekiah C. Tilton, an energetic young man, was sent here by the Methodist Conference, and he soon succeeded in establishing a church, which was joined by many persons the first year, as considerable interest was manifested. The building occupied by the Baptist Church was occupied by them until 1843, or 1844, when the Methodist meeting-house was built. Mr. Tilton remained till 1844, when he was succeeded by Rev. Charles Andrews, who made a favorable impression while here. After him came Rev. E. H. Small, another very worthy man, who made many friends while here. He resided here in 1845 and 1846 and, we think, in 1847. After his removal he preached in other places until, through infirmity, he became unable to preach, except occasionally. For several of the latter years of his life he resided in Winterport. Some years after, a house was built for the use of the ministers, standing near the house of the late Mr. Lemuel Small. The society and church have retrograded, as not much interest has been taken for a few years, and the house of worship bears marks of dilapidation.

CHURCH AT NORTH DEER ISLE.

Not far from the year 1858 a Congregational Church was established at North Deer Isle, as the members of that church found it inconvenient to go to the church at Northwest Harbor on account of the distance. A house of worship was built and dedicated, and in our notice of Mr. Merrill it was stated that he was the first pastor. In that of Mr. Drake, that he also was for a year or more pastor there, but as the society is small it is unable to support preaching. There has been some assistance from the Maine Missionary Society. A Mr. Closson preached there, sent by it, and later a Rev. Mr. Hart, but at present there is no preaching there.

FREE-WILL BAPTIST CHURCH.

At West Deer Isle a church of that denomination was established a few years since, but the society is small and unable to support preaching. A house of worship has been built, and most of the time Mr. Lafayette Collins, a lay preacher, has supplied the pulpit. At present the society and church are in a low condition, as no interest is manifested except by very few.

There are no other religious societies in the town, and occasionally preachers of the denomination known as "Adventists" have preached here, more particularly in that part of the town known as Stinson's Neck. A few years ago there were a number of persons who seemed to adhere to their principles, but at this time little or nothing is heard respecting that faith. There are at present five houses of worship which have been dedicated to the service of God, but at this time in only two of them is there public worship maintained, — at the church at the Northwest Harbor, occupied by the First Congregational Society, and the Methodist House at South Deer Isle. There is a house of worship in process of erection at Green's Landing, but in all probability it will be a Union Church, as no one denomination in that vicinity is able to support preaching. At the present time (1884) Rev. Charles H. Gates officiates at the Congregational Church and Rev. Israel Hathaway at the Methodist Church.

ORIGIN OF THE NAMES OF THE DIFFERENT LOCALITIES IN THE TOWN.

It may be of interest to the reader to know how some localities of the town came by the names assigned to them, — as we all know the different parts by the names which have been given them, — but very few have knowledge why they were so bestowed. On Little Deer Island there is a very convenient and safe harbor on the southwestern side known as Swain's Cove, and the farm of the late Daniel Billings, Esq., adjoins it. It was so named from Captain William Swain, whom we have noticed as an early occupant of the land in its vicinity. On Great Deer Island, about one mile south of its northern extremity, the harbor known as Thompson's Cove derived its name from Mr. Thomas Thompson, who lived near it and was the owner of the lands adjoining.

That body of water known as Webb's Cove was named for Mr. Webb, before mentioned, who lived near it after he left the Neck.

The harbor known as Allen's Cove was named from Rev. Samuel Allen who resided near it for many years.

The harbor known as Crockett's Cove derived its name from Mr. Josiah Crockett, as has been mentioned. He lived for many years near it.

Small's Cove was named from the two brothers of that name who settled near it. Mr. Thomas Small lived on the northern, and Mr. Job Small on the southern, side of it.

The harbor known as Burnt Cove derived its name from a fire which will be mentioned. The late Mr. Avery Fifield, Sr., lived near it for many years prior to his death, and was for some time the only settler there.

The cove or creek known as Fish Creek derived its name from the abundance of fish of the herring species which were taken in weirs by the early settlers in the vicinity.

The part of the town known as Greenlaw's Neck was probably named from Mr. William Greenlaw, who was an early settler in that vicinity; but we have no knowledge of his ever having resided upon the Neck, which we think was first settled by Mr. Nathaniel Bray.

That part of the town known as Stinson's Neck was named from its first settler, of whom mention has often been made — Thomas Stinson, Esq. Several of his descendants now reside there. That part of the island from Campbell's Neck to the steamboat landing is known as the Reach shore, as it borders on the passage known as Eggemoggin Reach, which lies between it and the towns of Sedgwick and Brooklin.

The tract of land known as Campbell's Neck, and the island near by, known as Campbell's Island, derived their name from Mr. John Campbell, who was their owner, with other lands in the vicinity, and who lived where his grandson, the present Mr. Samuel W. Campbell, now does.

The land known as Babbidge's Neck (now Oceanville),

was named from Mr. William Babbidge, who lived upon the southern part, but was not the first person there. The earliest was Mr. Seth Webb, who lived upon the land afterwards occupied by Mr. Joseph Whitmore.

The tract of land lying between Webb's Cove and Burnt Cove was for many years known as the "Burnt land," and the origin of the name, as we have been informed, was derived from its having been burnt over by a fire set by Mr. Joseph Colby, the early settler of that name. When he came the trees standing upon the tract had been blown down during a violent gale of wind. It was said that not many years before a fire had been set by some person who landed during a very dry time upon the shore, and, as it was not extinguished, it spread, and, remaining in the soil, weakened the hold of the roots of the trees as it spread, so as to render them liable to be blown down. As Mr. Colby was obliged to turn his cattle into the woods for pasturage, the trees were so entangled that it was very difficult for him to find them to drive home, and he set the fire for the purpose of clearing the obstructions. It spread all over the surface between the limits as before named, but since that time a large amount of wood and timber has grown upon it. That locality is now known as Green's Landing, named from Sullivan Green, Esq., the oldest resident now there.

The point known as Dunham's Point, the western extremity of the island (where mining operations have been made to a considerable extent), was named from Mr. Elijah Dunham, its earliest settler. The point of land on the southwestern side of the entrance to the Northwest Harbor is known as Pressey's Point, named from Mr. John Pressey, the first settler who lived near it. Dow's Point, on the northeastern entrance, was named from Mr. Nathan Dow, who settled there in 1767.

The island known as York's Island was named from Captain Benjamin York, its first settler and owner. The island known as Conary's Island was named from Mr. Thomas Conary who has been noticed, and who resided upon it.

The island known as Gibson's Island was named from Mr. James Gibson whom we have noticed as a soldier in the war of the Revolution, who made it his residence for some time.

The island now known as Thurlow's Island was named from the late Captain David Thurlow who resided there for sixty years or more before his death in 1857.

In the town of Isle au Haut, the island known as Merchant's Island was named from Mr. Anthony Merchant, the first settler in that town. He resided upon it till his death.

Kimball Island was named from Mr. Solomon Kimball, who was the purchaser from the State of Massachusetts. He occupied it after the removal of the family of Mr. Seth Webb, who died in 1785.

Cutter's Island, or, as it is now known, Fog Island, was named from a person by the name of Cutter who lived upon it for many years.

The harbor known as Douglass's Cove was named from Mr. Robert Douglass who settled near it, living there until he went thence to Nauvoo, Illinois, as a convert to Mormonism.

Head Harbor was named from the Eastern Head, the southeastern extremity of the island. I have given the origin of the name of Duck Harbor, in the description of the mode of " duck driving."

Moore's Harbor, on the western side of the island, was so named from Captain John Moore, one of the early settlers of the town of Castine, whose business in part was fishing in a small vessel in that vicinity and who frequently made that harbor an anchoring-place.

Conclusion.

I have now finished my work; I think I have recorded everything of consequence in early events here that has come to my knowledge. It has taken a wider range than was anticipated when I began it, and, from causes already named, it cannot be expected to be in all instances exactly correct, but I have given the reader the information I have received. I hope it may be of interest to us who are now here and those whose birthplace was in this town but who are not now residents. Here I have passed the active part of my life, and increasing years admonish me that I must soon follow those who have gone before. To my fellow-citizens of the town who have so many times bestowed upon me marks of their confidence, I tender my sincere thanks, and to them I dedicate this book.

STONINGTON.

In 1897 the southern part of Deer Isle was incorporated into another town, under the name of Stonington. Its taxable property at that time was about thirty-six per cent of the whole valuation, and some years of disagreement as to what share of the taxes should be expended in it for improvements led to its demand for a separation. The dissimilarity of conditions and pursuits between it and the northern part may be seen by a reference to 204 and the following pages. Its principal business is now the quarrying and cutting of granite.

INDEX.

Ackley, Mr., marriage of, 108.
Adams, George, marriage of, 52.
Adams, Rev. Jonathan, and family, 273.
Adams, U. S. frigate, affair of, in War of 1812, 224.
Alexander, Ezekiel, and family, 162.
Allen, Rev. Samuel, and family, 154.
Angell, Dr. David, and family, 143.
Annis, Benjamin, Rolf, and Simon, 265.
Babbidge, Courtney, Sr., and family, 109.
Babbidge, William, and family, 90.
Ball, Ebenezer, marriage of, 163.
Ball, Nathan, marriage of, 150.
Banks, Richard, and family, 176.
Barbour, Solomon, and family, 134.
Barter, Henry, and family, 187.
Barter, Peletiah, and family, 187.
Barter, William, and family, 188.
Benson, Jephtha, and family, 171.
Benson, Rufus, 169.
Billings, Daniel, and family, 173.
Billings, John, and family, 42.
Billings, Timothy, and family, 174.
Black, Shadrach, marriage of, 174.
Blaster, Noah, and family, 176.
Bray, Nathaniel, and family, 82.
Bray, William, and family, 137.
Brimhall, Cornelius, lot of, 107.
Brown, Rev. Joseph, and family, 148, 271.
Brown, Richard, marriage of, 106.
Bryant, Miss Betty, 135.
Buckminster, Thomas, and family, 122.

Bunker, Mr., great age of, 168.
Business, agricultural conditions, etc., 293.
Calef, Dr. John, 57.
Campbell, David, marriage of, 83.
Campbell, John, and family, 50.
Carlton, Jacob, and family, 200.
Carman, Levi, and family, 73.
Carney, Michael, settlement of, 39.
Census from 1790 to 1880, 38.
Chatto, Charles, and family, 166.
Children born of white parents, first, 22.
Childs, James, 184.
Choate, George G., and family, 167.
Church, allotment of land for support of, 37.
Church, building of, 269.
Church, early records of, 263.
Church, formation of Baptist, 149, 221, 275.
Church, notices of pastors of, 270.
Churches in town, other, 276.
Clarke, Ezekiel A., 169.
Clifton, Joseph, and family, 162.
Closson, Nathan, and family, 43.
Colby, Ambrose, and family, 81.
Colby, Joseph, Jr., and family, 115, 153.
Colby, Joseph, Sr., and family, 113.
Cole, Benjamin, and family, 91.
Collins, John, and family, 199.
Collins, Dr. William F., marriage of, 142.
Conary, Thomas, and family, 55.
Conclusion, 282.
Conley, Patrick, marriage of, 193.

Cornwallis, Lord, news of the surrender of, carried to Bagaduce, 29.
Coville, Judah, 25.
Crawford, Rev. William, 21.
Crockett, Isaac, marriage of, 190.
Crockett, John, drowning of, 180.
Crockett, Josiah, and family, 103.
Crockett, Robinson, and family, 103.
Cross, John, 184.
Curtis, Lot, settlement of, 87.
Cutter, Mr., drowning of, 179.
Davis, Roswell P., 263.
Discoverers, probable earliest, 6.
Douglass, John, 174.
Douglass, Robert, and family, 195.
Dow, Nathan, and family, 70.
"Duck-driving," description of, 17.
Duncan, James, and family, 155.
Dunham, Elijah, and family, 86.
Eaton, Asa B., and family, 65.
Eaton, Edward, and family, 65.
Eaton, Eliakim, and family, 168.
Eaton, Jeremiah, and family, 65.
Eaton, Jonathan, and family, 85.
Eaton, Solomon, and family, 170.
Eaton, Theophilus, and family, 71.
Eaton, William, Jr., and family, 67.
Eaton, William, Sr., and family, 39.
Emerson, Joshua, and family, 92.
Extent of town as incorporated in 1789, 203.
Ferguson, Benjamin F., 147.
Fifield, Avery, and family, 151.
Finney, John, and family, 166.
Foster, John, and family, 140.
Foster, William, and family, 48.
Freeze, Abraham, Isaac, and John 107.
Freeze, George, and family, 111.
Gibson, James, and family, 136.
Gilbert, Daniel, and family, 194.
Gordon, Amos, and family, 81.
Goss, John, 259.
Grant, Elisha, and family, 201.

Grant of one hundred acres each to settlers of Deer and Sheep Islands, 34.
Grant to Tyler brothers, 36.
Grants of territory in which Deer Island was included, 8, 34.
Gray, Isaac, and family, 172.
Gray, Jeremiah, and family, 132.
Gray, Josiah, and family, 132.
Green, Asa, and family, 62.
Green, Sullivan, marriage of, 153.
Greenlaw, Alexander, Charles, Ebenezer, Jonathan, and William, 41.
Greenlaw, Richard, and family, 136.
Greenlaw, William, 2d, and family, 59.
Gross, George, and family, 121.
Gross, Jacob, and family, 185.
Gross, Moses, and family, 156.
Grover, George and William, marriages of, 126.
Hallett, Henry W., marriage of, 52.
Hamilton, Solomon, 198.
Hardy, Peter, Jr., and family, 64, 177.
Hardy, Peter, Sr., and family, 63.
Harris, Joseph, and family, 172.
Harvey, John, and family, 201.
Haskell, Aaron S., and family, 145.
Haskell, Abijah, Jr., and family, 177.
Haskell, Abijah, Sr., and family, 68.
Haskell, Caleb, and family, 70.
Haskell, Francis, and family, 75, 76, 77.
Haskell, Ignatius, Jr., and family, 146.
Haskell, Ignatius, Sr., and family, 80.
Haskell, Joshua, and family, 90.
Haskell, Mark, Jr., and family, 78.
Haskell, Mark, Sr., and family, 74.
Haskell, Mark, 3d, and family, 146.
Haskell, Nathan, and family, 69.
Haskell, Solomon, and family, 147.
Hatch, Seth, and family, 127.

Index. 285

Hayden family, 150.
Hendrick, James, and family, 176.
Herrick, Dr. Amos A., marriage of, 142.
Holbrook, Elisha, and family, 193.
Holden, Amasa, and family, 138.
Holmes, Chauncey, and family, 190.
Holt, Stephen, 18.
Hooper, John and William, 88.
Horton, John, 128.
Hosmer, George L., marriage of, 159.
House, first framed, in town, 20.
Houses, oldest, now in town, 21, 266.
Howard, Edward, 72, 180.
Howard, Ezra, and family, 80.
Howard, John, and family, 66.
Incorporation Act of 1789, 36, 211.
Incorporation Act of 1868, 37.
Incorporation of Isle au Haut, 37, 178.
Indian occupancy, evidences of, 9.
Ingalls, Nathaniel, marriage of, 66.
Islands, settlement of other, 36, 178.
Isle au Haut, settlement of, 36, 178.
Johnson, Nathan, and family, 88.
Jordan, James, and family, 104.
Joyce, James, and family, 140.
Judkins, Leonard, marriage of, 114.
Kelsey, Robert, marriage of, 150.
Kempton, Charles, and family, 190.
Kench, Thomas, military record of, 171.
Kent, Nathaniel, and "Kent Claim," 18.
Kimball, George, and family, 186.
Knight, Mr., marriage of, 68.
Knowlton, Benjamin, and family, 197.
Knowlton, Robert, and prisoners of war, 224.
Lamson, Thomas, marriage of, 78.
Land-titles and surveys, 34.
Lane, Hezekiah, and family, 125.
Lane, Oliver, and family, 124.
Lanpher, Stephen, 199.

Lawry, John L., marriage of, 175.
Leland, Ebenezer, and family, 191.
Limeburner, Cunningham, 55.
Linn, Robert, settlement of, 46.
Little Deer Island, settlement of, 168.
Localities, origin of names of, 278.
Longevity, instances of, 22, 209.
Low, Nathan, and family, 137.
Loyalists among the first settlers, 25.
Loyalists, removal of, at close of war, 31.
Loyalists, cruelty to one of the, 33.
Lufkin, Benjamin, and family, 96.
Lufkin, Daniel, and family, 162.
Lufkin, Henry, and family, 161.
Lunt, Micajah, and family, 107.
Marble Company, the, 46.
Marriages, performance of earliest, 21.
Marshall, Ephraim, and family, 78.
Marshall, Ezekiel, and family, 75.
Matthews, Willard and William, marriages of, 184, 185.
McClintock, Samuel, marriage of, 125.
McDonald, John, 259.
McDonald, Laughlin, great age of, 169.
Merchant, Anthony, Sr., and family, 182.
Merithew, Aaron, and family, 199.
Merithew, Benjamin, and family, 198.
Mills, 18.
Morey, Elias, and family, 164.
Morey, Ezekiel, and family, 89.
Morey, Stephen B., marriage of, 152.
Municipal records from 1789 to 1882, 211.
Name, probable origin of, 9.
Nason, Robert, and family, 82.
Niles, Jesse, and family, 70.
Noyes, Joseph, and family, 148.
Noyes, Samuel, marriage of, 90.

Orono, 118.
Page, Noah, 193.
Parker, James, marriage of, 31.
Parker, James E., 172.
Parsonage lot, 37, 82.
Parsonage lot, building of house on, 219.
Perry, Peter, marriage of, 83.
Physicians, notices of, 208.
Pickering, Samuel, Sr., and family, 149.
Pittee, Samuel, marriage of, 173.
Powers, Rev. Peter, and family, 133.
Powers, Rev. Peter, call of, 264.
Powers, Rev. Peter, farm and house of, 264, 266.
Pressey, John, Sr., and family, 83, 87.
Pressey, John, 3d, and family, 179.
"Proprietors," 35.
Raynes, Benjamin, and family, 160.
Raynes, James, 96.
Raynes, John, Sr., and family, 94.
Raynes, Joseph, and family, 159.
Raynes, Samuel, 96.
Raynes, William, 2d, and family, 158.
Rea, Benjamin, 265.
Ready, Michael, and family, 166.
Redman, George W., 262.
Reed, Dr. Abiel, and family, 69, 208.
Revolutionary army, soldiers of, 25.
Revolution, conditions during, 26.
Rhodeisland, Reuben, 139.
Rich, John, and family, 197.
Richards, William, settlement of, 124.
Richardson, Asa, 52, 57.
Ring, William, marriage of, 58.
Robbins, Nathaniel, and family, 108.
Robbins, Thomas, Jr., and family, 57.
Robbins, Thomas, Sr., and family, 122.
Robertson, James, and family, 200.
Rowell, Hezekiah, and family, 144.

Russ, Charles A., 261.
Russell, Sidney, and family, 139.
Salt, early manufacture of, 15.
Saunders, James, and family, 85.
Sawyer, David, and family, 151.
Sawyer, Ebenezer, and family, 189.
Schools, allotment of land for support of, 37.
Scott, Nathaniel, and family, 60.
Sellers, Charles, and family, 101.
Sellers, Joseph, and family, 102.
Sellers, William, Jr., and family, 164.
Settlers, first, and early inhabitants, notices of, 39.
Settlers, life and hardships of first, 10.
Settlers, list of first, 24.
"Shaving mill," depredations of, 30.
Sheldon, Mr., and family, drowning of, 179.
Shipwrecks, men and vessels lost by, 206.
Simpson, Silvious, marriage of, 152.
Small, Andrew, and family, 106.
Small, Edward, and family, 116.
Small, Job, and family, 100.
Small, Michael, and family, 165.
Small, Naylor, and family, 165.
Small, Thomas, Sr., and family, 97.
Smith, Abiathar, and family, 192, 194.
Smith, David, and family, 127, 184.
Smith, Simon, and family, 163.
Snowman, Michael D., 175.
Spinney, Ebenezer, marriage of, 173.
Spofford, Pearl, and family, 141.
Sprowl, Mr., 193.
Staples, Mrs. Mercy, and family, 45.
Staples, Samuel, and family, 128.
Stinson, Benjamin, and family, 127.
Stinson, Thomas, Jr., and family, 115.
Stinson, Thomas, Sr., and family, 51.
Stockbridge, Benjamin, and family, 125.

Index.

Swain, William, and family, 175.
Switzer, William, marriage of, 152.
Sylvester, Edmund, and family, 120.
Tarr, Preston J., 262.
" Temperance riot, the," 234.
Territorial limits of town, 203.
Thompson, Thomas, and family, 44.
Thurlow, Carr, marriage of, 113.
Thurlow, David, and family, 152.
Thurston, John, and family, 126.
Tolman, George, marriage of, 142.
Toothaker, Elijah, and family, 58.
Torrey, David, and family, 157.
Torrey, John, and family, 157.
Torrey, Jonathan, Jr., and family, 156.
Torrey, Jonathan, Sr., and family, 46.
" Tour," working out of, 26.
Trundy, Samuel, and family, 93.
Turner, Calvin, and family, 192.
Turner, Samuel, and family, 188.
Tyler, Belcher, and family, 113.
Tyler, George, 112.
Tyler, Joseph, and family, 111.

Tyler, Thomas, and family, 195.
Van Meter, Oliver, and family, 139.
Walton, Charles, marriage of, 165.
War, Civil, list of men killed in, 254.
Wardwell, Eliakim, and family, 40.
Warren, Richard, and family, 57, 111.
Warren, Thomas, and family, 57.
Webb, Samuel, 116.
Webb, Seth, and family, 117, 185.
Webster, Ebenezer, and family, 97.
Webster, Jonathan, 90, 122.
Webster, Nathaniel, marriage of, 48.
Weed, Benjamin, and family, 129, 177.
Whitmore, Joseph, and family, 123.
Whitten, Joel, marriage of, 106.
Williams, Peter, and family, 139.
Wilson, Henry, and family, 199.
Witherspoon, Rodney K., 261.
Work, resources for this, 202.
Yeaton, William, and family, 189.
York, Benjamin, and family, 55.
" Young settlers," 35.
Young, William, 220.

CONNECTIONS WITH NON-RESIDENT FAMILIES BY MARRIAGES WITH:

Adams, Mr., 64.
Alexander, Edward, 92.
Alexander, Miss, 120.
Amazene, Lucretia, 186.
Arey, Joseph, 183.
Atwood, Frances, 198.
Austin, Mr., 208.
Averill, John, 85.
Babson, Abraham, 96.
Bagley, Betsey, 195.
Barnes, Edward, 45.
Barton, Betsey, 77.
Beal, John, 127.

Bell, William, 147.
Bickmore, Mr., 189.
Billings, Benjamin, 43.
Billings, Solomon, 72.
Black, Joab, 189.
Blunt, Mary, 50.
Briggs, Dr. Charles N., 74.
Bunker, Mary, 168.
Burrage, Benjamin, 196.
Calderwood, Mr., 89.
Calef, Polly, 53.
Candage, Gideon, 115.
Candage, Samuel, 44.

Carey, Ann, 93.
Carlton, Dudley, 51.
Carruth, Mr., 44.
Carter, John, 43.
Carter, Miss, 173.
Carter, Mr., 44.
Chase, Hepzibah, 84.
Chase, Miss, 83.
Clark, Mr., 184.
Clark, Robert, 158.
Clark, Willard, 186.
Clough, James, 74.
Coffin, Samuel, 194.
Collier, Charles, 153.
Coombs, Sarah, 198.
Cooper, James, 196.
Cooper, Thomas, 196.
Copp, Daniel G., 60.
Crockett, Solomon, 53.
Cross, Hannah Beck, 146.
Cummings, Mr., 92.
Curtis, George, 194.
Cushman, Deborah, 120.
Daggett, Elizabeth, 58.
Dale, Rev. Wigglesworth, 69.
Darling, Jedediah, 115.
Davenport, Mr., 149.
Davis, William, 110.
Day, Mr., 89.
Deering, Mr., 114.
Dexter, Mr., 65.
Doane, John, 193.
Dodge, Jonah, 96.
Doe, Dr. Theophilus, 80.
Dorr, Israel, 100.
Dorr, William, 187.
Drew, Alexander, 116.
Dyer, Isabel, 54.
Dyer, Miss, 191.
Eaton, Jonathan, 124.
Edson, Mr., 89.
Ellis, Lois, 194.
Faxon, Deborah, 134.
Fellows, Abigail, 72.
Ferguson, John, 74.

Ferrill, Mr., 130.
Fife, William, 164.
Foote, Mr., 163.
Foss, Mr., 51.
Fowles, Phebe, 111
Freeze, George, 53.
Full, Mr., 58.
Fuller, Joshua, 163.
Getchell, Daniel, 192
Gott family, 127.
Gray, John, 169.
Gray, Miss, 172.
Gray, Miss, 176.
Grover, Mr., 105.
Hall, Samuel, 167.
Harding, David, 127.
Harding, Isaac, 58.
Harding, Mr., 72.
Harmon, Abigail, 94.
Hazen, Enoch P., 61
Hazen, Mr., 45.
Hews, Paoli, 187.
Higgins, Mr., 191.
Hooper, Jeremiah, 54.
Hooper, Mr., 127.
Hopkins, Miss, 200.
Howard, Benjamin, 170
Howard, Edward, 83.
Jarvis, James, 73.
Johnson, Miss, 167.
Johnson, Mrs., 81.
Jones, Susan, 172.
Joy, Mr., 78.
Kellar, Henry, 115.
Kennison, Nathaniel, 45
Kent, Benjamin, 127.
Kettletas, Mr., 62.
Kidder, Stephen, 49.
Kimball, Francis, 119.
Kingsley, Mr., 94.
Leman, John, 156.
Littlefield, Thomas, 187
Long, Mr., 43.
Look, Lois, 154.
Lucas, J. P., 159.

Lunt, Mary, 99.
MacIntire, Mr., 49.
Manchester, Mr., 132.
Marks, Ebenezer, 55.
Matthews, Miss, 175.
McMullen, Mr., 96.
Merithew, Benajia, 187.
Merrill, John S., 187.
Moore, Daniel, 120.
Moulton, Rufus H., 66.
Norton, Patience, 114.
Obear, Samuel, 49.
Parker, John H., 134.
Parker, Timothy, 172.
Perkins, Deborah, 165.
Pettingill, Mr., 67.
Pierce, Josiah, 197.
Pritchard, Martha, 80.
Putnam, Miss, 64.
Randall, Joseph, 98.
Raymond, John, 112.
Raymond, Mr., 187.
Reed, Sarah, 194.
Rendell, Miss, 190.
Roberts, Amaziah, 55.
Robinson, the Misses, 95, 104.
Ross, Mrs. (Kench), 171.
Short, Mr., 67, 68.
Shute, Dorothy, 76.
Smith, Abigail, 193.
Smith, John, 183.

Smith, Miss, 197.
Smith, Mr., 49.
Snow, Larkin, 106.
Spencer, Mr., 58.
Stevens, Jonathan L., 80.
Stewart, Charles, 170.
Stickney, Mary, 80.
Stinson, Miss, 190, 192.
Stover, Jeremiah, 74.
Sweet, Mr., 89.
Thurlow, Betsey, 114.
Tibbetts, Mrs. Martha, 171.
Trott, John S., 106.
Trowbridge, Mr., 74.
Tuttle, Mr., 130.
Ward, Mr., 154.
Ware, Nathaniel, 115.
Waters, David J., 49.
Webster, Joseph, 84.
Wells, Miss, 174.
Wescott, Mercy, 100.
Wilkinson, Mr., 150.
Wilson, Jacob, 193.
Winship, Hannah, 117.
Winslow family, 120.
Woods, Josiah B., 85.
Wooster, Mr., 63, 89.
Wright, Mr., 115.
York, George, 124.
York, Solomon, 54.

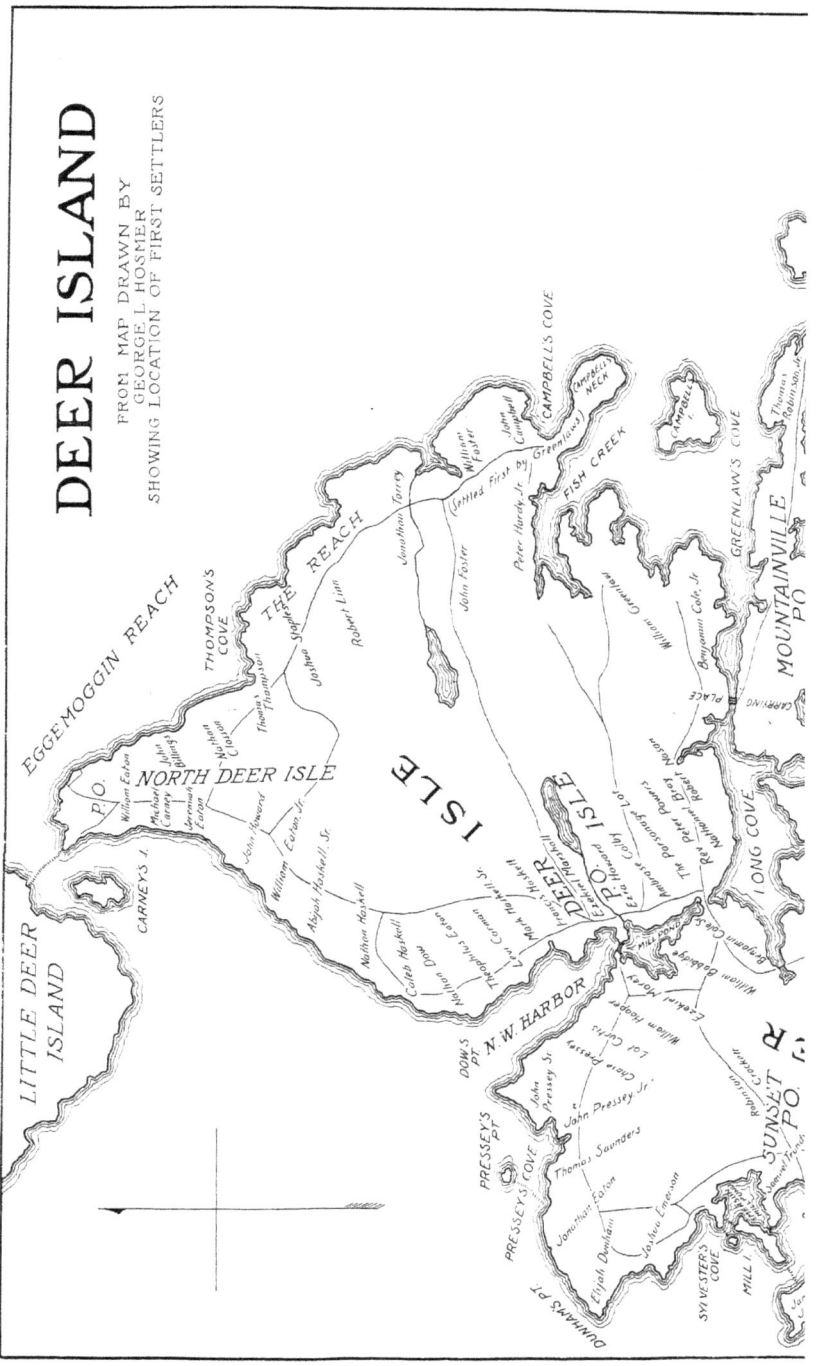

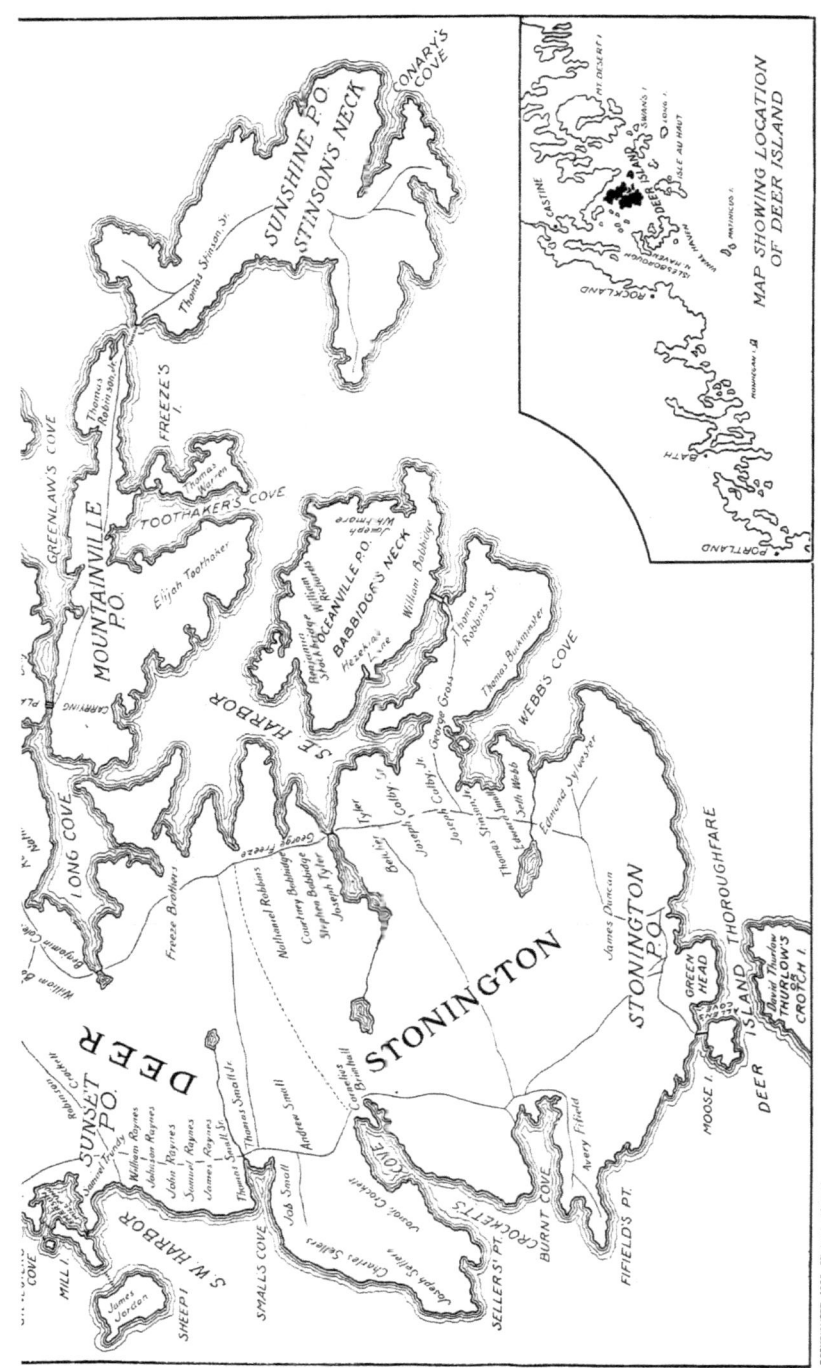

www.ingramcontent.com/pod-product-compliance
Lightning Source LLC
Chambersburg PA
CBHW071422150426
43191CB00008B/1015